ILLUMINATING COMPREHENSION
AND CLOSE READING

Also from Isabel L. Beck

Bringing Words to Life, Second Edition:
Robust Vocabulary Instruction
Isabel L. Beck, Margaret G. McKeown,
and Linda Kucan

Creating Robust Vocabulary:
Frequently Asked Questions and Extended Examples
Isabel L. Beck, Margaret G. McKeown,
and Linda Kucan

Making Sense of Phonics, Second Edition:
The Hows and Whys
Isabel L. Beck and Mark E. Beck

Illuminating Comprehension and Close Reading

Isabel L. Beck
Cheryl Sandora

THE GUILFORD PRESS
New York   London

Library of Congress Cataloging-in-Publication Data

Names: Beck, Isabel L. | Sandora, Cheryl.
Title: Illuminating comprehension and close reading / Isabel L. Beck, Cheryl
   Sandora.
Description: New York ; London : The Guilford Press, [2016] | Includes
   bibliographical references and index.
Identifiers: LCCN 2015025996| ISBN 9781462524853 (pbk.) | ISBN 9781462524860
   (hardcover)
Subjects: LCSH: Reading comprehension.
Classification: LCC LB1573.7 B43 2016 | DDC 372.47—dc23
LC record available at *http://lccn.loc.gov/2015025996*

For the teachers and students who have taught us so much—
and who continue to inspire us

About the Authors

Isabel L. Beck, PhD, is Professor Emerita of Education in the School of Education at the University of Pittsburgh. She has conducted research and published widely in the areas of decoding, vocabulary, and comprehension. Dr. Beck's contributions have been acknowledged by awards from the International Literacy Association, the Literacy Research Association, and the American Federation of Teachers. She is an elected member of the National Academy of Education.

Cheryl Sandora, PhD, is a Research Associate at the Learning Research and Development Center and a Fellow at the Institute for Learning, both at the University of Pittsburgh. Her work has included classroom-based research on comprehension and vocabulary instruction, the development of instructional materials for English/language arts classrooms, and professional development for districts around the United States. Dr. Sandora has taught in public, urban, and rural school districts and has served on the faculties of several universities.

Acknowledgments

We wish to thank the professional educators who read our manuscript and provided valuable feedback: Constance Nichols, Michelle Jo Sobolak, Lisa Yonek, and Mark E. Beck. Grateful acknowledgment is also made to ReadWorks, Inc., for permission to reprint the article "Pythons Invade the Florida Everglades."

Contents

Part Two. Text Lessons for Comprehension and Close Reading

PART ONE

The Hows and Whys of Comprehension and Close Reading

CHAPTER 1

Overview and Rationale

As many of us are aware, the Common Core State Standards (CCSS) initiative was launched in 2009 by state leaders from 48 states through their membership in the National Governors Association (NGA) Center for Best Practices and the Council of Chief State School Officers (CCSSO). Only 5 years later, "43 states, the Department of Defense Education Activity, Washington D.C., Guam, the Northern Mariana Islands and the U.S. Virgin Islands have adopted the CCSS/ELA [English Language Arts] . . . and are in the process of implementing the standards locally" (CCSS Initiative, 2015). We can't think of any other public school initiative that has come so far so fast.

The implications of the Common Core are a bigger deal than we had imagined. Before the CCSS became a reality in thousands of schools, we were cognizant, in the abstract, that they were a huge endeavor. Now that we realize the Common Core is actually in the hands of thousands of teachers, it kind of takes our breath away.

Beyond our awareness of the enormous scope of the Common Core, we share one motivation for undertaking the writing of this book—our positive reaction to seeing *close reading* front and center. Let us tell you what we knew at the time.

As an English major from undergraduate through graduate school, I (Cheryl) knew what close reading was to the extent that it was an area of literacy criticism under a New Criticism orientation. If asked about how it might be manifested in instruction, I would likely have mentioned "analyzing text." I also remembered clearly that close reading does not allow a reader to interpret authorial intent because a professor made that clear when he said something like, "You can't consider authorial intent unless you had dinner with the author last night."

I (Isabel) recognized that decades ago I had engaged with close reading in my ninth-grade English class with Ms. McFarland. At the time, I didn't know that what we sometimes did in English class was called close reading. If asked about what we *did* do in English class, I, too, probably would have said something about analyzing what we were reading.

When Ms. McFarland introduced a new novel to us, she usually read aloud the first chapter. I not only remembered, but I can see Ms. McFarland, at the front of the class, reading the beginning of *Great Expectations*. After Ms. McFarland had read Dickens's description of the convict— ". . . a man who had been soaked in water, and smothered in mud, and lamed by stones, and cut by flints, and stung by nettles, and torn by briars; who limped, and shivered, and glared, and growled . . ." —she stopped. Then she said something like, "Any time I read Dickens's description of the convict, I am in awe of Dickens's ability to bring a character to life." Look at the verbs: *soaked* and *smothered* and *lamed* and *stung* and *torn* and *glared* and *growled*. How different they are from *wet* and *hurt* and *injured* and *yelled*. Ms. McFarland also mentioned the rhythm: "Those staccato phrases— like the shots of a pistol or steady drumbeat. I'll read it again." And she did.

It is now clear to me that she was *modeling* close reading, which is a wonderful way to become acquainted with close reading. She did more than model it, and so did my other high school English teachers. I assume they had been trained when close reading was part of their preparation.

I searched my memory for other high school close reading activities and at first only remembered reading some sentences very slowly, word for word. But several years ago I came across a terrific book, which I shared with Cheryl, *Reading Like a Writer*, by Francine Prose (2006), a prolific novelist, journalist, and teacher. Her description of a close reading activity, hunting for words that had to do with vision and blindness in the two classics *Oedipus Rex* and *King Lear*, shook my memory, and I remember doing the same—but not for which words we hunted. Prose commented on her search for "eyes" words:

> It all seemed so dull, so mechanical. We felt we were way beyond it. Without this tedious, time-consuming exercise, all of us knew that blindness played a starring role in both dramas.
>
> Still we liked our English teacher, and we wanted to please him. And searching for every relevant word turned out to have an enjoyable treasure-hunt aspect, a Where's Waldo detective thrill. Once we started looking for eyes, we found them everywhere, glinting at us, winking from every page. (p. 4)

As the Common Core worked its way into the current scene, three issues, beyond our nostalgia for close reading, motivated our writing of this book. The first issue is confusion about the relationship between comprehension and close reading. The second is about the enormous difficulty of providing adequate quantity and quality of professional development in reading instruction. The third issue concerns the inconsistent quality of instructional materials available on the Internet. We hope this book will contribute to teachers' understanding of all three issues.

THE RELATIONSHIP BETWEEN COMPREHENSION AND CLOSE READING

We start with definitions of the two phenomena. *Comprehension* is, simply put, grasping the meaning of a text. *Close reading* is keen attention to the fine details of language and structure for the purpose of appreciating an author's craft and figuring out how broader-level meanings are developed.

The core of the confusion seems to be whether comprehension is an *outcome* of close reading or a *prerequisite* to close reading. Well, depending on what kind of comprehension, it's both! Surface or gist comprehension comes first and allows one to go on to close reading, which then enables deep or deeper comprehension. A very clear statement of the relationship comes from Jarrell D. Wright's (n.d.) essay "How to Teach Close Reading: Demystifying Literary Analysis for Undergraduates." Included in the essay is a link to a PowerPoint lecture that Dr. Wright gives on the first day of a literary analysis course he teaches that includes close reading.

In his essay, Dr. Wright declares that students must be able "to summarize or paraphrase [a text] accurately before they can go on to the more penetrating work of close reading. . . ." And in his PowerPoint presentation, he reminds students that close reading assumes initial comprehension. He explicitly declares, with what seemed like a little hesitation in his voice, that if students cannot comprehend adequately, they should "go to the resource center," a unit in his university that provides academic support to students having difficulty. This is a good example of the attitude behind the Common Core's concern that students be prepared to engage in college-level work. College professors are expert in their fields and teach and conduct research in their areas of expertise; they do not want to engage in, and most likely are not skilled at, remedial instruction. Thus, the point is that "surface" or "gist" comprehension is absolutely prerequisite to close reading.

Another clear example that comprehension is necessary for engagement in close reading is Timothy Shanahan's (2012) explication of the "first, second, and third reads." The first read should allow a reader to determine what a text says (comprehension). The second is to analyze how a text works (close reading). The third reading involves consideration of the quality and value of the text and connection to other texts (evaluation, integration).

Finally, it is logically clear that comprehension has to precede close reading. How could one consider an author's choices of words without knowledge of the extent to which a word choice fits or enhances the context, and the like? How can one identify clues to a problem unless one knows that a problem exists?

We have seen example lessons as well as noticed that several reading educators seem to suggest engaging in comprehension and close reading simultaneously. We are hesitant about that as a strategy that shifts attention from what is going on in the text to analyzing the impact of the author's use of particular words or the nature of the author's use of, say, peculiar syntax, that may reduce a reader's facility with both surface comprehension and depth of consideration of the author's craft and structure.

Related to the confusion is what we presently see as lots of attention to close reading—in articles, books, conferences, and conversations—with the sense that comprehension has been relegated to the back burner. All one has to do is look at the National Assessment of Educational Progress's most recent reading results to see that we put comprehension on the back burner to our peril.

So what have we done to reduce the confusion? We emphasize here and elsewhere that there is a sequence—comprehension of a text precedes close reading. We have adopted the notion of *gist before grist*, hoping that it might become a mantra. We view the gist of a text as its surface meaning. In the TV show *Dragnet*, the fictional detective Joe Friday frequently asks the women witnesses of a crime to give him "just the facts, ma'am." "Just the facts" is related to "just the *gist*." By contrast, a variation of the idiom "separating the wheat from the chaff" might be "separating the *grist* from the chaff"—with *grist* meaning something valuable. Given our view that close reading is valuable, we adopted *grist* to represent it. Of course this may be a stretch! But it allowed us to coin the idea of *gist before grist*, which we think is memorable.

PROFESSIONAL DEVELOPMENT

Given the scope of the CCSS, it is inevitable that there would be varying degrees of confusion. The confusions we are aware of come not from the standards themselves but from what has grown up around the standards. We have seen or been told about problematic matters that fall into two categories.

One category of complaints is about the quality of professional development (PD) offered to teachers. Although our knowledge is not limited to our locality in that comments have come from several regions, let us hasten to acknowledge that the number of our sources are miniscule. But the comments ring true in that they repeat, with more intensity, what has been discussed for several decades about the inadequate time allotted to PD and about trainers whose expertise on various topics was inadequate. Thus, with school resources especially limited at present, there is no reason to believe that the PD situation has changed. But the need for strong PD is especially important for the Common Core Initiative, given the many changes it entails, some of which are quite fundamental.

A major purpose of this book is to offer PD insofar as it can be done in a book. We model, explain, and provide opportunities to engage in developing components of a comprehension lesson—which involves identifying the content necessary to develop gist comprehension of a story and surface comprehension of informational pieces, transform such content into queries, determine where in the text to interrupt reading and initiate discussion, and more. We also provide texts for the teacher "to try it," that is, to plan the comprehension instruction for a text, which they can then compare with our version of a plan for comprehension that we developed for the same text. Then we suggest which specific features of a given text lend themselves to close reading analyses.

INSTRUCTIONAL MATERIALS

Another category of confusion about the Common Core concerns the inconsistent quality of the mountain of instructional materials for both teachers and students—all labeled as "Common Core aligned"—that are readily available on the Internet and that many teachers use. The CCSS architects made clear that the standards deal with *what* to teach: the *how* to teach had to remain with local control. Thus the *how* is still the prerogative of teachers, schools, and districts.

However, there are abundant resources that attempt to provide *hows* for the standards. Over the last several years, we have become concerned with the quality of these resources, in particular those from the Internet. Many websites offer examples of lessons, examples of text-dependent questions, templates for how to develop text-dependent questions, videos of readers engaging in close readings, examples of what "first read" questions look like, what "second reads" and "third reads" look like, and various additional *hows* for other topics associated with the Common Core.

Some of these websites offering how-to instruction were developed by existing organizations such as state education departments, while others were started for the specific purpose of supporting the Common Core, such as Student Achievement Partners, a nonprofit organization founded by David Coleman, Susan Pimentel, and Jason Zimba, lead writers of the CCSS. There are also many examples that come from teachers, and an abundance of *hows* from small commercial companies offering their wares.

Why is an abundance of resources not to the good? Obviously, quantity does not mean quality. And material that is not vetted, which is often the case on websites (we know of one exception), may be inconsistent or just plain inaccurate. Many teachers are new to the kind of instruction required by the Common Core and may take instructional suggestions from websites that are weak or that incorporate incorrect information into their lessons. Of course, the quality of websites about existing earlier practices is also highly variable. But teachers already know about these practices and thus are better equipped to choose stronger resources because they can judge information from their own experiences.

As to the quality of the lessons we provide in this book, you will be the judge. There are many lessons that you can review and decide for yourself. We have tried to keep it simple: *gist and grist*.

THE STRUCTURE OF THIS BOOK

The book is divided into two parts. Part One includes 10 chapters that cover background and the *hows* and *whys* of comprehension and close reading. Chapter 2 takes our readers on a sprint through the theoretical and research foundation in which our work in comprehension was grounded and the instructional practice that ensued—*Questioning the Author* (QtA; Beck & McKeown, 2006)—from which this book's approach to comprehension is derived. We then discuss the major features: queries, discussion, and interspersed reading.

Given the very important role that queries play in scaffolding comprehension, we devote Chapter 3 to the nature and purpose of queries. At the beginning of the chapter we explain the differences between the original QtA queries and the queries we recommend now, given that close reading follows comprehension. We emphasize that queries are *open,* in contrast to *constrained*, and show examples of differences in the kind of language students provide in their responses to those two different types of queries. Chapter 3 also has aspects of guiding a reader toward developing the kind of queries we recommend to the extent that we start to explain the choices we made.

Chapter 4 is devoted to guiding readers through the procedures involved in planning a comprehension lesson for a narrative, in this case the first chapter of

Alice in Wonderland, and for an informational article, "Black Death," about the bubonic plague. The four steps in planning a lesson are provided and applied to both texts with explanations for each instructional decision. Thus, complete comprehension lessons for both *Alice in Wonderland* (1865) and "Black Death" (2013) are presented for teachers to use. The goal of this chapter is to help readers gain some familiarity with the procedures involved in developing a gist, or surface, comprehension lesson.

Close reading is the focus in the next two chapters. In Chapter 5, we provide general comments about close reading. We clarify some definitions and present an example of a very competent reader engaging in close reading. We bring up the importance of a large vocabulary and suggest means for engaging with word meanings during close reading. We also offer examples of unpacking the meaning of complicated sentences from challenging text. In Chapter 6, we provide specific close reading activities for the two texts examined in Chapter 4, *Alice in Wonderland* and "Black Death." Taken together, the comprehension lessons in Chapter 4 and the close reading activities in Chapter 6 result in complete lessons for each text.

In Chapters 7 and 8 we implement what has so far been missing—opportunities to independently develop and apply the four lesson-planning steps and to compare your own version of the completed steps with a version developed by those who have more expertise—temporarily, we hope! Those opportunities are provided in Chapter 7 for a narrative, "The Two Brothers," by Leo Tolstoy (1878) and in Chapter 8 for an informational article, "Pythons Invade the Florida Everglades" (2013). Additionally, complete lessons of those stories—comprehension *plus* close reading—are available for use.

Chapter 9 deals with poetry—the ultimate text for close reading. The poet's use of rhythm, meter, rhyme; the extensive development of such figurative language techniques as metaphor or simile, personification, and imagery; and word choice and word order and the like make poetry a treasure chest for close reading.

Chapter 10 is titled "Younger Students: Last but Not Far from Least." The importance of kindergarten to second-grade students' comprehension of simple stories that they can read, and more complicated stories read aloud to them, should not be underestimated. Moreover, some attention to aspects of authors' language is appropriate and useful for younger students.

Part Two of this book presents completed lesson plans for eight texts: five narratives and three informational pieces, two of which are speeches.[1] By com-

---

[1] We did not include text lessons for kindergarten through second grade in Part Two, as to a large extent that is what Chapter 10 provides.

pleted we mean each lesson includes a copy of the text that can be duplicated for students' use, as well as queries, segmented text, and close reading activities for each selection.

The primary reason we provided completed text lessons is that they enable teachers to use the lessons designed as we have suggested with students. We think that the key to learning is examples. Examples enable a learner to first go through the "motions" and then to connect the motions with their rationale. Such practice enhances one's ability to develop similar lessons or adapt lessons or add their know-how to lessons.

So we developed the lessons in Part Two with the notion that teachers can use them with minimal preparation and for fairly short classroom time. This is in contrast with the extensive multiple text units found on some websites. We think arranging English language arts (ELA) materials into units is a positive thing, in that this adds coherence and depth to what students read, but these units legitimately require a lot of classroom time. What we do know is that the saying "there's not enough time" is widespread if not universal. What we don't know is how the use of a lot of classroom time for instruction "outside the core program" interacts with various schools' curricula and teachers' concerns about lack of time. Thus we have chosen the path of individual text material. As a result, you will notice that we do not provide separate suggestions for a "third read" because some of the close reading activities found in our lessons would be appropriate for a third read (and maybe beyond—particularly the writing suggestions). So we leave it to teachers to decide whether to work with a text, and the comprehension and close reading instructional plans for it, in two reads or if some activities should go on to a third read, or indeed beyond. Similarly, the suggestions we offer for close reading are only suggestions. It is up to the teacher, under whatever constraints he or she has, to determine whether to undertake all or just some of the close reading activities.

We would like to make explicit what we have implied so far: this book is written for teachers. We've tried to make it teacher-friendly by including all the materials you will need to teach any lesson between the covers of this book. We take the components slowly—first we model gist comprehension; next we ask our readers to develop a gist lesson while we provide prompts; and then we model close reading and ask our readers to develop lessons from beginning through close reading. Finally, we make more completed examples available in Part Two.

CHAPTER 2

A Sprint through Theory and Research

From Questioning the Author to the Present

Helping students to effectively read and learn from text arose as a focus for us some decades ago. In our attempts to understand how students comprehend text and to develop ways to support students' comprehension, we considered and studied two sources: the lessons that surrounded the textbooks that students read, which are intended to guide their reading, and of course our primary source: the students themselves and their efforts to comprehend their textbooks. We investigated these sources against a backdrop of theory and research on reading.

THEORY

The theoretical orientation that was central to our work is a cognitive-processing perspective that views comprehension as an active process of attending to information in text, making decisions about what is important, holding that information in memory as other information is encountered, and making connections to new relevant information—all toward building a coherent representation of what a text is trying to communicate. Kintsch and van Dijk (1978) and Kintsch (1998) were the most prominent researchers within this perspective, but many others also explicated aspects of the theory and its implications.

The cognitive-processing perspective made clear several aspects of reading not previously emphasized in earlier theory. First, reading requires the reader to be engaged in an active mental process of dealing with information rather than being a passive recipient of a completed message. Second, reading is more than accumulating information as one reads through a text. Instead, for comprehension to occur, information needs to be connected and integrated as the reader proceeds through a text. A reader attempts to make sense of information stated in the sentence being read, but making sense requires selecting relevant information to attend to and then connecting it to either information from preceding sentences in the text or relevant background knowledge. Successful comprehension depends on choosing the most relevant pieces of information to attend to, which the reader then carries over in memory to the next sentence. Skilled readers are better able to choose information that is likely to be relevant to subsequent information they encounter while reading.

Connecting information throughout the course of reading enables a reader to build a coherent representation. A key to successful comprehension is being able to recognize or construct logical relationships between ideas. Good readers are better at putting together text information and background knowledge to draw inferences that keep the flow of the text ideas building smoothly. Poor and novice readers are more likely either to fail to generate needed inferences or to jump to conclusions beyond what the text justifies.

BACKGROUND TO RESEARCH

Our foray into text-based comprehension research started several decades ago when our primary interest concerned questions as a key to supporting comprehension. At the time a prevalent instructional practice was to design questions in acccordance with taxonomies that represented levels of comprehension. Taxonomies were suggested as a guide to developing questions as well as a means to assess questions that appeared in basal readers and in classroom reading activities.[1] Most often the recommendation for instructional practice was that comprehension would be enhanced if more attention were given to higher levels of comprehension through questions that elicit evaluation and appreciation.

A large problem with questions based on taxonomies is that they do not consider the role within the text of information tapped by questions. As an illustration of this issue, consider two hypothetical questions for the story "The Three Little

---

[1]Presently, to the best of our knowledge, basal reading programs do not structure their questions in accordance with taxonomies. It is, however, the case that recommendations for their use are found in some method text books and instructional materials. Our point is that the use of taxonomies has not gone away.

Pigs": "What did the third little pig use to build his house?" and "How many bricks did the third little pig use?" The two questions would be equated in a taxonomic view since both query literal information from the story. Yet the question of the number of bricks is trivial while the question of the building material used is based on information of central importance to the story. Similarly, questions from higher taxonomic levels do not necessarily imply greater text comprehension. For example, less processing of text ideas would be required to answer an appreciation-level question such as "How would you have felt if you had been Goldilocks?" than to give a summary or synthesis of story events. Yet appreciation is a higher level in a comprehension taxonomy than is synthesis or reorganization.

Another problem with taxonomies is that they fail to account for the relationship among the questions for a particular text. If a set of questions for a story is useful to promote comprehension, the questions should not focus on isolated items, but need to be sequenced to help students consider the overall concept of the text. But questions developed and sequenced according to their taxonomic levels will likely not follow the sequence of events and ideas, and thus will not help the readers build a coherent representation of a text. In fact, a taxonomic sequence of questions may disrupt the flow of text ideas rather than promote their organization.

Faced with the above issues, we developed the notion of a text map[2] (Beck & McKeown, 1981). Our construct of a text map is one of a unified representation of a text based on a logical organization of events and ideas of central importance to a text and the interrelationships of these events and ideas. The design of questions around a text map begins with the determination of the important events that constitute the gist of a text and then the development of a series of questions that tap that information and match the progression of events and ideas in the text. The map requires the integration of both explicit and implicit ideas, since even the most basic understanding of a text requires the making of inferences as well as recall of explicit events.

RESEARCH

We engaged in several studies to test our notions of the influence on comprehension of taxonomic-based questions or text map-based questions and coherent or

---

[2] The original label was story map, but given that we applied the notion to expository material too, we changed the label to text map.

less coherent text, and background knowledge. Basal teachers' editions provided instructional suggestions for dealing with many such areas.

A comparison of two third-grade groups, reading the same stories, assessed the influence on comprehension of questions based on taxonomic categories and questions based on a text map. Children who received the text map questions recalled significantly more of the stories and correctly answered more questions than children receiving taxonomic questions (Beck, Omanson, & McKeown, 1982).

We studied coherent and less coherent passages to determine the extent to which more coherent text enhanced comprehension. There was a strong finding that they did (Beck, McKeown, Omanson, & Pople, 1984).

Later we developed a processing description of the way in which the background knowledge and questions components of the basal and text map versions of those components influenced the children's comprehension (Omanson, Beck, Voss, & McKeown, 1984). Processing descriptions were developed for each group by tracing responses children gave in recalls to the particular lesson they had received. The most important conclusion from this work was that an account of what children do *during* a reading lesson gave us more insight into how to design reading lessons than a description of what children do *after* the lesson.

The studies that we mentioned above showed that students' comprehension can be upgraded by carefully crafting lessons and texts to match what we know about influences on comprehension. That is, lesson features such as a logical sequence of questions, relevant knowledge, and coherent texts have a positive influence on comprehension. It is important, however, to keep in mind that although students who receive the various manipulations did better than students who did not, the positive effect rarely approaches optimal or ideal comprehension.

Our general observations of students' comprehension of texts were that although some students developed coherent representations of what they had read, many students developed only a superficial understanding by simply gathering words from the text, and a disheartening number did not seem to even approach an understanding of what they had read.

USING RESEARCH

Given the kind of responses that students provided to text in our studies and the text-processing perspective on comprehension, we began to formulate what was needed to assist students' understanding of text. Clearly the answer lay in helping them in the course of reading the text. That is, we needed to intervene in what they were doing when they were casting their eyes on text, and require them to consider and attend to what the text offered and use that to make sense for themselves. Our first attempts to intervene in students' processing involved trying to figure out what students were thinking as they went through a text, using a think-aloud procedure. We gave students a text to read and stopped them after a sentence or two to ask them to talk about what they had read. As we proceeded, we began to alter the probes we asked the students to see if we could get more verbiage and more thoughtful verbiage. It was in that round of exploration that we discovered that when we asked open questions, such as "What's going on now?" and "What's the main point in this section?" we were more likely to get useful information or to get the students to take a further look at the text content.

THEORY AND RESEARCH INTO INSTRUCTION

The approach to comprehension that we present in this book was adapted and further developed from Questioning the Author (QtA; Beck & McKeown, 2006), a method for text-based instruction that was designed to facilitate developing comprehension of text ideas. More recently we have characterized QtA as a *content approach* to distinguish it from a *strategies approach* (McKeown, Beck, & Blake, 2009). Strategies instruction encourages students to think about their mental processses and, on that basis, to execute specific strategies with which to interact with text. In contrast, content instruction attempts to engage students in the process of attending to text ideas and building a mental representation of the ideas, with no direction to consider specific mental processes. Thus, before the CCSS were published, our focus has always been on the text.

Building understanding and developing comprehension are synonomous; they are what a reader needs to do to read successfully. They involve figuring out what information one needs to pay particular attention to and connecting that to other information. According to this view, a learner must actively deal with the information in a text in order to make sense of it (Kintsch, 1998). We had taken those well-researched propositions seriously and incorported them in QtA's major features and adjusted them for our purposes here.

QUESTIONING THE AUTHOR: A CONTENT APPROACH

QtA takes in the context of reading as it initially occurs, by going back and forth between reading portions of text, and discussing ideas encountered in the text.

Text is read and the teacher stops the reading at certain points and poses questions to initiate discussion. We provide an illustration of how QtA plays itself out in a classroom. Below is an excerpt from a social studies textbook used in a sixth-grade class about manor life during the Middle Ages. Following the excerpt is a transcript of a classroom lesson as it unfolded.

> Around A.D. 800 a system called feudalism was put to use. This system mandated that people behave in particular ways. Manors were so large that many people never had to leave them their entire lives. The manors were made up of villages which were inhabited by people who provide everything they needed to live right on the manor. Because of this there was no need for money.

Ms. L: OK. So what has the author told us about these manors?

Anna: That everything was there for you. But I just want to say that before [earlier in the text] they said that the economy was decreasing. So was that maybe because they didn't, like, have any money and never really had to leave a manor in your whole life?

As shown, the teacher began with an open-ended query designed to elicit a characterization of manors. Notice that Anna not only portrays an important feature of manors, but also proposes a connection to prior text. This illustrates that students in this classroom were quite accustomed to producing thoughtful responses to queries. They were adept at making connections to earlier readings and portions of text, as they had been engaged with QtA for some time. Let's continue:

Ms. L: Did everybody hear Anna?

Kathy: Can you say that again, Anna? [Anna repeats her comment]

Ms. L: Okay, did they say the economy decreased?

Student: It was altered.

Ms. L: Altered, which means what?

Students: Change.

Ms. L: But what do you think about Anna's question that not having money might be connected with that economy change?

The teacher has quickly cleared up a confusion between *decreased* and *altered* and then moves right back to the important concept that Anna has raised.

LAUREN: I agree with her because you wouldn't have trade if you didn't use money.

Lauren is referring to discussion of earlier text that explains that trade as a source of power declined in the Middle Ages. Notice now how the teacher poses queries that encourage students to elaborate on Lauren's line of discussion about trade.

MS. L: So now there's not this trade? So what happens when you don't trade goods?

NICK: You don't trade ideas or goods or anything.

MS. L: So what happens when you don't trade ideas?

The teacher pounces on Nick's wonderful insight that ideas wouldn't be traded either. Nick provided the teacher with an opening for a major idea she wanted students to consider: the insularity of the manors and its effects.

LEAH: Well, people will kinda stay stupid because they wouldn't have any other different ideas.

MS. L: We don't want to stay stupid. So how does that connect to what Nick said?

TYLER: I think they're kind of connected because they're all like the same thing. People just don't really have smart new ideas.

Leah's and Tyler's responses indicate that students are extending the notion of insularity to its effects on the spread of ideas in a society.

MS. L: Smart new ideas. Hmm . . . Nick?

NICK: I think intelligence equals power.

MS. L: Intelligence equals power. Okay, keep that thought in mind as we read on about life in the Middle Ages.

The students had integrated features of life on the manor with the broader economic situation they had read about earlier. These understandings will serve them well as they read further about the social and political developments of the period in history.

Now we discuss specific features of QtA below and comment about changes we made over the years.

Text

QtA was designed to be and has been successfully used with both informational and narrative texts. This includes social studies textbooks, as shown earlier, science textbooks, basal reading selections both fiction and nonfiction, novels, short stories, informational articles, poems, and more. It is especially useful for challenging texts. This is because reading portions of texts that are interspersed with questions that prompt short discussions can untangle difficult portions of text. We discuss interspersed reading toward the end of this chapter.

Discussion

The activity structure used for developing meaning is short discussion of what is read. Classroom discussion is certainly not a new idea. But the purpose for discussion that we derived from QtA and the kind of interactions students engage in during discussion depart from what perhaps is conventionally viewed as classroom discussions. Classroom discussions are typically characterized by students sharing ideas after they have already read a text and formulated their own thoughts and opinions about what the text says. The goal of the kind of discussion that we propose is to assist students in the process of understanding what the text says. Therefore, as mentioned earlier, discussion takes place in the course of reading the text for the first time so students can share in the experience of learning how to develop comprehension.

Perhaps one of the ways to best understand discussion in the service of gist comprehension, and other kinds of discussions, is to encourage the teacher to be actively involved, as exemplified by Ms. L in the transcript on pages 16–17. This is different from a discussion in which a teacher sets a discussion in motion and the students explore an issue with little teacher involvement. In contrast, in the kind of discussion that we propose for the first read, the teacher is right in there the whole time, as a facilitator, guide, initiator, and responder. However, after gist comprehension has been established, we are very much in favor of broader and deeper discussion in which the teacher plays, at most, a minor role.

Queries[3]

As we already have mentioned, the value of a question depends on the role within a text of the information tapped by the question. As another example, given a story about a young boy who rides the rails from Virginia to California, the role of the question "What did we find out [from a portion of the text just read] about how the boy is getting across the country?" is important because it tells how the boy expects to achieve his goal. On the one hand, the question, "What did the boy take with him?" may well not be important for comprehension, if the response connects to nothing else in the text. On the other hand, what the boy takes with him may be central to the gist if the boy was able to barter for food that he needed with a small tarpaulin he had taken. Thus a major characteristic of a query is that it taps information that is important to the gist of a text.

In QtA lessons the interaction of text and discussion is accomplished through queries. Queries are text-based open (in contrast to closed or constrained) probes the teacher uses to initiate and develop discussion. The goal of queries is to prompt students to deal with the meaning of text ideas. These open questions were designed to make public the important idea in a text segment (e.g., "What's going on here?"; "How does all this connect with what we read earlier?").

Of course, students respond to these queries in a variety of ways. Sometimes what they say is sparse, or their response simply reiterates text words and it doesn't appear that there is understanding, so the teacher is encouraged to follow up. For example:

- If the student merely reports words from the text and it doesn't appear that there is understanding, the teacher might ask: "That's what the author said but tell us what the author meant by what he said?"
- If the student's response has some good kernels in it, but is incomplete, the teacher may say something like, "Can someone tell us more about that point?"
- To prompt thinking about how ideas relate to the text as a whole, the teacher may ask, "How does that fit in with what we've been talking about?"

---

[3]Queries *are* questions. But when we developed QtA, we thought that giving them a different label might inhibit some preconceived ideas of what questions are, especially tendencies to think of questions in taxonomic terms. In particular, we were concerned that some inferential questions are essential to understanding the gist of a text and literal questions are not equivalent to text-dependent questions.

The purpose of the follow-ups is not merely to invite student participation, but to move the discussion toward a meaningful goal. That is, engaging students shouldn't be directed solely toward participation, but toward engaging their processing so they are intentionally pursuing the goal of understanding.

We will talk more about queries in the next chapter, but for now it is important to know that queries are a key instructional tool in QtA discussions that assist students to comprehend text ideas.

Given the importance of building meaning as one reads, how does one get students to do that? How does one get students to become actively involved as they read, to dive into even difficult information and grapple to make sense of it? An important means is collaboration, which we discuss below.

Collaboration

Except when a student works alone, virtually every other classroom activity structure—partners, small group, whole class with teacher, or whole class with another leader—can facilitate collaboration. Our encouragment of a variety of activity structures is so students know that their voices are being heard and that they hear their peers' voices, as they grapple with text. To accomplish this, we have to involve students in thinking and talking. But besides their peers hearing their voices, we need to hear their voices to encourage their contributions, and urge them to wrestle with ideas. Students need to learn the power of collaborating with their peers and teachers in constructing meaning.

Consider an example of discussing and collaborating. Think of the last really good movie you went to. When you came out of the theater and headed to your cars with your friends, you were probably discussing the film, arguing with each other about what it really meant, offering reasons about why you liked it or did not, why it made you cry, what the true significance and message of the film was. Such interaction is natural and valuable in developing meaning. Students need to engage in these same kinds of interactions when they read, considering and reacting to their peers' ideas and supporting their own arguments.

Public grappling with text gives students the opportunity to hear from each other, to question and consider alternative possibilities, and to test their own ideas in a safe environment. Everyone is engaged in building meaning, and everyone understands that the author, not the teacher, has presented them with this challenge. The chance for cumulative misconceptions diminishes, and the opportunity for some authentic wrestling with ideas and meaningful discussion increases.

Responding to Students

In the kind of discussion we propose, the teacher has an important interactive role. Everyone contributes to the development of meaning during a lesson, including the teacher. The teacher has the important task of dealing with student responses in ways that highlight the aspects of what students say that contribute to meaning making. In doing so, teachers help students to both recognize and build on the aspects of their responses that are productive for comprehension. To accomplish this, teachers need to be particularly attentive to what students say and then consider how to use students' contributions to move the discussion productively.

Interspersed Reading

As mentioned in the beginning of this chapter, QtA takes place in the context of reading as it initially occurs by going back and forth between reading portions of text, and then discussing the ideas encountered. Text is read and the teacher stops the reading at certain points and poses questions to initiate discussion. This framework models for students that comprehension of text is an iterative process in which one takes in text and deals with the meaning of the ideas it offers, as they are offered. Reading doesn't mean reaching the end of a text by keeping one's mind on the words and then trying to think about what it said. Studies have demonstrated that readers deal with meaning in the course of reading. In fact they do so as soon as they have accessed meaning for the content word[4] upon which their eyes are fixating and before they start processing the next word. This is known as the immediacy assumption in which "readers attempt to integrate content words as soon as possible while fixating on the word they are processing" (Carpenter & Daneman, 1981, p. 158).

Thus, we teach students that readers should "take on" a text little by little and try to understand, while they are reading, what ideas are there and how they might connect or relate those ideas to what they've already read. We do this to simulate what a competent reader does in the course of reading. While you are reading, you are making sense of it as you go along, even though it may seem like one smooth seamless process. The reader does not hold up understanding until he or she has completed a section of text.

---

[4]In this context, content words refer to words that have meaning—nouns, verbs, adjectives, etc., virtually all word forms except articles, conjunctions, and prepositions.

Now let's consider what is often done in classrooms when teaching from a text. It is fairly typical teaching practice to assign material to be read and then to pose questions to evaluate student comprehension. This is basically an after-the-fact procedure. Because students are left on their own until reading is complete, this may not lead to productive reading for several reasons. First, students may have questions in their minds as they read or simply finish a text knowing only that they are lost but not sure why. Moreover, there is no way for teachers to know if some students have constructed misconceptions about the passage but think they have understood. Second, even though students hear "right" answers in after-reading questioning, they may never understand what makes them right. But in QtA the goal is to assist students to understand what a portion of text is about at the point of reading that portion for the first time.

There is older research that shows that there is advantage to intevening with questions during reading. Studies by Watts and Anderson (1971) and Rothkopf (1966, 1972) demonstrated that when students respond to questions during reading, their understanding of the text is stronger than it is if they read the text through.

Relatedly, Sandora, Beck, and McKeown (1999) compared the effects of two discussion techniques on students' comprehension and interpretation of complex literature. Sixth- and seventh-grade students in a school with a predominantly African American, lower socioeconomic status (SES) enrollment were involved in a study in which half of the students engaged in reading interspersed with short discussions prompted by open queries about portions of four selections from a Junior Great Books series. The other half of the students engaged in discussion of the same texts after the whole text was completed. In order to eliminate decoding and fluency issues all stories were read aloud.

At the completion of each text lesson students provided a free recall about what they remembered from the text and responded to questions for each story. Across all four stories, scores on both the recalls and responses to questions were higher for the students who participated in the query-prompted interspersed discussions than for those students who participated in the after-reading discussions. Further analyses revealed that students in the query-prompted, interspersed discussions provided longer recalls and the recalls included more of the complex story elements than students in after-reading discussions. Thus our findings are a pretty good assessment of comprehension unfettered from inadequate lower-level skills that can play havoc with comprehension.

IS INTERSPERSED READING THE ONLY WAY?

Of course not! But the question raises some important matters: Who reads first—the teacher or student/s? In what mode—aloud or independently? As we reviewed example lessons from such groups as Achieve the Core, the National Board of Certified Teachers, and other respectable groups, there did seem to be a favored sequence about who should read first. The preferred order is that (1) students read an entire text independently, and then (2) the teacher or a good reader reads the text aloud and students follow along in their texts. However, the option of reversing the two steps was offered, depending on the difficulty of a given text and teachers' knowledge of students.

The stated goal of those groups is to enable all students to interact with challenging text. We could not agree more with that goal. But beyond the option of having the teacher read first with the students following along, and then having students read the text independently, there are no suggestions about what to do to enable all students to interact with challenging text. Reversing the two steps above is not enough scaffolding. Indeed, the 2013 national reading results suggest that asking almost 60% of students to read challenging text independently is wishful thinking.[5] Although following along while a good reader reads is helpful, that is not enough scaffolding for many students.

The approach we present for reading segmented text with interspersed, open-query prompted discussion could contribute to much needed scaffolding. We have seen many teachers engage in various forms of segmented-interspersed reading. Sometimes teachers ask students to read a segment aloud; sometimes they ask students to read a segment independently; sometimes the teacher reads aloud; and there are other such activity structures. But after every segment the open-query prompted brief discussion makes the information public. From these public short discussions of text ideas—and *only* text ideas during the first read—those students who might not successfully read some segments independently are able to learn what's going on. As a result, they might not be left behind when they enter the next text segment. By making the text information public, poor readers can interact with challenging text.

---

[5]The most recent results available at this writing, those of the National Assessment of Educational Progress (NAEP) at fourth, eighth, and 12th grades report percentages proficient or above for each grade, respectively, of 42, 36, and 38 percent (National Center for Education Statistics, 2013).

CHAPTER 3

Queries and the Role They Play in Discussion

Queries are a driving force in helping students comprehend text ideas. Given the important role they play, we examine them in some detail in this chapter. We start, however, by clarifying a difference between the queries we present in this chapter and the original queries we published (Beck, McKeown, Hamilton, & Kucan, 1997). We do so because the original QtA queries have been discussed in other publications and are in use in some schools, so readers may still encounter them. Let's look at why we changed from an earlier version of the queries to the ones we offer in this book.

ORIGINAL QUERIES AND JUST-FOR-GIST QUERIES

When we developed QtA, close reading was not a priority in educational research or school environments, so we folded "close reading" analyses into our original queries for the first reading. For instance, our original queries for the novel *Tuck Everlasting* (Babbitt, 1985) included, "How is the author making you feel right now about [character]?" [More sympathetic to the character.] Here the query asks the students to go beyond the words to the message the author was communicating about the character. Now that close reading is part of the current landscape, we would bring up such a query in a second read and pursue it more fully by discussing what the author did—his word choices and the like—to encourage your sympathy.

Similarly, the query "So how does [the character] think things are going for her?" goes beyond a simple prediction question such as "What's going to happen?" The query implies taking the character's perspective to reflect on not only what might occur but on how the character is being affected by an ongoing or changing situation. Again, that kind of analysis belongs in *close reading* analyses, and should be dealt with in a second read.

Our recommendation—comprehension first, close reading second—is far from new, yet we have sensed from conversations with practitioners and some instructional materials on the Internet that this idea is not very clearly understood. Toward clarifying the matter, let's consider several issues. First, how can one consider an author's techniques that, for instance, provide a frightening mood, if one hasn't comprehended that the mood is tense and fearsome? Or how can a reader perceive that a particular word captures a character's disquieted demeanor, if the reader hasn't understood that that character was alarmed? Second, if close reading is as promising as we think it could be, it should be given more time and focus than simply being "folded in." Third, as we noted in the first chapter, let's not have another endeavor that competes with scaffolding surface comprehension—especially given that the 2013 NAEP showed that fourth, eighth, and 12th graders' comprehension to be 65%, 64%, and 62%, respectively, *below* proficient, respectively (National Center for Education Statistics, 2013). Fourth, beyond our own positive opinion of close reading, we have paid attention to other educated opinions, especially from two professors we referred to in Chapter 1: Jarrell Wright, who teaches close reading as part of a literary analysis course at the university level, and Timothy Shanahan, a reading researcher and educator. Both Wright and Shanahan clearly make the point that surface comprehension is the prerequisite to close reading. We strongly agree.

Close reading will be taken up in later chapters of this book. First we deal with just-for-gist queries.

DEVELOPING QUERIES FOR A NARRATIVE

Toward elaborating gist queries, we here provide a story and show how an experienced teacher thinks through the story for what students need to understand and develops queries to bring that information to the front.

The story "The Raven and the Whale" is an Inuit folktale, retold by Lawrence Millman (1987), among others, about a raven—an extravagant, self-interested character—who flies into a whale's belly. Inside he sees a woman tending a lamp, who tells him he can stay but never to touch the lamp. Eventually, even with the kindness and care the woman gives him, he touches the lamp and both the woman and the whale die. The raven makes his way to a village in which humans live and turns himself into a man. He boasts that he has killed a whale without using a harpoon. The villagers don't believe him, but eventually a herd of narwhales are sighted. The raven paddles to them in his kayak, which is knocked over and pierced by a narwhale's horns. When he dies he is turned back into a raven and eaten by one of the narwhales. "Thus did the mighty hunter die" twice.

Queries Are Open

A feature that distinguishes queries is their open characteristic. Here we provide the first five segments of "The Raven and the Whale" and the text-dependent open gist queries that an experienced teacher developed.

Text	Open queries
1. There was once a raven who by accident flew into the mouth of a big bow-headed whale. He flew right down the throat and ended up in the belly. There he saw a little house built of ribs and soft hides; a shabby little house, just like a human dwelling.	1. **How has the author started things off?**
2. Inside this house was a young woman minding a blubber lamp. "You may stay here as long as you like," she told him, "but you must never touch this lamp." For the lamp was the whale's heart.	2. **What has the author told us now?**
3. The raven decided to stay there for quite a while. The woman was very pleasant company. Likewise she did all the work. "Eat," she'd say, and offer him some fish, mussels, or crabs which the whale had swallowed. There would be more fish than he could eat in a dozen lifetimes.	3. **What kind of life is the whale having?** 3a. The teacher expected many students to respond "good," so she planned the follow-up query: **What's good about it?**

4. "Is there anything you would like?" the woman would ask him.
    "Yes," said the raven. "I would like to touch the lamp."
    "You must never, never touch the lamp," she told him.
    But this made the raven all the more curious. More than anything else, he wanted to touch that lamp. He gazed at it for long hours.
	4. **What's this all about?**
	
	4a. **What's the author doing here by giving us this little scene?**

5. And once, while the woman's back was turned, he walked up and pecked at it. Instantly the lamp went out and the woman fell down dead.	5. **What do you see going on here?**

Teacher's Thinking

Below we share the teacher's thinking that led her to develop the queries in the table above. The initiating query the teacher decided on was, "How has the author started things off?" Notice that the query doesn't ask, "What's the setting?" because in her experiences this question tended to draw one-dimensional answers, such as "in a whale." In contrast, the more open query of "How has the author started things off?" prompted students to put together the information in the first segment in their own words. Paraphrasing and synthesizing information are vital skills, so when there is an opportunity to ask a query that requires putting several pieces of information together, we take advantage of it.

The teacher's query for the second segment, "What has the author told us now?," was designed to bring forth the very important information that the lamp was the whale's heart and should never be touched. Again notice that the question requires bringing ideas together, rather than simply retrieving information, which could well be asked within a framework of traditional literal questions such as "What is the lamp?"

The query for the third segment is about the raven's present life, "What kind of life is the raven having?," and is meant to establish that the raven is enjoying living in the body of the whale. However, the teacher anticipated that students might respond by "good" so she planned the follow-up query: "What's good about it?"

The teacher's intention for the fourth query, "What's this all about?," is for students to see that the seeds of a problem have been presented. If students do not see that this portends an important conflict, the teacher planned to follow up with "What's the author doing here by giving us this little scene?" The purpose of the fifth query was to dramatize that "the plot thickens." The teacher planned to ask, "What do you see going on here?"

COMPARISON BETWEEN TYPES OF QUESTIONS AND TARGETED RESPONSES

Keep in mind that both constrained questions and open queries can be text-dependent. Thus the text-dependency characteristic does not deal with the nature of how a question is constructed. Most of the time open queries require students

Constrained questions	Open queries
1. **What is the setting?** (In a whale's belly.)	1. **How has the author started things off?** (A raven flew into a whale's belly where there was a little house.)
2. **What is the lamp?** (The whale's heart.)	2. **What has the author told us now?** (There was a woman who told the raven that he could stay, but not to touch the lamp because it was the whale's heart.)
3. **What does the lady do for the raven?** (She gives him lots of fish, mussels, and crabs to eat.)	3. **What kind of life is the raven having?** (Very good.) 3a. **What's good about it?** (The woman is pleasant and she gives him lots to eat.)

FIGURE 3.1. Constrained questions and open queries and resultant responses.

Questions	Responses
"As they started scrubbing, what came off?"	"Dirt"
"How have things turned out for Harry?"	"Good"
"The mole found a new what?"	"Home"
"The mitten will be colored like snow, so would be hard to what?"	"Find"
"Who needed the dress?"	"The duchess"
"Where did the wind blow the dress to?"	"A tree"

FIGURE 3.2. Examples of children's responses to constrained questions.

to paraphrase text language and often to synthesize text ideas—arguably the two most important comprehension skills. Figure 3.1 above enables a close-up comparison of the differences between constrained questions and open queries, and the resultant targeted responses.

All Text-Dependent Questions Are Not Created Equally

The differences in the kinds of responses young children give to constrained questions and open questions about read-alouds mirror what intermediate grades students did with "The Raven and the Whale" as seen on pages 26–27. The examples in Figure 3.2 above come from first graders engaging in read-alouds for *Harry the Dirty Dog* (Zion, 1956), *The Mitten* (Brett, 1996), and *Brave Irene* (Steig, 1986).

In contrast, the responses in Figure 3.3 also come from first graders listening to read-alouds and demonstrate the kind of responses that open queries prompt. In this case the responses were drawn from two of the same books as those used for responses in Figure 3.1.

Questions	Responses
"How does what Harry did fit in with what we already know about him?"	"He doesn't really want to get clean, he just wants to stay dirty."
"When the family looked out and said, 'There's a strange dog in the backyard,' why did they call Harry a strange dog?"	"Because when he got all dirty, his family didn't know who he was."
"What's Harry up to now?"	"He decided to dig a hole and get the brush so he could wash, and then they would know him."
"They called Harry 'this little doggie.' What does that tell us?"	"That means that they don't know that it's their doggie. They don't know its name, so they just call him little doggie."
"It says that 'the mitten swelled and bulged, but Baba's good knitting held fast.' What does that mean?"	"That it was strong, and she's a good knitter."
"What do you think Baba meant when she said, 'If you drop one in the snow you'll never find it'?"	"The gloves are the same color as the snow. That if you drop it in the snow it's colored like snow."
"What happened when the bear sneezed?"	"All the animals were pushed out of the mitten and they ran away."

FIGURE 3.3. Examples of children's responses to open queries.

DEVELOPING QUERIES FOR EXPOSITORY TEXTS

As we noted in Chapter 2, QtA was designed to be and has been successfully used with both narrative and expository texts. (We use "expository text" and "information text" synonymously.) Expository texts are those that transmit new information and discuss new topics and ideas (Black, 1985). In fact the impetus to develop QtA was both our observations and teachers' reports of the difficulty students had with understanding their social studies textbooks. Toward understanding the problem, we engaged in in-depth analyses of several social studies textbooks (Beck, McKeown, & Gromoll, 1989). Among the problems for students is that the books are crammed with facts, but there is a paucity of explanations. Our view of explanations echoes Hallden's (1986) point that facts must be interpeted and given meaning if they are to serve as elements in an explanation. Of course, the teacher is the primary source of explaining and discussing facts. But students do use these textbooks, and the overall message applies to both oral and printed discourse. That is, for effective learning to occur, instruction should help students develop a model of the situation that is the target of instruction. It is not enough to give students the facts; discourse should promote the building of ideas.

For expository text, we start thinking about a text lesson by articulating the major understandings that we want students to take away from the lesson. In the next section we share what an experienced teacher wanted her students to understand at the end of the lesson.

Major Understanding

The teacher was discussing the events surrounding Britain's passage of the Stamp Act and wanted students to understand that this represented a turning point in relations between Britain and the American colonies; the colonists didn't think the British Parliament had a right to tax them, and the concept of "no taxation without representation" came upon the scene. The rift with Britain widened as the colonists worked together across the colonies in protest.

We should mention two important points about queries and history texts before we look at those used for the Stamp Act text. First, given the narrative nature of history, the type of queries we use are the same as those we offer for stories. And as mentioned earlier, our first iteration of queries were for history texts. Second, you will notice that the ratio of queries to text is higher for this expository text book selection. That's because so many important ideas were merely touched upon, a problem often found in textbooks. As such we interrogate most of them toward getting the basic facts established. Were the text complete with the details needed to understand the situation, the ratio of queries to text would be lower.

Below, we provide several paragraphs about events along the route to the colonists initiating the Revolutionary War, and the queries for each text segment. The text comes from the history section of a fifth-grade social studies book.

Text	Queries
1. **A New Tax for the Colonies.** After the French and Indian War ended in 1763, Britain was having financial difficulties. The war had been expensive. So the British came up with a plan to make money by taxing the colonists. There had been taxes on the colonists before, but most of them had not been enforced. Britain just didn't collect the money.	1. **What has the author given us so far?** 1a. **What's going on with the British?**
2. The idea of taxes made sense to the British. Since the French and Indian War had taken place in the colonies, they thought the colonists should help pay for it. The colonists did not see it this way. They thought they had	2. **What's going on between Britain and the colonies?**

paid enough. Many colonists had fought and
died in the war.

3. Besides, the colonists didn't think that the British Parliament had the right to tax them for purchases they made inside the colonies. Parliament is Britain's law-making body, and the colonists were not represented in Parliament.	**3. What did we learn about Parliament?** **3a. What was the problem?** **3b. What was it about Parliament that made the colonists feel that way?** **3c. What does it mean to be represented in a law-making body?**
4. In 1765, the British government passed the Stamp Act, which put a new tax on printed materials. They made everyone who bought things like newspapers, calendars, and marriage licenses, even playing cards, buy a special tax stamp. The colonists became very angry over this tax. The list of items to be taxed was six pages long.	**4. What did we learn about this new tax?** **4a. What did the colonists think of this new tax?**
5. **Colonists Protest.** The colonists began to act against the tax. They decided they would rather do without things than pay Britain. They organized a boycott of British goods. A boycott means people refused to buy anything made in Britain.	**5. Now, what's going on with the colonists?** **5a. How does that connect to what we read about the taxes?**
6. Not buying British goods caused hardship for the colonists. They had to do without many items, or make their own. But even though the clothes they made themselves were not as nice as they could buy from Britain, the colonists believed it was worth it.	**6. The text states that not buying British goods caused hardship for the colonists. So what do you think it means that they would make all this trouble for themselves?**

Teacher's Thinking

The teacher's thinking about queries interacts with her thinking about where to
stop reading and initiate discussion. At the first stop, the teacher began with a
general query to get the information on the table: "What has the author given us
so far?" The teacher also wanted students to understand that Britain was going
to enforce taxes, which they hadn't done before, so she asked, "What's going on
with the British?" The second stop was to help students glimpse the conflict that

is developing before the complication of "taxation without representation" comes in, so she asked, "What's going on between Britain and the colonies?"

At the third stop, to make sure students understand a "law-making body" and that this is located in Britain, she asked, "What did we learn about Parliament?" and "What was the problem?" To move students beyond just repeating text phrases, the teacher thought a follow-up question might be needed, such as "What was it about Parliament that made the colonists feel that way?" And to help students connect the idea of representation with electing officials, "What does it mean to be represented in a law-making body?"

The teacher's fourth query was "What did we learn about this new tax?" Having taught the Stamp Act text in previous years, the teacher wanted to reduce students' tendencies to simply reiterate the difficulty caused by this law, so she used a follow-up question to connect the boycott to the feelings about the taxes: "What did the colonists think of this new tax?"

To establish the basics of a boycott and its relationship to taxes, at the fifth segment the teacher asked, "Now what's going on with the colonists?" and "How does that connect to what we read about the taxes?" To emphasize that the boycott was a sacrifice to the colonists, at the sixth segment her query was, "The text states that not buying British goods caused hardship for the colonists. What do you think it means that they would make all this trouble for themselves?"

TRANSFER

Getting students to transfer what they have learned during instruction to real-life situations is the goal of instruction. This explains why the anecdote below is one of our favorites.

A fifth-grade class, whose language arts and social studies teachers had implemented QtA, was in a science class, in which QtA had not been implemented. While pairs of students were silently reading two pages that the teacher had assigned, one member of a pair blurted out "I don't get this." And another responded, "Yeah. What's this dude trying to tell us?"

We were elated by the comment because the students did what all teachers want them to do. The first student recognized that he wasn't understanding what he was reading, and the other offered a tool to dig into what was not being understood—a just-for-gist-query. In this case it was a functional version of "What's the author telling us?"

CHAPTER 4

Just the Gist
Developing Instruction
for Basic Comprehension

A gain we want to raise the point that we have made in previous chapters: comprehension of a text is prerequisite to engaging in close reading of that text—but this does not imply just any comprehension instruction. Valencia and Wixson (2013) note the importance of educators' "ability to carefully *craft* instruction" (p. 184; emphasis ours). Toward that goal, in this chapter we model and discuss how we developed comprehension instruction for gist or surface comprehension for two texts, one narrative and one informational.

Our objective for this chapter is that your engagement with the procedures that follow will provide you with facility in developing good comprehension instruction. What's more, the lessons provided are complete plans for the first read (gist comprehension)[1] for *Alice's Adventures in Wonderland* (hereafter *Alice in Wonderland*; Carroll, 1865) and "Black Death" (Callahan, 2013).[2]

FOUR STEPS IN PLANNING A COMPREHENSION LESSON

In this section we discuss each step in planning a comprehension lesson and then apply the steps to the two texts in this chapter. The steps are as follows:

---

[1]Note also that in Chapter 5 we provide some general suggestions about close reading, and in Chapter 6 we provide specific close reading activities for the two texts used in this chapter.

[2]Copies of the *Alice and Wonderland* and "Black Death" selections, and all other texts included in Part One of this book for students to engage with, can be found in the Appendix for duplication and distribution.

1. Read the story carefully.
2. List important content.
3. Develop queries.
4. Segment the text.

Step 1: Read the Story Carefully

Planning for any text-based lesson always begins with reading the text carefully. One reason for doing this, of course, is to know the content and identify important ideas and events necessary for students to comprehend the text. But another reason is so the teacher can anticipate potential problems in the text that could get in the way of his or her students' comprehension and plan how to scaffold such matters.

As adult skilled readers, we don't usually have problems comprehending a text, even if it is poorly written. We are skilled at making inferences about ideas not explicitly stated and making connections among ideas in a text. For the most part we do these things with little overt attention, but in order to anticipate and plan for problematic portions of a text, teachers need to predict where students are most likely to have trouble.

Reading to anticipate problems students may have understanding a text means being aware of parts of the text that are potentially difficult. One way to develop that awareness is to read the text and consciously monitor your comprehension, noticing when you're doing extra work. This might mean having to reread a portion of text, or stopping to think about how one idea follows from another. Teachers who find themselves going off "automatic pilot" when they read (i.e., doing extra work) can be reasonably confident that their students will also have to do extra work.

Composition teachers often talk about the importance of being aware of your audience. We suggest that a way to operationalize "being aware of your audience" is to bring several students to mind as you read. For example:

"Some students, especially Loretta, will be overwhelmed with the long sentences. I'll have to model reading some sentences and have students read with me."

"Nehemiah is one of the few students who might immediately understand that the material in parenthesis is the narrator's voice."

"I bet a number of students will not understand that Alice's adventures take place when she is dreaming."

Keep these ideas in mind as you read the story below.

Alice in Wonderland[3]
by Lewis Carroll

Alice was beginning to get very tired of sitting by her sister on the bank, and of having nothing to do: once or twice she had peeped into the book her sister was reading, but it had no pictures or conversations in it, 'and what is the use of a book,' thought Alice 'without pictures or conversations?' So she was considering in her own mind (as well as she could, for the hot day made her feel very sleepy and stupid), whether the pleasure of making a daisy-chain would be worth the trouble of getting up and picking the daisies.

Suddenly a White Rabbit with pink eyes ran close by her. There was nothing so VERY remarkable in that; nor did Alice think it so VERY much out of the way to hear the Rabbit say to itself, 'Oh dear! Oh dear! I shall be late!' (when she thought it over afterwards, it occurred to her that she ought to have wondered at this, but at the time it all seemed quite natural); but when the Rabbit actually TOOK A WATCH OUT OF ITS WAISTCOAT-POCKET, and looked at it, and then hurried on, Alice started to her feet, for it flashed across her mind that she had never before seen a rabbit with either a waistcoat-pocket, or a watch to take out of it and burning with curiosity, she ran across the field after it, and fortunately was just in time to see it pop down a large rabbit-hole under the hedge.

Alice started after the rabbit, never once considering how in the world she was to get out again. The rabbit-hole went straight on like a tunnel for some way, and then dipped suddenly down, so suddenly that Alice had not a moment to think about stopping herself before she found herself falling down a very deep well. Either the well was very deep, or she fell very slowly, for she had plenty of time as she went down to look about her to make out what she was coming to, but it was too dark to see anything. Then she looked at the sides of the well, and noticed that they were filled with cupboards and book-shelves; here and there she saw maps and pictures hung upon pegs. She took down a jar from one of the shelves as she passed; it was labeled 'ORANGE MARMALADE', but to her great disappointment it was empty: she did not like to drop the jar for fear of killing somebody, so managed to put it into one of the cupboards as she fell past it.

Down, down, down. Would the fall NEVER come to an end! 'I wonder how many miles I've fallen by this time?' she said aloud. 'I must be getting somewhere near the center of the earth. Let me see: that would be four thousand miles down, I think—' (for, you see, Alice had learnt several things of this sort in her lessons in the schoolroom, and though this was not a VERY good opportunity for showing off her knowledge, as there was no one to listen to her, still it was good practice to say it over) '—yes, that's about the right distance—but then I wonder what Latitude or Longitude I've got to?'

---

[3]There are many versions of *Alice in Wonderland* that are retold from the original story by Lewis Carroll. We use Carroll's original version here. From quantitative and qualitative analyses, this text falls into the seventh- to eighth-grade band.

(Alice had no idea what Latitude was, or Longitude either, but thought they were nice grand words to say.)

Presently she began again. 'I wonder if I shall fall right THROUGH the earth! How funny it'll seem to come out among the people that walk with their heads downward! I shall have to ask them what the name of the country is. Please, Ma'am, is this New Zealand or Australia?' (and she tried to curtsey as she spoke—fancy CURTSEYING as you're falling through the air! Do you think you could manage it?) 'And what an ignorant little girl she'll think me for asking! No, it'll never do to ask: perhaps I shall see it written up somewhere.'

Down, down, down. There was nothing else to do, so Alice soon began talking again. 'Dinah'll miss me very much to-night, I should think!' (Dinah was the cat.) 'I hope they'll remember her saucer of milk at tea-time. Dinah my dear! I wish you were down here with me! There are no mice in the air, I'm afraid, but you might catch a bat, and that's very like a mouse, you know. But do cats eat bats, I wonder?' And here Alice began to get rather sleepy, and went on saying to herself, in a dreamy sort of way, 'Do cats eat bats? Do cats eat bats?' and sometimes, 'Do bats eat cats?' for, you see, as she couldn't answer either question, it didn't much matter which way she put it.

She felt that she was dozing off, and had just begun to dream that she was walking hand in hand with Dinah, and saying to her very earnestly, 'Now, Dinah, tell me the truth: did you ever eat a bat?' when suddenly, thump! thump! down she came upon a heap of sticks and dry leaves, and the fall was over. Alice was not a bit hurt, and she jumped up in a moment. She looked up, but it was all dark overhead; before her was another long passage and the White Rabbit was still in sight, hurrying down it. Away went Alice like the wind and was just in time to hear it say, as it turned a corner, "Oh, my ears and whiskers, how late it's getting!" She was close behind it when she turned the corner, but the Rabbit was no longer to be seen.

She found herself in a long, low hall, which was lit up by a row of lamps hanging from the roof. There were doors all 'round the hall, but they were all locked; and when Alice had been all the way down one side and up the other, trying every door, she walked sadly down the middle, wondering how she was ever to get out again. Suddenly she came upon a little table, all made of solid glass. There was nothing on it but a tiny golden key, and Alice's first idea was that this might belong to one of the doors of the hall; but, alas! either the locks were too large, or the key was too small, but, at any rate, it would not open any of them. However, on the second time 'round, she came upon a low curtain she had not noticed before, and behind it was a little door about fifteen inches high. She tried the little golden key in the lock, and to her great delight, it fitted!

Step 2: List Important Content

At this step we think about the content of the story that is important for developing a coherent representation of the gist and jot down those items. You might want to try it for this story, but you will also have another opportunity in Chapter 7. The list should include both content taken directly from the text as well as ideas not explicitly stated in the text.

Our list follows, but be aware that usually no two lists are exactly the same, either in content or wording. By comparing your list with ours, you may find on second view that you included something that does not actually contribute to the gist of the story. On the other hand, you may well find some items that you think should be included, although we did not. Just keep in mind that it is just the gist that we want to identify during the first read. Here is our list of important content:

1. Alice, sitting on a bank with sister, is bored.
2. A talking rabbit appears.
3. Alice runs after rabbit and follows it down a hole.
4. Alice tries to figure out her location.
5. Alice's concern for her cat.
6. Alice lands in a hall with doors all around.
7. Alice finds key that opened a little door.

Take a moment to note that text information can be recast as a summary statement. As an example, the fourth item on our list was derived from the following information from the story:

> 'I must be getting somewhere near the center of the earth. Let me see: that would be four thousand miles down, I think—yes, that's about the right distance—but then I wonder what Latitude or Longitude I've got to?'—

That information can then be recast in a summary statement: "Alice tries to figure out her location."

Step 3: Develop Queries

The next step is to develop queries that will bring out the content in your list. Sometimes there will be places where it is necessary to address more than one issue or draw attention to more than one idea at a single stop. It is fine to ask one or two more queries that address additional ideas at the same stop. The key is to include queries that tap all of the ideas from your content list. Below we present the important content we identified for *Alice in Wonderland* and the queries we developed to bring the content to the front. Please look at it carefully. What do you think about our choices?

Content to be questioned	Questions/targeted responses
1. Alice, sitting on a bank, is bored.	1. **What did we learn about Alice?** (She is sitting on a bank and doesn't have anything to do.)
2. Talking rabbit appears and Alice doesn't think it unusual.	2. **Now, what happened?** (A talking rabbit ran past Alice.) 2a. **At first what did Alice think about the rabbit?** (It was not unusual that the rabbit could talk.)
3. Alice follows rabbit down hole, remains nonchalant as she falls.	3. **What's Alice up to?** (She runs after the rabbit and follows it down a hole.) 3a. **How does Alice seem to be feeling as she keeps falling down?** (She seems fine. She is calm.) 3b. **What does this tell us about Alice?** (She's not afraid.)
4. Alice tries to figure out where she is located and narrator tells about some things related to location that she learned in school.	4. **What is Alice thinking about as she is falling?** (Where on the earth she is located.) 4a. **What does the narrator tell us?** (What she learned in school and wanted to practice.) 4b. **Alice says, that if she kept digging to the center of the earth she might come out "among the people that walk with their heads downward!" Why might Alice think that?** *We offer the following explanation as needed:* (Maybe she thinks that when you dig down to the bottom center of the earth, and then go up from the center on the other side, everything is opposite, and that would mean the people walk opposite from us which would be on their hands.)
5. Alice thinks about and is worried about her cat.	5. **What is Alice thinking in this section?** (She is worried about her cat and hoping someone will remember to give her milk.)
6. Alice lands in a hall with locked doors.	6. **What happened to Alice?** (She landed in a long, low hall with locked doors all around the hall.) 6a. **What's going on with the white rabbit at the end of this section?** (It turned a corner and Alice could no longer see it.)
7. She tries and then finds a key that opens a door.	7. **What's Alice up to in this section?** (She came across a key that opened a little door.)

7a. **How does this section connect with what we know about Alice?**

(She's curious and not afraid.)

7b. **What makes you say that?**

(Although she is in a strange place, she doesn't seem to be bothered.)

Developing a Map of the Gist from Queries and Responses

An appropriate set of responses to queries should enable the development of a map of the gist of the story. As a way of checking whether a set of queries has tapped the important information in a story and produced a coherent representation, you can see whether appropriate responses to the queries when strung together form a brief synopsis of the gist. The content for a map uses the targeted responses, any information in a query because when the teacher asks a query that information is public, and small transitions added to make the map grammatical. We strung targeted responses, information from queries, and some small transitions into paragraph form to emphasize that the content does provide a map of the gist.

Gist Map for Alice in Wonderland

Alice was sitting on a bank and didn't have anything to do. Suddenly, a talking rabbit ran past her. She ran after the rabbit and followed it down a hole. While Alice was falling down the hole, she had many thoughts including trying to use the information she learned in school to figure out her location on earth. She thought about her cat while falling and hoped that someone would remember to give Dinah her milk. Alice finally landed in a long hall. She searched to find an unlocked door and eventually found a key that unlocked a little door.

Step 4: Segment the Text

By segmenting, we mean determining where to stop reading to ask a query. In segmenting, it is important that content drives decisions about where to stop reading and start discussions, not necessarily paragraph breaks in a text or where the text ends on a page. Sometimes a single sentence needs attention because the information it presents is key to developing comprehension. In other cases, a series of paragraphs can be dealt with all at once because there's not much of importance in the paragraphs or because the paragraphs are all about the same idea.

Below we provide our segmented version of *Alice in Wonderland*. Each text segment is shown on the left, and the numbers indicate where we suggest stopping the reading. On the right *in italics* is our explanation for why we stop at this point in each segment (i.e., to prompt discussion or ask queries).

Text segment	Explanation for stopping
Alice was beginning to get very tired of sitting by her sister on the bank, and of having nothing to do: once or twice she had peeped into the book her sister was reading, but it had no pictures or conversations in it, 'and what is the use of a book,' thought Alice 'without pictures or conversations?' So she was considering in her own mind (as well as she could, for the hot day made her feel very sleepy and stupid), whether the pleasure of making a daisy-chain would be worth the trouble of getting up and picking the daisies. **1**	**1** *This is a good place to stop as the students are immediately confronted with Carroll's long sentences and his technique of placing the narrator's voice in parentheses. The content is not difficult, it just sets the scene, but here at the beginning of the story students need to learn who talks in the parentheses, and hear and practice reading the long sentences. Toward that end, you read the first paragraph and ask the first query. Then ask students to locate the parentheses and to read the words aloud. Ask who is talking (a narrator). As needed, discuss what a narrator is. Then tell students that you will reread the first paragraph and they should follow along, but when you get to the parentheses, the words are the narrator's voice and they should read those words aloud. Then switch: have the group read the straight text and you read the narrator's words.*
Suddenly a White Rabbit with pink eyes ran close by her. There was nothing so VERY remarkable in that; nor did Alice think it so VERY much out of the way to hear the Rabbit say to itself, 'Oh dear! Oh dear! I shall be late!' (when she thought it over afterwards, it occurred to her that she ought to have wondered at this, but at the time it all seemed quite natural); but when the Rabbit actually TOOK A WATCH OUT OF ITS WAISTCOAT-POCKET, and looked at it, and then hurried on, Alice started to her feet, for it flashed across her mind that she had never before seen a rabbit with either a waistcoat-pocket, or a watch to take out of it and burning with	**2** *There are two important ideas in this paragraph. First, the appearance of the talking rabbit, although strange, is clear. Second, Alice is not surprised that the rabbit speaks, which introduces students to Alice's fascinating mind.*

curiosity, she ran across the field after it, and fortunately was just in time to see it pop down a large rabbit-hole under the hedge. **2**

Alice started after the rabbit, never once considering how in the world she was to get out again. The rabbit-hole went straight on like a tunnel for some way, and then dipped suddenly down, so suddenly that Alice had not a moment to think about stopping herself before she found herself falling down a very deep well. Either the well was very deep, or she fell very slowly, for she had plenty of time as she went down to look about her to make out what she was coming to, but it was too dark to see anything. Then she looked at the sides of the well, and noticed that they were filled with cupboards and book-shelves; here and there she saw maps and pictures hung upon pegs. She took down a jar from one of the shelves as she passed; it was labeled 'ORANGE MARMALADE', but to her great disappointment it was empty: she did not like to drop the jar for fear of killing somebody, so managed to put it into one of the cupboards as she fell past it. **3**

Down, down, down. Would the fall NEVER come to an end! 'I wonder how many miles I've fallen by this time?' she said aloud. 'I must be getting somewhere near the center of the earth. Let me see: that would be four thousand miles down, I think—' (for, you see, Alice had learnt several things of this sort in her lessons in the schoolroom, and though this was not a VERY good opportunity for showing off her knowledge, as there was no one to listen to her, still it was good practice to say it over) '—yes, that's about the right distance—but then I wonder what Latitude or Longitude I've got to?' (Alice had no idea what Latitude was, or Longitude either, but thought they were nice grand words to say.)

Presently she began again. 'I wonder if I shall fall right THROUGH the earth! How funny it'll seem to come out among the people that walk with their heads downward! I shall have to ask them what the name of the country is. Please, Ma'am, is this New Zealand or Australia?' (and she tried to curtsey as she spoke—fancy CURTSEYING as you're falling

3 *Here, there are two important points. First, Alice is falling down a rabbit hole and doesn't want to drop the jar for fear of killing somebody— both clear ideas. Again, the reader is getting a glimpse into Alice's mind. Although Alice is falling, she doesn't seem to be afraid or to think that her predicament is anything out of the ordinary.*

4 *This section is a bit confusing, as random thoughts seem to float around Alice's mind as she is falling. Although the information is confusing, it gives the reader insight into Alice's character.*

through the air! Do you think you could manage it?)
'And what an ignorant little girl she'll think me for
asking! No, it'll never do to ask: perhaps I shall see
it written up somewhere.' **4**

She found herself in a long, low hall, which

Down, down, down. There was nothing else
to do, so Alice soon began talking again. 'Dinah
will miss me very much to-night, I should think!'
(Dinah was the cat.) 'I hope they'll remember her
saucer of milk at tea-time. Dinah my dear! I wish
you were down here with me! There are no mice in
the air, I'm afraid, but you might catch a bat, and
that's very like a mouse, you know. But do cats eat
bats, I wonder?' And here Alice began to get rather
sleepy, and went on saying to herself, in a dreamy
sort of way, 'Do cats eat bats? Do cats eat bats?'
and sometimes, 'Do bats eat cats?' for, you see, as
she couldn't answer either question, it didn't much
matter which way she put it. **5**

5 *This paragraph introduces Alice's relationship with her cat, Dinah.*

She felt that she was dozing off, and had just
begun to dream that she was walking hand in hand
with Dinah, and saying to her very earnestly, 'Now,
Dinah, tell me the truth: did you ever eat a bat?'
when suddenly, thump! thump! down she came
upon a heap of sticks and dry leaves, and the fall
was over. Alice was not a bit hurt, and she jumped
up in a moment. She looked up, but it was all dark
overhead; before her was another long passage and
the White Rabbit was still in sight, hurrying down it.
Away went Alice like the wind and was just in time
to hear it say, as it turned a corner, "Oh, my ears
and whiskers, how late it's getting!" She was close
behind it when she turned the corner, but the Rabbit
was no longer to be seen. **6**

6 *It's a good idea to stop here so students recognize that Alice's long drop has finally ended, and that she has lost sight of the rabbit.*

She found herself in a long, low hall, which
was lit up by a row of lamps hanging from the roof.
There were doors all 'round the hall, but they were
all locked; and when Alice had been all the way
down one side and up the other, trying every door,
she walked sadly down the middle, wondering how
she was ever to get out again. Suddenly she came
upon a little table, all made of solid glass. There was
nothing on it but a tiny golden key, and Alice's first
idea was that this might belong to one of the doors
of the hall; but, alas! either the locks were too large,

7 *From a literal perspective, this section is easy to understand— Alice is searching for an open door, doesn't find one, but does find a key that opens a door. However, a larger idea is that Alice does not seem to be afraid.*

or the key was too small, but, at any rate, it would not open any of them. However, on the second time 'round, she came upon a low curtain she had not noticed before, and behind it was a little door about fifteen inches high. She tried the little golden key in the lock, and to her great delight, it fitted! **7**

A CAVEAT

We have presented the four steps in planning as independent steps: (1) read the text carefully, (2) list important content, (3) develop queries for the important content, and (4) segment the text. Viewing them individually is clearer, but this is misleading because the steps are more integrated than we presented them. Many experienced teachers integrate Steps 1 and 2 as they are reading the text. Similarly they integrate Steps 3 and 4. Relating the queries to identifying segments is essential because one has to segment the text so that the material students need to respond to a query is available in the segment. One caution: when first developing queries and segments, teachers have a tendency to put the stop immediately after the material needed to respond to the query has been provided. As our stops and queries for *Alice in Wonderland* show, there is almost always more content in a segment than will be queried, and the content right before a stop is not necessarily what is queried. Remember that queries are used for the most important content that moves the ideas forward.

PLANNING A COMPREHENSION LESSON
FOR AN INFORMATIONAL TEXT

Informational texts, also known as expository texts, do what their label suggests—they inform readers, usually about new material. Although the structure of informational texts may be different from one text to another, they most often include *main ideas* and *details* that support those ideas. It is important to recognize that some authors spell out the main idea, but sometimes the reader needs to derive the main idea from the details the author provides. Additionally, *theories* and *evidence*, and the ways in which they are presented in a text, are important features of informational texts. Thus it is important to design activities that target these areas.

The text provided in this section is an informational selection about the bubonic plague, also known as the "Black Death." It describes the disease—what caused it, how it was transmitted, the lack of ways to cure it, and its spread across Europe and devastation to communities—and provides a historical account of its first appearance until its disappearance. The content of "Black Death" is informational, but its structure is narrative like many other historical accounts, and so the same four steps discussed for *Alice in Wonderland* apply to this text.

Step 1: Read the Story Carefully

Black Death[4]
by Janet Callahan

In 1347, a deadly disease swept across Europe. People did not know what caused it. They did not know how to treat it, either. As a result, 25 million people died within five years. About 40 percent of Europe's population was wiped out.

This terrible disease became known as the Black Death. This name suggests the fear that gripped Europe as the disease spread. It also describes the disease's most unmistakable sign: the black or dark purple spots that appeared on victims' bodies just before they died. The disease is also referred to as Bubonic Plague from swellings, called "buboes," that spread over the entire body.

Most experts believed the Black Death was caused by a germ called *Yersinia pestis*. In 2011, scientists studying centuries-old skeletons confirmed that the experts were right about this germ. The germ lived in the bodies of fleas that attached themselves to rats. In the 1300s, rats were a part of everyday life in the cities and villages of people's homes. Infected fleas that bit people passed the disease on to them. People could also catch the disease by coming in close contact with someone who had already fallen ill.

Historians have studied how Black Death germs arrived in Europe. Many believe the flea-ridden rats came from China to Europe on trade ships. Why do they think so? They know that just a few years before the Black Death struck Europe, the same deadly disease broke out in China. Historians think that the flea-ridden rats got aboard European trade ships that visited Chinese ports. When the ships returned to Europe, they brought the rats—with fleas on their bodies—with them.

There is a convincing piece of evidence for this theory. It is an account of an eyewitness from Sicily, an island in Europe off the coast of Italy in the Mediterranean Sea. According to this account, a fleet of trade ships arrived in Sicily in October 1347. Many of the ships' crewmen were already dead when the ships docked. Many more were sick with the disease. When the people of Sicily realized that the Black Death had reached their shores, they ordered the ships out of the harbor. This action came too late to save the people of Sicily, however. Within days, Sicilians began to come down with the disease.

Before long, the Black Death reached other cities along the Mediterranean coast. Historical documents record that the disease spread inland with terrifying speed. In

---

[4]"Black Death" is appropriate for the fourth and fifth grades. From Callahan (2013). Copyright 2013 by the International Reading Association. Reprinted by permission.

Europe it spread through France, Germany, Spain, and Portugal. It moved on to the British Isles and Scandinavia. It even reached the island of Greenland, near the North Pole, almost wiping out its population.

People felt helpless in the face of such a deadly disease. Although they did not know how to prevent the Black Death, they were willing to try almost anything. Some people washed walls and furniture and even their bodies with rose water or vinegar. Others tried to ward off the illness by wearing garlands of flowers. Many people believed they could stay healthy if they did not eat, drink, or exercise too much. None of these precautions worked. Although a tiny fraction of people who fell ill with the disease were able to recover, most died within a week after their first symptoms appeared.

People who practiced medicine in the 1300s did not know much about diseases or how to treat them. The Black Death was often treated with a warm preparation of butter, onion, and garlic applied to the skin, but it did not help. The most popular remedy of the time was bloodletting, or leeching. In this treatment, the doctor tried to get rid of a disease by taking blood from the patient's body. But this procedure had no effect on the Black Death.

The fear and panic that came with the Black Death was almost as destructive as the death toll. When the Black Death struck a town or village, those who were still healthy often fled for their lives. In the blink of an eye, a town would be left without its shop owners, craftsmen, and other workers. In this way, the Black Death wiped out whole communities.

By 1351, the Black Death had mostly vanished from Europe. In the next 150 years, there would be several more outbreaks of the disease, but none was as bad as the first. Yet fearful memories of the disease's first wave lingered for many years before Europeans finally believed that they had put the Black Death behind them for good.

Step 2: List Important Content

Here the task is to think about the content that is important to understanding the gist of this informational text and jot down those items. Here is our list:

1. Meaning of "Black Death" and symptoms of the disease.
2. Where disease originated and how transmitted to people.
3. Theory that flea-ridden rats on ships brought disease from China to Europe.
4. Proof of theory.
5. Disease spreads and kills many people.
6. People went to great lengths to try to avoid disease.
7. Doctors lacked knowledge and used strange remedies.
8. Disease wiped out communities and even when it had left, people were fearful for years.

Step 3: Develop Queries

Content to be questioned	Questions/targeted responses
1. Meaning of the Black Death and symptoms.	1. **What did we learn about the Black Death?** (It was a disease that killed a lot of people in Europe.)
	1a. **How did someone know if they were infected with the disease?** (They got dark black or purple spots and swellings, called "buboes," that spread over the entire body.)
2. Origin of disease and how transmitted to people.	2. **What new information did we learn about the Black Death?** (The germ that caused the disease lived in fleas and when fleas bit someone the person got infected.)
3. Disease came to Europe by flea-ridden rats on ships from China.	3. **How did Europe end up with this dreadful disease?** (Fleas attached themselves to rats, and rats on ships brought the disease to Europe.)
	3a. **Find the sentence that tells why people thought that the infected fleas came from China.** (. . . a few years before the Black Death struck Europe, the same deadly disease broke out in China.)
4. Proof for theory that rats on ships brought disease to Europe.	4. **How does the fleet's arrival in Sicily connect with the information in the previous paragraph?** (The ships' arrival supports the theory that rats on trade ships brought the disease to Europe. An eyewitness actually saw the ships come in with dead crewmen from the disease.)
5. Disease spreads rapidly and kills many people.	5. **Now, what is happening with the Black Death?** (It is spreading very rapidly and killing a lot of people. It almost wiped out Greenland.)
6. Lengths people went to try to avoid the Black Death with no results.	6. **What's going on with the people?** (They try anything to avoid getting the disease, including washing with rose water and wearing garlands of flowers.)
	6a. **How did their remedies work?** (Not well. Most still died.)
7. Doctors didn't know how to treat the disease and tried strange remedies.	7. **How does the information connect with what we just read?** (They didn't know how to treat it. So, they tried things like mixing butter, onion, and garlic and rubbing it on the skin, or trying to take blood from the patient's body.)

8. Black Death wiped out entire communities and kept people frightened for many years.

8. **What did we find out here?**
    (When the Black Death struck, people fled their towns. This wiped out many communities.)

8a. **What lasting effect did the Black Death have on the people of Europe?**
    (They remained fearful for many years and took a long time before they were able to put it behind them.)

Step 4: Segment the Text

Text segment	Explanation for stopping
In 1347, a deadly disease swept across Europe. People did not know what caused it. They did not know how to treat it, either. As a result, 25 million people died within five years. About 40 percent of Europe's population was wiped out. This terrible disease became known as the Black Death. This name suggests the fear that gripped Europe as the disease spread. It also describes the disease's most unmistakable sign: the black or dark purple spots that appeared on victims' bodies just before they died. The disease is also referred to as Bubonic Plague from swellings, called "buboes," that spread over the entire body. **1**	**1** *Students are introduced to the Black Death, what it is, and its symptoms. It's important to stop here so that students establish an understanding of this basic information.*
Most experts believed the Black Death was caused by a germ called *Yersinia pestis*. In 2011, scientists studying centuries-old skeletons confirmed that the experts were right about this germ. The germ lived in the bodies of fleas that attached themselves to rats. In the 1300s, rats were a part of everyday life in the cities and villages of people's homes. Infected fleas that bit people passed the disease on to them. People could also catch the disease by coming in close contact with someone who had already fallen ill. **2**	**2** *Here, students are provided with a theory about what caused the disease so it is important to stop to bring attention to the theory.*
Historians have studied how Black Death germs arrived in Europe. Many believe the flea-ridden rats came from China to Europe on trade ships. Why do they think so? They know that	**3** *This paragraph explains that the disease made its way to Europe from China. It also introduces the theory as to why historians believe that's how*

just a few years before the Black Death struck Europe, the same deadly disease broke out in China. Historians think that the flea-ridden rats got aboard European trade ships that visited Chinese ports. When the ships returned to Europe, they brought the rats—with fleas on their bodies—with them. **3**

the disease ended up in Europe. It's important for students to be able to identify theories and evidence, so this is a good place to stop to allow students to begin that work.

There is a convincing piece of evidence for this theory. It is an account of an eyewitness from Sicily, an island in Europe off the coast of Italy in the Mediterranean Sea. According to this account, a fleet of trade ships arrived in Sicily in October 1347. Many of the ships' crewmen were already dead when the ships docked. Many more were sick with the disease. When the people of Sicily realized that the Black Death had reached their shores, they ordered the ships out of the harbor. This action came too late to save the people of Sicily, however. Within days, Sicilians began to come down with the disease. **4**

4 *This is a good place to stop to allow students to work with the evidence presented here that supports the theory presented in the previous paragraph.*

Before long, the Black Death reached other cities along the Mediterranean coast. Historical documents record that the disease spread inland with terrifying speed. In Europe it spread through France, Germany, Spain, and Portugal. It moved on to the British Isles and Scandinavia. It even reached the island of Greenland, near the North Pole, almost wiping out its population. **5**

5 *The important, but simple, point to emphasize here is that the disease is spreading rapidly. However, this also is another place to draw attention to the idea of the importance of supporting evidence as historical documents support the idea that the disease spread rapidly.*

People felt helpless in the face of such a deadly disease. Although they did not know how to prevent the Black Death, they were willing to try almost anything. Some people washed walls and furniture and even their bodies with rose water or vinegar. Others tried to ward off the illness by wearing garlands of flowers. Many people believed they could stay healthy if they did not eat, drink, or exercise too much. None of these precautions worked. Although a tiny fraction of people who fell ill with the disease were able to recover, most died within a week after their first symptoms appeared. **6**

6 *Although this section is pretty simple to understand (the various things people tried in order to avoid getting the disease), it speaks to their panic and feelings of helplessness.*

People who practiced medicine in the 1300s did not know much about diseases or how to treat them. The Black Death was often treated with a warm preparation of butter, onion, and garlic applied to the skin, but it did not help. The most popular remedy of the time was bloodletting, or leeching. In this treatment, the doctor tried to get rid of a disease by taking blood from the patient's body. But this procedure had no effect on the Black Death. **7**

7 This section reinforces the frustration people had with the disease. Even the doctors didn't know how to treat it and tried some strange remedies. This concept might be difficult for students to grasp, as their experience with doctors is quite different—in most cases, their doctors know exactly what to do.

The fear and panic that came with the Black Death was almost as destructive as the death toll. When the Black Death struck a town or village, those who were still healthy often fled for their lives. In the blink of an eye, a town would be left without its shop owners, craftsmen, and other workers. In this way, the Black Death wiped out whole communities. By 1351, the Black Death had mostly vanished from Europe. In the next 150 years, there would be several more outbreaks of the disease, but none was as bad as the first. Yet fearful memories of the disease's first wave lingered for many years before Europeans finally believed that they had put the Black Death behind them for good. **8**

8 This section highlights an important concept—it wasn't just the disease itself that wiped out communities; it also was the fear of the disease. That point might be difficult for students to grasp, as most students are unfamiliar with the panic associated with such a deadly disease. It's also important to draw students' attention to the idea that the fear of such a deadly disease doesn't go away easily, so people feared the disease for many years.

Gist Map for "Black Death"

The Black Death was a disease that killed a lot of people in Europe. People knew they were infected with the disease when they got dark black or purple spots and swellings over the entire body. The germ that caused the disease came from fleas and people got infected if a flea bit them. Fleas attached themselves to rats, and rats on ships brought the disease to Europe. People thought the disease came from China because it had broken out there before the disease came to Europe. An eyewitness who saw a ship from China when it arrived in Sicily noticed some crewmen dead from the disease. The Black Death spread rapidly, even to Greenland. People tried to avoid the disease, including washing with rose water and wearing garlands of garlic. They didn't work. Doctors didn't know how to treat it and tried remedies that didn't work. People fled their towns when the disease arrived, so many communities were wiped out. It took a long time for people to put what happened behind them.

BEFORE ALL OF THE ABOVE!

Given the way we intentionally organized this book, this chapter (and all other chapters) start "ahead of the game." Specifically, we provided the texts to use. We did this because we wanted to explain planning with actual texts and start by modeling how we would plan for the first read. Then we would bring in other components, such as close reading, after we had modeled how to approach the first read. This is ahead of the game because we had already decided which texts to use—mostly challenging texts—and we did the analyses for establishing at which grade levels each text was appropriate. However, the first step a teacher must take when planning a text-based lesson is deciding what text he or she will use.

CHALLENGING TEXTS

The CCSS underscore the importance of making sure that students read challenging text. For example, one of three key shifts (changes from previous practices to Common Core practices) specifies that students engage in "regular practice with complex texts and their academic language" (*www.corestandards.org/other-resources/key-shifts-in-english-language-arts/*). As such, it is important that we provide some comments about identifying challenging material.[5]

Of course, one cannot think about designing lessons until a text has been identified. The Common Core provides a three-part model of the factors that need to be considered. It is often shown as a triangle-like graphic, with the three sides of the triangle of equal length. Each of the three sides is labeled with a dimension to be considered when determining complexity: quantitative, qualitative, and reader and task.

- Quantitative evaluation of text considers word and sentence length and word frequency, which are the features that have traditionally been measured in reading formulas. Lexile analyses have added other features, such as cohesion and word concreteness, and presently appear to be the quantitative measure most popular. Appendix A of the Common Core lists the major formulas. Most, if not all, of the formulas have computer programs that analyze texts.

---

[5]Appendix A of the CCSS has a lot of information and resources for obtaining quantitative information.

- Qualitative evaluation of text has to be done by a human, as consideration must be given to matters such as levels of meaning, text structure, language conventionality and clarity, and knowledge demands.
- Text and reader factors consider the reader (his or her skill, motivation, and knowledge). Task factors bring to bear the kind of tasks that teachers assign students to do in relation to text (e.g., what kinds of questions do they need to answer, how complex are the requirements students need to complete when writing from sources).

The Common Core has concluded that all three factors are of equal importance and need to come into play when identifying complex text and determining text appropriateness. Also, the CCSS make the point that "sometimes qualitative considerations will trump quantitative measures in identifying the grade band of a text" (CCSS Initiative, 2015, Appendix A, p. 8). We agree and offer a recent example.

"A Tribute to Dogs" (Vest, 1855) is a speech that we include in Part Two of this book. I (Cheryl) didn't yet know that its Lexile score was 1190L, which corresponds with ninth grade, when I successfully taught both gist comprehension and close reading to fourth-grade students!

Another issue that likely trumps quantitative analysis is whether a text is rich enough to be worthy of close reading. Are some of the sentences so complex as to require parsing them into parts? Is there sophisticated vocabulary? Is there something about the text's structure that relates to the theme? The mood? Does the tone of the story change from beginning to end? What aspects of the author's language made you aware that the tone changes throughout the text? Are there layers of meaning that should be further analyzed? Most importantly, keep in mind that not all texts are worthy of close reading. Don't try to find something when there is little to find.

Finally, we must acknowledge that the kind of work needed to identify appropriate texts is far from trivial, especially given everything else teachers are asked to do. There is, however, some help. Results of analyses of the quantitative dimension can be found on some websites. Look for the listing of quantitative measures in Appendix A of the Common Core and Google them for directions. Additionally, MetaMetrix has a large database of English fiction books that have been analyzed and have Lexile scores. Finally, commercial school publishing companies are likely to provide the information you need in their newer products. But a teacher will always have the responsibility to engage in qualitative analyses. Since reading a text is necessary to plan a lesson, qualitative features may emerge at that time. Qualitative assessments are not so hard to do and as one gains experience, we have found them easy to determine. Again, information about engaging in qualitative analyses is readily available in Appendix A of the Common Core document.

Careful judgment and available information from classroom experience with students make the teacher an excellent judge of the reader and the task.

WHO READS? WHEN? HOW?

The first thing that has to happen in a text-based lesson is to expose the content. That is, the teacher or student/s read the text, or a portion of the text, aloud or independently. We have already noted that with the CCSS initiative the preferred approach is for students to read an entire text independently, and then for the teacher to read it as the students follow along.

Our concerns about that routine stem from the legitimate worry that students who cannot read text independently will not make it to college or indeed through high school. But requiring that some students read a new text independently will not help those who are in most need of developing comprehension skills.

Because we recognize the importance of providing students with opportunities to read independently, as well as recognizing its limitations, we offer a couple of options that address both. First is to begin the selection by reading and discussing the text with the entire class, using the queries and designated stops. Then, after several segments of interspersed reading, divide the class into groups and give one student a copy of the gist queries and the text that has the segments marked and ask that student to act as facilitator. You also might place a couple of students in the role of recorder and have them jot down the important points made during the group's discussion. When you bring the class together, you can ask the recorder and remaining students in the group to report to the class what they discussed. In this manner, each group will be equipped to share their thoughts from the discussion and you can gauge their understanding of the text.

A second option is to provide students with opportunities to read independently. Again, we suggest that you begin reading and discussing the text with the entire class and then at some appropriate point (e.g., halfway through or with only a fourth of the text remaining) have students continue the reading independently. As with the small-group discussions, you might provide each student with the remaining queries and tell students that when they finish reading the group will come together and discuss their responses to the queries.

As a third option, you might provide students with another copy of the text and ask them to mark places of importance—say, by underlining—and points of confusion—say, with squiggly underlining. Since it is important for students to be able to recognize the important ideas in a text and to be aware of their confusion, providing students with opportunities to read and mark texts as suggested will support those goals. After students have read the text independently and either responded to the gist queries or marked the text on their own, have them share their ideas with the class. Again, this provides you with an opportunity to gauge their understanding of the text and you can make note of students who seemed to struggle and identify specific places that caused their confusion.

There are certainly some exceptions to the suggestion that an entire text be read all the way through, whether by teacher or student/s. For instance, in the case of a mystery, the impact of a surprise ending will be reduced. In the case of such texts as the "Gettysburg Address" and *Alice in Wonderland*, we certainly prefer that the texts are first read by the teacher.

Who reads and how much of a text is initially read needs to be considered in light of the nature of the text, as well as readers' reading skill. As we mentioned in Chapter 2, the notion of interspersed reading of segments that is interrupted for short discussion enables different configurations of oral or silent reading, and scaffolded or independent reading.

In the next chapter, we resume our discussion of close reading. In Chapter 6, we offer specific ideas for close reading activities for the two texts presented in Chapter 4, *Alice in Wonderland* and "Black Death."

CHAPTER 5

Close Reading
Gist to Grist

We start this chapter by looking at several definitions of *close reading* and then viewing an example of an accomplished writer engaging in close reading. We then pick up the importance of words for a writer as well as for a reader. Learning words from context is our next topic, followed by interrogating context toward revealing word meaning, which can be undertaken as a close reading activity. Next we provide examples of unpacking complex sentences, and end with a discussion of some literary techniques that may trigger close reading ideas.

WHAT IS CLOSE READING?

Shanahan explains that close reading places a "substantial emphasis on readers figuring out a high quality text." He further points out that the "figuring out" [should be done] "primarily by reading and discussing the text" (2012, p. 1).

Fisher and Frey point to the notion that "close reading is the practice of having students critically examine a text, especially through multiple readings" (2012, p. 179).

Burkins and Yaris (2013) characterize close reading as "rereading for the purpose of recognizing details and nuances of text that may go unnoticed during a cursory first read so that new understandings and insights may reveal themselves."

We consider all these views as valid and offer our own characterization of close reading as *the purposeful examination of text through multiple reads, and follow-up analytic analyses, that encourages readers to penetrate the text so that they become conscious of how authors use language to create works that are loved for decades, if not centuries.*

THE ART OF WRITING

Writing is one of the creative arts, and every art has its tools. Painting has the most obvious ones—paints, brushes, and the like—but writing has its tools too (and not just pencils and pens!). Words, punctuation, sentences, and text structure are examples of writers' tools. The importance of words to writing is highlighted in Francine Prose's (2006) wonderful book, *Reading like a Writer*, where she asserts that "all the elements of good writing depend on the writer's skill in choosing one word instead of another. And what grabs and keeps our interest has everything to do with those choices" (p. 16).

Prose emphasizes the importance of slowing down when reading and cautions that, if a reader doesn't, he or she will miss the author's techniques that contribute to a masterpiece or just an ordinary book. She then asks us to consider the wealth of information provided by the first paragraph of Flannery O'Connor's short story "A Good Man Is Hard to Find" (1953). Here we will look at just the first sentence and what Prose learns from that sentence.

> The grandmother didn't want to go to Florida. . . .

> The first simple declarative sentence could hardly be more plain: subject, verb, infinitive, preposition. There is not one adjective or adverb to distract us from the central fact. But how much is contained in these eight little words!
>
> Here, as in the openings of many stories and novels, we are confronted by one important choice that a writer of fiction needs to make: the question of what to call her characters. Joe, Joe Smith, Mr. Smith? Not, in this case, Grandma or Grandma Smith (no one in this story has a last name) or, let's say, Ethel or Ethel Smith or Mrs. Smith, or any of the myriad terms of address that might have established different degrees of psychic distance and sympathy between the reader and the old woman.
>
> Calling her "the grandmother" at once reduces her to her role in the family. . . . At the same time, the title gives her . . . an archetypal, mythic role that elevates her and keeps us from getting too chummy with this woman whose name we never learn, even as the writer is preparing our hearts to break. . . .

The first sentence is a refusal, which, in its very simplicity, emphasizes the force with which the old woman is digging in her heels. It's a concentrated act of negative will, which we will come to understand in all its tragic folly. . . . And finally, the no-nonsense austerity of the sentence's construction gives a kind of authority that—like *Moby Dick*'s first sentence, "Call me Ishmael"—makes us feel that the author is in control, an authority that draw us farther into the story.[1]

VOCABULARY

Prose's assertion that "skill in choosing one word instead of another" is a significant feature of good writing means that a good writer must know a lot of words. Correspondingly, a good reader must know a lot of words. In fact there is strong empirical evidence that one's vocabulary knowledge is a reliable predictor of comprehension as early as first grade and continuing through the school years. So how do people learn words?

Acquiring Vocabulary

At first vocabulary comes through oral contexts. These are the words that typically appear in conversation, so children are exposed to them at high frequency and most often in shared physical surroundings. As a result, these words rarely require instructional attention in school. Later written language—what people read—is the major source of vocabulary learning. But written language is not usually about the immediate present, and it lacks many of the prosodic features of oral language, such as intonation and stress, that support word meaning. Thus learning word meanings in the course of reading is far more difficult. In fact, although reading is the major source of acquiring new words, this doesn't happen as often as one might think. Studies estimate that of 100 unfamiliar words met in reading, between 5 and 15 of them will be learned (Nagy, Herman, & Anderson,1985). Less than 80% of unfamiliar words encountered in reading will be learned. This means that to acquire a large vocabulary one needs to read a lot, and to read material that uses challenging vocabulary—a big problem for our less skilled readers.

---

[1] Excerpts from Prose (2006, p. 17). Copyright 2006 by Francine Prose. Reprinted by permission of HarperCollins.

The Three-Tier Framework

To get a perspective on the kinds of words that need instructional attention, we conceptualized a three-tier framework (Beck, McKeown, & Omanson, 1987). Tier One words are high frequency words that typically appear in oral conversations—*dog, tired, talk, party*—and rarely require instruction about their meanings in school. Tier Three words are those that have a low frequency and are often limited to specific topics and domains, such as *filibuster, pantheon*, and *epidermis*. In general, a rich understanding of these words would not be of high utility for most learners. These words are probably best learned when a specific need arises, such as introducing *filibuster* during a unit about the U.S. Congress. The content words of science and social studies reside in this tier.

Tier Two contains words that are of high utility and are found across a variety of domains. Examples include *auspicious, fervent,* and *retrospect.* These words are characteristic of written text and are found only infrequently in conversation (Hayes & Ahrens, 1988), which means that students are less likely to learn these words independently. Thus, instruction directed toward learning Tier Two words can be most productive, and challenging literature is among the best sources of Tier Two words.

Support for Using Context Clues during Close Reading

Given that only about 5–15 out of 100 unknown words will be learned in the course of reading (Nagy et al., 1985; Swanborn & de Glopper, 1999), how might we increase those numbers? There is some indication that scaffolding students toward deriving word meanings from what they read can be helpful (Goerss, Beck, & McKeown, 1999), and there is no better time to do so than during close reading, when the teacher and students are discussing features of written language. So how does one do it?

Arguably, the most important part of successfully using context clues to reveal word meaning is to arrange conditions that require students to deal deeply with the context. A useful way to access the context is for students to respond to another's interrogation of the context. To start with, the other person should be the teacher. On the next page we provide two examples of interrogating contexts toward deriving word meaning, both from *Treasure Island* (1883) by Robert Louis Stevenson. In both cases, the narrator, Jim Hawkins, is speaking. (The interrogator's questions and comment are in bold.)

The captain had been struck dead by thundering apoplexy.

What happened in this sentence?
   (The captain died.)

What did he die of?
   (Thundering apoplexy.)

Apoplexy is a sudden stroke. What word describes the kind of apoplexy he died of?
   (Thundering.)

What would something thundering be like?
   (Loud, scary, intense, powerful.)

What would be the difference between dying of apoplexy or being struck dead by thundering apoplexy?
   Hopefully students will mention a characteristic of thundering.

In another context, Jim Hawkins, the narrator, describes his dreams:

How that person haunted my dreams. . . . On stormy nights, when the wind shook the four corners of the house and the surface roared along the cove and up the cliffs, I would see him in a thousand forms, and with a thousand diabolical expressions.

What are some of the phrases the narrator uses to describe stormy nights?
   (*Wind shook the house*; *surface roared*.)

What feeling do you get when you read the description of the stormy nights?
   (Loud, dark, scary.)

What does the narrator say he sees on stormy nights?
   (A thousand forms with a thousand diabolical expressions.)

What kind of expression is a diabolical expression?
   (No response.)

Think about the story's description of a storm—wind shook, surface roared. Does that give you an idea of what a diabolical expression might be?
   (Mean, scary.)

***Diabolical* does mean scary and mean. In fact, something diabolical is extremely evil.**

I (Isabel) did this kind of interrogation with fifth and sixth graders many years ago. Since then I have passed it on to other teachers and received feedback that students learn from it and like it, especially when they can be the interrogator. That matches my experiences. One of the best things about this method is that it benefits both the interrogator and the one being interrogated. Engaging in the exercise just a few times with the teacher as interrogator is all it takes for students to become good interrogators. This activity is made for partner work. Again, the goal is to burrow into the context.[2]

ALL CONTEXTS ARE NOT CREATED EQUAL

Many contexts that give a clue to a target word's meaning also contain information that can distract and lead to other possible interpretations of the word. The following example comes from a scene in *Charlotte's Web* (White, 1952) in which Templeton, the rat, goes into a tunnel that he has dug:

> Templeton was a crafty rat and he had things pretty much his own way. The tunnel was an example of his skill and *cunning*. The tunnel enabled him to get from the barn to his hiding place under the pig trough without coming out into the open.

The following exchange is how one teacher pursued the meaning of *cunning*.

MS. J: What's happening here?

[*Four students talk about Templeton digging the tunnel and going into it.*]

PERRY: Nobody sees him.

MS. J: What's it mean, "The tunnel was an example of his skill and cunning"?

MELIA: He was good at making the tunnel.

MS. J: OK, so that's an example of his skill, but what do you think *cunning* means?

MARTIN: His digging skill.

MS. J: Well, he did dig the tunnel, but *cunning* is telling us something more about Templeton. Remember when Perry [first student mentioned in the transcript above] told us that he goes into the tunnel so nobody sees him. So, what's that say about Templeton?

MARTIN: He goes in the tunnel. He's smart.

SHANNEL: He's sneaky.

MS. J: Great! Templeton is smart and sneaky! And that's what *cunning* means. *Cunning* means "to be clever and sneaky."

---

[2] Such interrogation is also useful for supporting comprehension of complicated portions of text.

The *cunning* example is an instance of going through the process of using a context that has several clues to the word's meaning, as well as information that could distract and lead to other possible meanings. In other cases, a text might not have enough information to provide direction for the target word's meaning, as in the example of *glutton* below. After Templeton declines to play with Wilbur, he explains:

> [I want] to spend . . . [my] time eating, gnawing, spying and hiding.
> I'm a glutton but not a merry-maker.

Ms. J: What does this tell us about Templeton?

[*Three students enter the conversation characterizing Templeton as not a merry-maker and a spy. The teacher stops the "name calling," repeats the context, and asks about the word directly.*]

Ms. J: What do you think a *glutton* is?

SHIKIA: Somebody who doesn't like to have fun.

MARTIN: Like somebody who spies and steals things.

Ms. J: Those ideas show good thinking because those points did come through about Templeton. But *glutton* means somebody who likes to eat a lot and is very greedy about food. You know, there really was no way for you to figure that out for sure because there was other information about Templeton, and it was hard to tell what information would have been useful for figuring out *glutton*.

Given the students' inability to determine the meaning of *glutton* from context, one could suggest that the teacher should have simply told them what a glutton is. But students need to learn that although they can *sometimes* gather meaning from context, they may not be able to get potentially useful information from all contexts.

MEANING OF PHRASES AND SENTENCES

Another consideration for close reading activities is to examine the overall meaning of a phrase or sentence. Sometimes a reader knows the meaning of individual words in a phrase or sentence but finds them challenging collectively. As an example, we will consider several lines from *The Lady, Or The Tiger* (Stockton, 1882), a story that we include in Part Two of this book.

First a synopsis of the story: A barbaric king decided that guilt or innocence should be determined by chance. If someone was accused of a crime, the king arranged a trial to which the populace came. The accused had to open one of two exactly identical doors. If he opened the door behind which there was a lady, he would be declared innocent and would have to marry the lady. If he opened the door behind which there was a tiger, he would be declared guilty and the tiger would tear him to pieces.

Early in the story, when the crowd who attended the trial is discussed, the following sentence comes up: *And the thinking part of the community would bring no charge of unfairness against [the king's] plan.* At this point the teacher asks:

"What's the meaning of 'And the thinking part of the community would bring no charge of unfairness against [the king's] plan?'" (**The intelligent members of the community would not accuse the king of unfairness.**)

Prompt as needed:

"Who are 'the thinking part of the community'?"

Tell students to suggest some characteristics of someone whom they consider to be a "thinking person." Responses such as (**intelligent, smart, educated**) are likely.

"What does 'bring no charge' mean?" (**not accuse someone**)

Prompt as needed:

"What does it mean 'when someone is charged with a crime'?" (**Some people say they are guilty of something.**)

Tell students to use the information they have discussed and paraphrase the original sentence. If needed, remind them that to paraphrase is to say something in your own words that still communicates the meaning of the original sentence.

"What does it mean that 'some of [the king's] ideas were progressive, but others caused people to suffer'?" (**Some of the king's ideas were modern and forward-thinking, but others hurt people.**)

Prompt as needed:

> "How many kinds of ideas does the king have?" (**Two**)
>
> "Which idea—the first or second—was mean?" (**The second.**)
>
> "What does the word *but* at the beginning of the second part of the sentence tell you about the second idea?" (**The second idea will not be like the first idea.**)
>
> "So what might it mean that 'some of the king's ideas were progressive'?" (**Forward-thinking.**)

Students are likely to say that progressive ideas are "good," "not mean." Tell them that they are close and that progressive means forward-looking, which is a good way to look at the world.

Over time many students may only remember that *progressive* is in a "good" category. But that is a leg up in coming to know the precise meaning of *progressive*. Next time the student meets *progressive*, he or she will likely consider whatever is labeled as progressive as something positive and from the new context add to his or her knowledge of the word. It is important to keep in mind that one rarely learns everything there is to know about a word with one encounter, unless it is a very simple word. Rather, each encounter adds to its meaning.

UNPACKING THE MEANING OF LONG, FORMAL SENTENCES

In Part Two of this book, we include the first chapter of *The Hound of the Baskervilles* by Sir Arthur Conan Doyle, whose prose is complex, old-fashioned, and formal. Working to unpack meaning in such prose is important in that many classics use similar language. The paragraph below presents some difficulties, so it offers grist to work at unpacking meaning.

The story has established that Holmes and Watson have had a visitor who left behind a walking stick. Holmes and Watson examine the stick for clues to who the visitor might have been. Watson makes an observation about the stick, and Holmes is impressed with Watson's suggestion. Then the following sentence appears: *Really, Watson, you excel yourself.* At this point the teacher asks:

> "What does Holmes mean when he says *'Really, Watson, you excel yourself'*?" (**You did something better than you usually do.**)

Prompt as needed:

> "Which word might be a clue?" (*excel*)
>
> "Why?" (**It starts like** *excellent*.)

If needed, ask

> "What's a word that you know that starts like *excel*?" (***Excellent.***) Excel not only has something to do with doing something excellent—*excel* means doing something better than somebody else. Who is the somebody that Watson excels?" (**Himself.**)
>
> "Put that information together and tell what Holmes means when he says, 'Really, Watson, you excel yourself.'"
>
> "What does Holmes mean when he tells Watson, 'It may be that you are not yourself luminous, but you are a conductor of light'?" (**Watson might not be brilliant himself, but he brings out the brilliance in others.**)

Prompt as needed:

> "If we divided that sentence into two parts, what would the first part be . . . ?" (**It may be that you are not yourself luminous.**)
>
> "What would the second part be?" (**But you are a conductor of light.**)
>
> "Read the first part aloud. What do you think *luminous* means?" (**Light up, bright.**)

Prompt as needed:

> "*Luminous* has something to do with 'light up.' We couldn't say, 'It may be that you are not yourself *light up*.' But it wouldn't be hard to figure out that *luminous* is related to *illuminate*, which means light up. What does something that is lit up look like?" (**Bright, brilliant, dazzling, shining.**)
>
> "So with that information, what do you think the first part of the sentence means?" (**It may be that you yourself are not brilliant or shining.**)

Read the second part of the sentence: "but you are a conductor of light."

"What's a conductor? Someone who directs an orchestra, or who directs people on a train? In science a conductor is material that lets heat and electricity flow through it. How could you paraphrase the second part?" (**You are a director of light.**)

"So put the two parts together." (**You may not be brilliant yourself, but you are a director of light.**)

"What does 'Some people without possessing genius have a remarkable power of stimulating it' mean?" (**Some people who are not geniuses have an exceptional way to encourage [spark, trigger] it.**)

Sentences like the one above are a good place for students to work independently. We might assume that they understand what *remarkable* means and the only potentially problematic word would be *stimulating*. If needed, you could suggest that they go to an outside source. For appropriate paraphrases, make the point that there is not necessarily one way to paraphrase something. The only rule is that the paraphrase needs to communicate the same thing as the original sentence.

APPRECIATING SOME LITERARY TECHNIQUES DURING CLOSE READING

A major purpose of close reading is to help students become cognizant of and hopefully appreciative of an author's writing. One point of entry to that cognition and appreciation is to become aware of some literary techniques that authors use and the effects of those techniques on the text.

We say *some* techniques in this section to indicate that there are other techniques beyond the ones we discuss here. All one has to do is look at two or three lists of techniques for author's structure and craft, often called literary or stylistic devices, to find that there is no universal list, or even universal labels. But this is in fact a positive thing. The reader can go far beyond what any list offers and look at any techniques that he or she notices or wants to consider about an author's language.

Here we list some stylistic devices and examples that may be helpful to teachers to trigger close reading ideas for specific texts. We begin by drawing examples from the lessons included in this book. When these texts did not include a technique that we wanted to explicate, we include examples from other sources.

Figurative Language

Authors use figurative language to enhance their writing. Figurative language goes beyond the literal meaning of words. It enables an author to "paint" a scene vividly and a character's emotions more deeply than might be possible without manipulating language. It is used in creative and imaginative ways and often appeals to the senses.

Metaphor

A metaphor compares two things that are different from each other, except there is some characteristic that they have in common. Unlike similes that include the signal words *like* and *as* in their comparisons, metaphors can be kind of hidden so they can be hard to recognize. Consider the poem "Advice to a Young Author" by Arthur Conan Doyle that we include in Chapter 9 of this book. The first stanza introduces a ship that is being filled with cargo and then emptied. The ship is compared with the young writer's mind and cargo with his ideas. This is a rather distant comparison so it would be important to work with it in the first stanza.

Personification

Older students typically notice personification, as they can recognize when an author has given human traits to a nonhuman character or object. However, younger students sometimes are confused by the idea that an inanimate object can have human-like traits. So we include an example that is perfect for introducing young readers to the concept of personification. The very short poem "Who Has Seen the Wind?" by Christina Rossetti that we include in Chapter 10 makes clear, through the use of personification, the power of the wind. The teacher might model and point out personification in the first stanza and then ask students to identify personification in the second stanza. A discussion of how the poet's use of personification provides a better sense of what was happening in the poem would be useful.

Foreshadowing

A literary device that is particularly appropriate for a second read is foreshadowing; on a first read, students might miss the clues the author has provided. However, once they complete the first read and realize they were given multiple clues to the ending, students seem to enjoy working through the text to find the clues they missed. Let's look at an example from the story "The Birds" by Daphne du Maurier (1952), a story about birds that suddenly attack a community. In a paragraph early in the story, the author explains that there are more birds than usual, they are more restless, and they are following the farmers' plows with more vigor and noise than usual. Those clues and others foreshadow the eventual attacks by the birds.

Flashback

Flashback is sometimes confusing to students as it interrupts an ongoing story line to let the reader learn about something that happened at an earlier time. Sometimes, students don't understand this unexpected change in time. Daniel Keyes's *Flowers for Algernon* (1966), a fascinating novel, is filled with flashbacks for the main character Charlie, a mentally challenged adult who undergoes a surgical procedure to increase his intelligence. As Charlie's intelligence increases, he suffers from disturbing flashbacks that connect his past to his changing present.

Mood

Another element students recognize but may have difficulty putting into words is the notion of mood. They know how a story makes them feel, but they might not recognize what the author has done to make them feel that way. Moods can range from happy and cheerful to gloomy and miserable. Let's consider one of the greatest authors of all time at creating a suspenseful and frightening mood, Edgar Allan Poe. One of his classics, "The Tell-Tale Heart," is included in Part Two of this book and tells the story of a man who commits murder simply because he can't tolerate an old man's eye. This story is perfect for having students work with the element of mood. There are words that express actions, sounds, and sights that contribute to the dark and grotesque mood.

Simile

The simile is one of the easiest forms of figurative language for students to recognize and understand, as they typically can find the "like" or "as" between the two objects or ideas being compared. Consider the famous poem "Harlem" by Langston Hughes (1951). The poet begins with the line "What happens to a dream deferred?" His first response, "Does it dry up like a raisin in the sun?" provides a simile that creates a vivid image of what happens when a dream is lost. It doesn't just fade away, but, like a raisin, it completely dries up and no longer exists as it once was. The rest of the poem provides similar similes that create vivid images of what happens when a dream is lost.

Irony

Ironic situations are unexpected twists of events that may give the reader a moment of pause and encourage an "Oh" reaction. They range from the humorous to the tragic. An example of irony is taken from the well-known O. Henry short story "The Gift of the Magi" (1906). In the story a husband and wife, who live in poverty, each have a treasured possession—the wife's beautiful hair and the husband's pocket watch. To show their love for one another, each sells their own prized possessions in order to purchase the perfect Christmas gift for the other. The husband sells his pocket watch to buy his wife an ornate comb for her beautiful long locks, and the wife sells her gorgeous hair to buy her husband a chain for his pocket watch. Ironically, they now have gifts neither can use.

GENRE STUDY

A genre is a category in which things belong. In music there are such genres as pop, rock, and classical. Written material is also categorized into genres, with the two broadest categories being fiction and nonfiction. Within these broad categories there are subcategories, including the examples of common genres for both fiction and nonfiction listed here:

Fiction	Nonfiction
Historical fiction	Speech
Myth	Biography
Mystery	Autobiography
Folk tale	Narrative nonfiction
Science fiction	Essay
Poetry	Eulogy
	Reference texts

It is useful for students to engage in close reading activities that encourage them to examine texts in light of how their characteristics represent a text's particular genre. For example, in *Arachne, the Spinner*, an old Greek myth included in Part Two of this book, students engage in a close reading activity that targets genre study. Although students may know what a myth is, they may not be familiar with the characteristics of a myth. We recommend spending some time discussing common elements frequently found in myths. Then, we would have students return to the text to find examples that reflect those characteristics, reinforcing their understanding of a myth.

FINAL COMMENT

We want to emphasize that as students gain some experience with engaging in close reading it is essential to encourage them to indicate aspects of an author's craft, or deeper meaning of a part of a text, as they notice these things. Do encourage them to bring up ideas for further examination and discussion.

We hope our examples provide grist for when you and your students engage in close reading by digging into the author's craft and subtle meanings of text. In the next chapter, we provide specific close reading ideas for the two texts discussed in Chapter 4, *Alice in Wonderland* and "Black Death."

CHAPTER 6

A Closer Look at Close Reading
Modeling the Development
of Close Reading Activities

In this chapter we discuss and model our approach to close reading and provide close reading activities for two texts, *Alice in Wonderland* and "Black Death."[1] We start, however, by making the point that the nature of close reading activities for any text depends on whether students have (1) not yet engaged with close reading, (2) somewhat engaged with close reading, or (3) had frequent opportunities to engage.

In the first case, the teacher will likely need to model how to analyze portions of text. In the second case, toward reducing his or her role, the teacher might provide a category (e.g., words that frighten) and ask students to look for instances of those, or he or she may have students examine the author's use of figurative language and discuss how those choices contribute to the mood of a story. In the third case, students would independently decide which aspects of the author's craft and structure they find interesting, unusual, important, thought-provoking, and more. Then they would do their analyses of whatever features they want to deal with independently, and complete a paper explaining their thinking.

It is important to recognize that these three approaches do not have strict boundaries. For instance, although students may be quite familiar with close reading, there well could be a particular section of a text that has a subtle feature that might not be readily noticed (e.g., a repeating pattern of two short sentences,

---

[1] Students will need their copies of *Alice in Wonderland* and "Black Death."

followed by one long sentence) and the teacher may need to model or direct students to notice the pattern. Or, the teacher may direct students to a paragraph and ask them what they notice about the author's language. The latter is essential and should happen after students have had a few experiences with more directed close reading activities. Moving toward greater independence, the teacher could start every close reading session by asking students what they notice in the text and then follow through with a worthwhile feature identified by a student before moving to the lesson plan. These suggestions are examples of teaching for transfer.

AN INITIAL APPROACH TO THINKING ABOUT CLOSE READING

When first attempting to develop activities to engage your students in close reading, we suggest you start by thinking about two elements of a text: the content and the language by which the content is presented. These two elements are simple to keep in mind and, with a little deeper consideration, can probably take you fairly far into a text. When considering close reading for narratives, various aspects of the author's language have greater importance and content takes a back seat, although it must still be considered in close reading. For informational materials, content weighs more heavily, which makes obvious sense in that the purpose of informational text is to inform and convey new information. Both of these elements—the content and the author's language—will be considered for close reading activities for the two texts we discuss in this chapter. We begin by modeling our thinking and close reading plans for *Alice in Wonderland*.

CLOSE READING ACTIVITIES FOR *ALICE IN WONDERLAND*

Close reading opportunities for both language and content reveal themselves quickly in *Alice in Wonderland*, but there is little doubt that language plays the leading role. When considering which language details to pursue, we first made a beeline to usage or misusage—capitalized words and phrases in the middle of sentences.[2] Then we went to the frequent use of parentheses—in which the narrator's voice is provided. Both of these aspects of language add meaning and charm to Carroll's prose.

---

[2]Capitalization is sometimes discussed under punctuation or grammar. For the case at hand we prefer the definition "the way a word is used in a language."

When we considered whether there was content that should be given attention, we were fairly certain that more than a few students would not realize that Alice's adventures take place during her dreams. This is a key element, so we pursued it before dealing with the opportunities to delve into Carroll's rich language.

Content

Is It a Dream?

Toward understanding that Alice's adventures are a dream, point out to students that Alice seems to be pretty sleepy during this part of the book. Then ask students to reread the text and mark places where the author indicates that Alice is sleepy or tired. (If needed, tell students there are three places where the author talks about Alice being sleepy.) When students indicate they have found the three places, call on several students to read one of the "sleepy" phrases:

> *. . . as well as she could, for the hot day made her feel very sleepy and stupid . . .* Paragraph 1
>
> *And here Alice began to get rather sleepy . . .* Paragraph 7
>
> *She felt that she was dozing off, and had just begun to dream . . .* Paragraph 8

Ask students what conclusion they can make about Alice's adventures. (They occurred while she was dreaming.)

Proving That It's a Dream

Ask students to read the second, third, and fourth paragraphs with a partner and underline the parts that provide evidence to support the conclusion that the story is too fantastic to be real. Then, bring students together and have them share their evidence and explain how their examples prove that Alice's adventure really is a dream.

> Paragraph 2:
>
> *Suddenly a White Rabbit with pink eyes ran close by . . .*
>
> *[Alice heard] the Rabbit say to itself, 'Oh dear! Oh dear! I shall be late!' . . .*
>
> *The Rabbit actually TOOK A WATCH OUT OF ITS WAISTCOAT-POCKET. . . .*

Paragraph 3:

she found herself falling down a very deep well . . .

she looked at the sides of the well, and noticed that they were filled with cupboards and book-shelves; here and there she saw maps and pictures hung upon pegs.

Paragraph 4:

She took down a jar from one of the shelves as she passed; it was labeled 'ORANGE MARMALADE' . . .

Language

Lewis Carroll has an interesting and unconventional style of writing, and we thought it important to draw students' attention to those features. Tell students to look at some of the pages of the story for a minute and look for some unusual features that the author uses in his writing (e.g., capital letters in the middle of sentences and a lot of parentheses).

Why the Use of Capital Letters?

Tell students that we are going to try to understand why the author uses capital letters in the middle of sentences.

Ask them to follow along as you read the second paragraph aloud: "When suddenly a White Rabbit with pink eyes ran close by her. . . ."

Skipping the two capitalized *very*s at this point, read aloud, "TOOK A WATCH OUT OF ITS WAIST-COAT-POCKET," and ask why the author capitalized that phrase. Students will probably say it is a way of emphasizing that Alice was really very surprised to see a rabbit take a watch out of its pocket—an appropriate response here. But the two capitalized *very*s have a different purpose.

Go back and read aloud "There was nothing VERY remarkable in that; nor did Alice think it so VERY much out of the way to hear the Rabbit say to itself, 'Oh dear! Oh dear! I shall be late.'" Tell students that the two *very*s are not actually emphasizing that it was *especially* remarkable that a rabbit ran by her, nor that it was *especially* much out of the way to hear the rabbit speak. In fact, they are being used to have the opposite effect on the sentence.

Read the sentence again, this time stretching out the word *VERY* slightly: "There was nothing VEERRY remarkable in that; nor did Alice think it VEERRY much out of the way." If the *very*s are not there to emphasize *remarkable* and *much* *out of the way*, ask students if they have any ideas why they were capitalized. It is likely that students will not get the idea that the capitalization is actually reducing *remarkable* and *out of the way*. You might then provide the following example:

> "If your mother was angry that your brother was late for dinner and you were trying to help him out for being late, you might say, 'Terrill wasn't so very late,' rather than 'Terrill wasn't so late.' The *very* reduces how late Terrill was. He wasn't VEERRY late, he was just late."

You could ask students to apply this example to the two *very*s in the text sentence, but if the students are unable to do this, you can explain it thus:

> "Alice didn't think it was VEERRY remarkable that the rabbit ran by, it was just remarkable. Similarly Alice didn't think it was VEERRY much out of the way. It was just out of the way."

Have students work with a partner and go through the rest of the text and find all the places where the author capitalized words. Tell them to consider the contexts surrounding each of the capitalized words and to be ready to suggest why the author might have chosen to capitalize those words, and what point the author is making with each context. Then bring the groups together to discuss their ideas. The table below is offered to help you organize the activity that follows, but is not meant to be used by the students.

Direct students to find the sentence(s) in each paragraph (shown in the table) that include a capitalized word or words. Call on various students to read the sentences with appropriate expression. Then call on a student to explain in his or her own words what the sentence means.

Text	Explanation
Paragraph 3: She took down a jar from one of the shelves . . . it was labeled 'ORANGE MARMALADE,' but to her great disappointment it was empty.	Alice must love orange marmalade and later it even said that she was disappointed that the jar was empty.
Paragraph 4: *Would the fall NEVER come to an end!*	It's a way of saying that the fall is taking so long. Someone listening to a long and boring speech might think, *Will this speech NEVER end?*

Paragraph 4: As Alice is falling, the narrator says something about what Alice had learned in school but that . . . *this was not a VERY good opportunity for showing off her knowledge.*

Maybe the narrator was being sarcastic, really meaning something like, "this would be a terrible time for showing off her knowledge."

Paragraph 5: *I wonder if I shall fall right THROUGH the earth!*

Since Alice doesn't know where she is going she offers a kind of far-fetched possibility of where she might end up.

The Narrator's Voice

We think it is particularly important for students to understand that it is the narrator who speaks within the parentheses. Have students find the second sentence in the first paragraph and follow along as you read it aloud. Now tell them that you will read the sentence again, but when you get to the part that is in parentheses, you will stop reading and *they* should read that part. Then you will read the rest of the sentence.

> "So she was considering in her own mind (as well as she could, for the hot day made her feel very sleepy and stupid), whether the pleasure of making a daisy-chain would be worth the trouble of getting up and picking the daisies."

Ask students what they learned from the information in the parentheses. Students probably will respond that **Alice felt sleepy and stupid**. You might need to draw attention to how the author used the word *stupid* by asking, "What does stupid mean in this context?" **(Probably that Alice is feeling "out of it," or not thinking clearly.)**

Then ask students who is providing the information in the parentheses? If they say the author, make the point that the author is providing *all* the information but also gives the narrator the additional role to make comments about what's happening in the story, which the author puts in parentheses.

One teacher that we observed explained the material in the parentheses as the narrator "putting in his two cents." Another teacher called the information in the parentheses "asides." It's as if the narrator knows that we readers are involved with the story, so sometimes he gives us additional information by talking to us directly.

As the next step, divide students into five small groups and have each group find the places in the text where the author's voice provides information in the parentheses. Ask the groups to discuss what more they learn about Alice through this additional information. Then have each student select one of the parentheses. (They can volunteer, choose a leader to assign each person with a specific parentheses, put numbers on five slips of paper, etc.) Each student is instructed to write an explanation and interpretation of the information in the parenthesis. Bring the class together and discuss all the parentheses, giving each of the students who selected the same parenthesis an opportunity to offer their interpretation of its purpose (see the examples in the table).

Text	Explanation and interpretation
Paragraph 2: *(when she thought it over afterwards, it occurred to her that she ought to have wondered at this, but at the time it all seemed quite natural)*	The narrator seems to want us to know that after thinking about it, Alice realized she should have been surprised. Maybe the narrator wanted us to know that Alice isn't so foolish to believe the fantastic things the rabbit does.
Paragraph 4: *(for, you see, Alice had learnt several things of this sort in her lessons in the schoolroom, and though this was not a VERY good opportunity for showing off her knowledge, as there was no one to listen to her, still it was good practice to say it over)*	The narrator lets the reader know that this isn't a good time to share knowledge because there's no one there. Then he kind of says, "Oh, well it's OK to practice."
Paragraph 4: *(Alice had no idea what Latitude was, or Longitude either, but thought they were nice grand words to say.)*	The narrator gives us a reason why Alice liked to say the words.
Paragraph 5: *(and she tried to curtsey as she spoke—fancy CURTSEYING as you're falling through the air! Do you think you could manage it?)*	The narrator emphasizes how impossible it would be to be falling, having a conversation, and trying to curtsey at the same time by asking us whether we could be falling, talking, and curtseying at the same time.
Paragraph 6: *(Dinah was the cat.)*	As readers we don't know who Dinah is, so the narrator tells us.

Because it is such an important point, discuss again why Lewis Carroll might have decided to include a narrator who provides various comments to us, the readers. Make the point that the story is not in first-person point of view; it is the narrator, not Alice, who tells the story. The comments in parentheses seem to allow the narrator to speak directly to us about various things that may not be necessary to move the story forward, such as Alice's thoughts and feelings, why she does or doesn't do something, what she worries about, or what she learns in school. This creates a kind of intimacy between narrator and reader.

So, What Can We Say about Alice?

Alice is an engaging and unusual little girl, and we want students to appreciate and understand her curious nature and her well-mannered and accepting personality. As a final close reading activity, we thought we could spend some time making certain aspects of her personality more concrete by having students offer words that characterize her, and then ask them to write several paragraphs in which text evidence is provided in support of one or two of the descriptive words.

Given that our students have read all of *Alice in Wonderland* several times (and parts of it even more often) we thought it would be a good idea for them to think about what Alice is like—her personality, nature, spirit, and makeup.

To establish some descriptors, write the words *nice*, *mean*, and *curious* on the board. Ask students if they think *nice* is a good description of Alice. If yes, tell students that Alice does seem nice but that she is unusual, and there are stronger words that describe her. Cross *nice* out. Then ask whether *mean* is a good description. Students should say no, so cross out *mean*. Finally ask whether Alice is *curious* and students should agree. Write "<u>Alice Is</u>," on the board, as the title to a list, and write *curious* as the first word on the list. Tell students to find an example of Alice's curiosity in the first paragraph (*once or twice she had peeped into the book her sister was reading*). Ask students to offer some other words that describe Alice. It might be helpful to prompt students by saying something like, "What would you say if someone came up to you and said, 'Tell me one word that describes Alice?'" A final list could include *curious, brave, thoughtful, good mannered*.

Writing Activity

Now that students have analyzed Alice's character, it is important to move them further by having them think about the role these traits play in the story. Ask them to write an essay where they respond to the following prompt: Describe how Alice's character traits contribute to the sequence of events in the story. Remind students that they must support their ideas with evidence from the text. Explain that when they find a part of the text that is evidence for their thinking, they should write about that evidence but present it in their own words. For example, tell students to find the part at the end of the second paragraph that starts with *she ran across the field*. Have them follow along as you read:

"She ran across the field after it, and fortunately was just in time to see it pop down a large rabbit-hole under the hedge. Alice started after the rabbit, never once considering how in the world she was to get out again."

Ask students how they might say that part in their own words. As needed, offer the example: *Alice went down a rabbit hole and wasn't worried how she would get out.* Make the point that there is no one way to say something in your own words. For example, you could have said: *Alice followed the rabbit down a hole and didn't think about how to get out.* Tell students that when you describe something that someone has written, but in your own words, it's called paraphrasing.

CLOSE READING ACTIVITIES FOR "BLACK DEATH"

When preparing close reading activities for informational texts, the two categories of *content* and *language* still hold, but content is the primary focus. Even though language is secondary in informational texts, it should also be considered.

In this text, students are introduced to a dreadful disease referred to as the "Black Death." The author uses both literal and figurative language to represent the meaning of that name, and this story provides an excellent opportunity for students to engage with the distinction between these terms. Here we start with language as it seems appropriate to deal with the name of the disease before getting into details of the topic.

Language

"People Felt Helpless"

An important idea in the text is that *people felt helpless in the face of such a deadly disease.*

- Ask students to offer words or phrases that represent what it means to feel helpless. Write their suggestions on the board. If needed, provide some examples (e.g., *desperate, incapable, vulnerable, nothing I can do, powerless, unable*).
- Have students work with a partner to underline places in the text that reflect how and why people felt helpless. Bring the class together and discuss the places they found that support the idea that people felt helpless.

WRITING ACTIVITY

To encourage students to think about the role these vivid descriptions play in the text and the way they were able to influence the reader's thinking, have them respond to the following prompt: You identified and explained the ways in which the author described the feeling of helplessness. Write some paragraphs and explain how these phrases influenced your thinking about the disease Black Death. Cite specific examples and explain the role they played in your understanding of the disease and the helplessness felt by the people.

Personification

Begin by reading the following line to students: *This name suggests the fear that gripped Europe as the disease spread.* Ask them to explain the meaning behind that sentence. (**People in Europe were very afraid of the disease.**)

• Ask, "Why didn't the author just say, 'People in Europe were very afraid of the disease?'" "Why did she choose to use the word *grip* in her description?" (**Saying that the fear *gripped* makes it sound stronger because if you grip something you hold on to it very tightly. People were so afraid that their fear was not going anywhere. It had a tight hold on them.**) Tell students that using *grip* the way she did is called *personification* because fear can't really grip something. Personification is when an author uses human-like traits to describe a nonhuman object trying to bring that object to life.

• Explain that the author used personification to bring the Black Death to life. Reread the following paragraph with students: *Before long, the Black Death reached other cities along the Mediterranean coast. Historical documents record that the disease spread inland with terrifying speed. In Europe it spread through France, Germany, Spain, and Portugal. It moved on to the British Isles and Scandinavia. It even reached the island of Greenland, near the North Pole, almost wiping out its population.*

• Read the first sentence again: *Before long, the Black Death reached other cities along the Mediterranean coast.* Tell students that by saying that the Black Death "reached," it gives the sense that Black Death is a person who is physically moving. Then, have students read the rest of the paragraph and find additional descriptions, especially verb choices, of what the Black Death did (**spread inland with terrifying speed, moved on to the British Isles, even reached the island. . . .**). Ask students what picture these descriptions give them of the disease.

- Have students work with a partner to go through the rest of the text and identify places where the author uses personification to describe the Black Death **(the Black Death struck, the Black Death wiped out, the Black Death had mostly vanished . . .).**

- Bring the class together and ask them to discuss how the author's choice of words, especially through the action verbs, brought the Black Death to life.

WRITING ACTIVITY

To conclude the activity, have students respond to the following prompt: "What did you learn about personification, in general, and the role it played in this text?"

Content

Theories and Evidence

As already noted, theories and evidence are important features in informational text. Several theories with supporting evidence are presented in "Black Death," so it is important to include an activity that provides students with the opportunity to locate these theories and find the supporting evidence.

- Remind students that theories and evidence are important elements in expository texts. A theory is an idea, but it needs evidence to make it a fact. Have students work with a partner to find the theories and evidence presented in the text. Remind students that two sources of evidence provided in this text are documents and eyewitness accounts.

- To help students understand the task, work through an example with them. Read the first line of the third paragraph: *Most experts believed the Black Death was caused by a germ called Yersinia pestis.* Tell students that the theory is that the germ Yersinia pestis caused the disease called the Black Death. Then read the following sentences: *In 2011, scientists studying centuries-old skeletons confirmed that the experts were right about this germ. The germ lived in the bodies of fleas that attached themselves to rats.* Point out that those lines provide the evidence. Reinforce the idea that the first experts just had a theory as to what germ caused the Black Death, but in 2011, scientists found evidence to confirm the theory.

After talking through the first example, have students work with a partner to find the two additional theories presented in the text and the evidence to support these theories. Have them underline the theory with a pencil and underline the evidence with another color. When students have completed the task, bring them together and have them present the two theories and the supporting evidence (see examples in the table below).

Theory	Evidence
Paragraph 4: *Many believe the flea-ridden rats came from China to Europe on trade ships.*	**Paragraph 4:** *They know that just a few years before the Black Death struck . . . they brought the rats—with fleas on their bodies— with them.*
	Paragraph 5: *There is a convincing piece of evidence. . . . Many more were sick with the disease.*
Paragraph 6: *Before long, the Black Death reached other cities along the Mediterranean coast.*	**Paragraph 6:** *Historical documents record that the disease spread inland with terrifying speed.*
Paragraph 6: *It spread through France . . . almost wiping out its population.*	

Main Ideas and Supporting Details

It is important that students differentiate the main idea from supporting details. This is especially true in informational texts. Because informational texts include facts, theories, and evidence, students may mix up the big idea with interesting, but supportive details.

As a group, discuss what the main idea of the text is. (**The Black Death was a terrible disease that spread far and caused 25 million people to die.**) Then, have students list the supporting details that led them to that conclusion. It might be helpful to provide a chart like the one shown below with just the titles and let students complete the rest of the chart. Or you can develop a group chart together.

Main Idea: The Black Death Was a Terrible Disease That Spread Far and Caused 25 Million People to Die

Detail	Connection to Main Idea
Paragraph 1: *About 40 percent of Europe's population was wiped out.*	It wiped out a lot of people.
Paragraph 6: *Before long, the Black Death reached . . . wiping out its population.*	The disease spread across many countries.
Paragraph 8: *The Black Death began with fever and chills . . . death was very near.*	The symptoms were awful, and it was a terrible way to die.
Paragraph 10: *The fear and panic . . . fled for their lives.*	The Black Death held power over all people, even ones who were not ill.
Paragraph 11: *Yet, fearful memories . . . behind them for good.*	The power of Black Death lingered in people's memories for many years.

Writing Activity

The Black Death was a terrible disease that killed many people, but the damage it did to communities goes well beyond the disease itself. To reinforce this important understanding, have them respond to the following prompt:

> "The text states that the disease Black Death wiped out entire communities. One of the obvious reasons is the disease itself, but the text points to other reasons for this deadly disease wiping out entire towns. Find the places in the text that point to these reasons and then write an essay discussing these reasons and the role they played in the destruction of these towns."

CHAPTER 7

Your Turn for a Narrative

In this chapter we take on an important feature of professional development—the opportunity for you to engage in developing a lesson and to receive feedback on it. The best scenario would be if someone skilled in developing and conducting the kind of text-based lesson we are suggesting could watch you conduct a lesson and provide direct feedback. Since that is not possible, we offer you the opportunity to develop a lesson—both the comprehension component and the close reading component—and then to compare your lesson with the one we developed for the same story. We hope you will afford yourself of this opportunity. Finally, if it can be arranged, it would be great if you could conduct the lesson as you designed it with an appropriate group of students.

The narrative text we've chosen for this lesson is the story "The Two Brothers" by Leo Tolstoy. The story text and our prompts to support your completion of the lesson follow here.

STEP 1: READ THE TEXT CAREFULLY
The Two Brothers[1]
by Leo Tolstoy

Two brothers set out on a journey together. At noon they lay down in a forest to rest. When they woke up they saw a stone lying next to them. There was something written on the stone. It said, "Whoever finds this stone," they read, "let him go straight into the forest at sunrise. In the forest a river will appear; let him swim across the river to

---

[1] Analyses of "The Two Brothers" puts it at the fourth- and fifth-grade band.

the other side. There he will find a she-bear and her cubs. Let him take the cubs from her and run up the mountain with them, without once looking back. On the top of the mountain he will see a house, and in that house he will find happiness."

When they had read what was written on the stone, the younger brother said: "Let us go together. We can swim across the river, carry off the bear cubs, take them to the house on the mountain, and together find happiness."

"I am not going into the forest after bear cubs," said the elder brother. "And I advise you not to go. In the first place, no one can know whether what is written on this stone is the truth; perhaps it was written in jest. It is even possible that we have not read it correctly. In the second place, even if what is written here is the truth, suppose we go into the forest and night comes, and we cannot find the river. We shall be lost. And if we do find the river, how are we going to swim across it? It may be broad and swift. In the third place, even if we swim across the river, do you think it is an easy thing to take her cubs away from the she-bear? She will seize us, and, instead of finding happiness, we shall perish, and all for nothing. In the fourth place, even if we succeeded in carrying off the bear cubs, we could not run up a mountain without stopping to rest. And, most important of all, the stone does not tell us what kind of happiness we should find in that house. It may be that the happiness awaiting us there is not at all the sort of happiness we would want."

"In my opinion," said the younger brother, "you are wrong. What is written on the stone could not have been put there without reason. And it is all perfectly clear. In the first place, no harm will come to us if we try. In the second place, if we do not go, someone else will read the inscription on the stone. Then they will find happiness, and we shall have lost it all. In the third place, if you do not make an effort and try hard, nothing in the world will succeed. In the fourth place, I should not want it thought that I was afraid of anything."

The elder brother answered him by saying, "A proverb says: 'In seeking great happiness small pleasures may be lost.' And also: 'A bird in the hand is worth two in the bush.'" The younger brother then said, "I have heard: 'He who is afraid of the leaves must not go into the forest.' And also: 'Beneath a stone no water flows.'

The younger brother set off, and the elder remained behind. No sooner had the younger brother gone into the forest, than he found the river, swam across it. And there on the other side was the she-bear, fast asleep. He took her cubs, and ran up the mountain without looking back. When he reached the top of the mountain the people came out to meet him. They had a carriage to take him into the city, where they made him their king.

He ruled for five years. In the sixth year, another king, who was stronger than he, waged war against him. The city was conquered, and he was driven out.

Again the younger brother became a wanderer. One day he arrived at the house of the elder brother. The elder brother was living in a village and had grown neither rich nor poor. The two brothers rejoiced at seeing each other. And at once began telling of all that had happened to them.

"You see," said the elder brother, "I was right. Here I have lived quietly and well, while you, though you may have been a king, have seen a great deal of trouble." The younger brother replied, "I do not regret having gone into the forest and up the mountain. I may have nothing now, but I shall always have something to remember, while you have no memories at all."

Jot down anything you notice that may be difficult or confusing for your students. Consider those issues when you develop queries.

STEP 2: LIST IMPORTANT CONTENT

This is a dense story, so the content list will be fairly long for such a short story. You may want to combine two ideas into one item on your list, when they go together.

Below are examples of two ideas from our list of important items. We show them where we numbered them on our list, but rarely do two people use the same wording for content items or have the same number of items.

1. Two brothers find a stone saying if they accomplish several challenges they will find happiness.
5. Brothers support their reasons about whether to take up the challenges with proverbs.

When your list is complete, compare it with ours:

1. Two brothers find a stone saying if they accomplish several challenges they will find happiness.
2. Younger brother wants them to attempt the challenges together.
3. Older brother does not want to and gives reasons why.
4. Younger brother gives counterreasons for why they should go.
5. Brothers support their reasons about whether to take up the challenges with proverbs.
6. Younger brother attempts challenges by himself, succeeds, and becomes king.
7. Younger brother is overtaken by stronger king and loses everything.
8. Brothers reunite and share how they've lived.
9. Brothers try to convince each other that each lived a better life.

After you compare your list of important content with the one above, you may decide to eliminate or add items. Make any changes that you think are needed as your list of important content triggers the queries.

STEP 3: DEVELOP QUERIES

Tips When Developing Queries

As you develop your queries, keep the text and your list of important content available. Usually teachers report that they first look at the list of content, then write the query, and then segment the text. Teachers who know the procedures report that they always develop a query and segment the text as one step. We have learned that some teachers skip the list of important content after a while and go right to developing the queries. Having read the text carefully, they already know what is needed to capture the gist. When we ask experienced teachers if we should skip the step of having teachers list the important content, they mostly say that the listing is needed when teachers are getting started, but that it can fade fairly soon.

You will see in the following section that there are eight queries, but two of those have several parts to them. Some people might have made those parts into individual queries. You need to organize your queries so they make sense for you and meet the needs of your students.

Compare your queries to ours. You may have worded your queries differently, but we strongly recommend that for the most part you keep them open in terms of specific content. For example, with our first query below, "What did we find out in this first paragraph?," a closed version might be "What did the brothers find?" Keeping queries open requires students to decide what was important, to synthesize information, and to respond in their own language. Keeping the queries open seems to be the most difficult aspect for teachers just beginning to develop queries.

You may have split the content differently and developed 10 queries rather than eight. That does not matter; the main thing is to consider whether you have left out content that is important to developing the gist, or included content that could be left out. The gold standard for queries does not exist. Rather, the goal is to develop a sequence of queries that focus on what is important for identifying a coherent gist.

Queries for "The Two Brothers"

1. **What did we find out in this first paragraph?**
   (Two brothers found a stone that told them how to find happiness.)

1a. *If students haven't given the details of the challenges, follow with:* **So, tell us about these challenges**.
   (They had to go into a forest, swim across a river, take cubs from a mama

bear, run up a mountain with the cubs, and go into a house where they will find happiness.)

2. **Now what did we learn?**
   (The younger brother suggests that they attempt the tasks and find happiness together.)

3. **What's going on with the older brother?**
   (He doesn't think it's a good idea.)

3a. **Why doesn't he agree?**
   (He gives five reasons. Tell students that they can look at the story to remind them or you may want students to read the reasons as they can't remember them. What's written on the stone might not be true; they could get lost in the forest looking for the river, or if they find the river, it might be too dangerous to cross; it would be quite a challenge to take cubs from a mama bear; they wouldn't be able to run up a mountain carrying cubs; and finally, even if they were able to accomplish all of these tasks, the happiness awaiting them might not be the kind of happiness they want.)

4. **What about the younger brother?**
   (He also finds five specific reasons for why they should go: the writing on the stone had to be put there for a reason; no harm will come to them if they try; if they don't, someone else will read the inscription, and they will try; if you don't try, you can't succeed; he doesn't want it to appear that he was afraid.)

5. **What's going on with these two brothers?**
   (Each is trying to persuade the other to see his point of view.)

5a. **How do their actions connect to what we read previously?**
   (First, they tried using reasons to support their views. This time they are using proverbs.)

6. **What did we learn in this section?**
   (The younger brother goes on the adventure on his own and becomes a king.)

7. **What happened now?**
   (A stronger king took over the younger brother's kingdom.)

8. **What happened with the brothers in this section?**
   (The younger brother showed up at the older brother's house, and they shared their stories of how they've been living.)

8a. **What do the brothers think of how each has lived his life?**
   (The older brother thinks that although the younger brother got to be king, he had to deal with trouble, so it wasn't worth it. The younger brother thinks that although he had to deal with some adversity, he always will have the memories of being a king, but his brother has no memories of such a fantastic life.)

STEP 4: SEGMENT THE TEXT

You can place your numbers on the copy of the text that is included in this chapter, or you can duplicate another copy from the Appendix.

Segmented Text for "The Two Brothers"

Two brothers set out on a journey together. At noon they lay down in a forest to rest. When they woke up they saw a stone lying next to them. There was something written on the stone. It said, "Whoever finds this stone," they read, "let him go straight into the forest at sunrise. In the forest a river will appear; let him swim across the river to the other side. There he will find a she-bear and her cubs. Let him take the cubs from her and run up the mountain with them, without once looking back. On the top of the mountain he will see a house, and in that house he will find happiness." **1**

When they had read what was written on the stone, the younger brother said: "Let us go together. We can swim across the river, carry off the bear cubs, take them to the house on the mountain, and together find happiness." **2**

"I am not going into the forest after bear cubs," said the elder brother. "And I advise you not to go. In the first place, no one can know whether what is written on this stone is the truth; perhaps it was written in jest. It is even possible that we have not read it correctly. In the second place, even if what is written here is the truth, suppose we go into the forest and night comes, and we cannot find the river. We shall be lost. And if we do find the river, how are we going to swim across it? It may be broad and swift. In the third place, even if we swim across the river, do you think it is an easy thing to take her cubs away from the she-bear? She will seize us, and, instead of finding happiness, we shall perish, and all for nothing. In the fourth place, even if we succeeded in carrying off the bear cubs, we could not run up a mountain without stopping to rest. And, most important of all, the stone does not tell us what kind of happiness we should find in that house. It may be that the happiness awaiting us there is not at all the sort of happiness we would want." **3**

"In my opinion," said the younger brother, "you are wrong. What is written on the stone could not have been put there without reason. And it is all perfectly clear. In the first place, no harm will come to us if we try. In the second place, if we do not go, someone else will read the inscription on the stone. Then they will find happiness, and we shall have lost it all. In the third place, if you do not make an effort and try hard, nothing in the world will succeed. In the fourth place, I should not want it thought that I was afraid of anything." **4**

The elder brother answered him by saying, "A proverb says: 'In seeking great happiness small pleasures may be lost.' And also: 'A bird in the hand is worth two in the bush.'" The younger brother then said, "I have heard: 'He who is afraid of the leaves must not go into the forest.' And also: 'Beneath a stone no water flows.'" **5**

The younger brother sets off, and the elder remained behind. No sooner had the younger brother gone into the forest, than he found the river, swam across it. And there on the other side was the she-bear, fast asleep. He took her cubs, and ran up the mountain without looking back. When he reached the top of the mountain the people came out to meet him. They had a carriage to take him into the city, where they made him their king. **6**

He ruled for five years. In the sixth year, another king, who was stronger than he, waged war against him. The city was conquered, and he was driven out. **7**

Again the younger brother became a wanderer. One day he arrived at the house of the elder brother. The elder brother was living in a village and had grown neither rich nor poor. The two brothers rejoiced at seeing each other. And at once began telling of all that had happened to them.

"You see," said the elder brother, "I was right. Here I have lived quietly and well, while you, though you may have been a king, have seen a great deal of trouble." The younger brother replied, "I do not regret having gone into the forest and up the mountain. I may have nothing now, but I shall always have something to remember, while you have no memories at all." **8**

After you have segmented your text, compare your stopping points with our segmented text above.

CLOSE READING ACTIVITIES FOR "THE TWO BROTHERS"

We did not find anything in the language, craft, and structure of this story that was particularly noteworthy. Tolstoy, one of the greatest writers of all time, uses simple, straightforward language in this story, and much may have been lost in the translation from Russian to English. Of course, you may see something in the text that we did not that offers an opportunity to deal with craft and structure. But the story does provide an excellent opportunity for students to learn about proverbs and the role they played in it, so that's what we decided to work with. Before you look at how we dealt with the proverbs, try to think about how you would approach them. The next section shares our ideas for working with proverbs.

Proverbs

Toward understanding the role proverbs play in the story, explain that a proverb is a short saying that reflects words of wisdom or suggests advice. Provide a proverb that most students probably have heard (e.g., "Two wrongs don't make a right") and ask students to share their thoughts on what that proverb means. Together, come to the understanding that it means if someone does something wrong to you, it isn't acceptable to do something bad to them; it won't make the situation better.

Have students read the story independently and underline the proverbs spoken by the two brothers. Then, have them work with a partner to figure out the meaning of each proverb. You might have them create a chart similar to the one in Figure 7.1.

After sharing student responses, ask students what role the proverbs play in the story. **(They reflect the two brothers' philosophies of life.)** Then, discuss how these proverbs reflect each brother's philosophy. **(The older brother thinks one should be happy with what he has, and the younger brother thinks one should strive for more.)**

Writing Activity

Write the following proverb on the board: "'Tis better to have loved and lost than never to have loved at all." Ask students to explain the meaning of that proverb, in writing, and then explain which brother's philosophy they believe it best reflects. Tell them to cite at least two specific examples from the text to support their ideas.

SOME HINTS FOR IDENTIFYING CLOSE READING MATERIAL

Step 1: Reread the Text

Reread the text paying close attention to the language and structure, marking places that are particularly unusual, important, or confusing. Think about one

Brother	Proverb	Explanation
Younger	I have heard: 'He who is afraid of the leaves must not go into the forest.'	If you are afraid of the little things, you won't be able to accomplish the big things.
Younger	Beneath a stone no water flows.	In order to make something happen, sometimes you have to overcome an obstacle.
Older	In seeking great happiness small pleasures may be lost.	In trying to get more than you need, you might lose the good things you already have.
Older	A bird in the hand is worth two in the bush.	It's better to be satisfied with what you have than try to get more of what you don't have.

FIGURE 7.1. Chart of proverbs in "The Two Brothers."

or two of the following questions while rereading. Or ask yourself some of the questions below and search for them in the text.

- Are there words, phrases, or sentences that you noticed? What is it that made you notice them?
- Do any of the words have double meanings? What does the author achieve with double meanings?
- Has the author deliberately and intentionally played with some of the language?
- Has the author used any figurative language? Which? What does the author achieve with the kind of figurative language used?
- Is there something interesting about the structure of the text?
- Have you noticed any patterns? Word repetition? Word order? Long sentences? Short sentences? Deliberative mixing?
- Are there metaphors? Any that represent the whole piece? Any local metaphors and similes?
- Are there places in the text that are confusing and need to be unpacked?

Step 2: Think about the Content

- What events and characters lend themselves to further analysis?
- What portions of the text play a critical role and should be further examined?
- Are there layers of meaning? How can you uncover the subtle meaning of an event or idea?
- Is there a theme? A moral?

Step 3: Narrow Your List

Keep in mind that some texts lend themselves more to language analysis, while others may be more challenging conceptually. Review your notes and decide on which areas of the text you will focus. Also, keep in mind that not all texts are worthy of close reads, so be careful not to try to make something out of nothing. When narrowing your list, think about one very important question, "From what analyses will my students benefit the most?" Once you have narrowed your list, begin designing activities.

Step 4: Design Activities

When you have identified the content you want to bring attention to, the issue becomes how to accomplish this. What should you do? What should the class do? We think examples are the best way to break into the design of close reading activities. We have many activities for close reading in the lessons in Chapters 6 through 10.

Additionally, there is close reading material for the eight texts in Part Two. Some people have told us they think the material in Part Two is more challenging. Although we do include complex material in Part One, our major goal is teaching teachers, so in a couple of places we use less challenging text in order to focus on teaching procedures for developing instruction. Don't get us wrong; there are challenging materials in both parts of the book, but Part Two has more of them.

Some General Questions about Activities

When designing activities, ask yourself:

- "How much scaffolding will be required before students can do this work independently?"
- "How can I design this activity so students are working with pencil in hand?"
- "How much time will I need to spend on each activity?"
- "Have I utilized the key literacy components of an ELA classroom? Are students reading, writing, thinking, and discussing?"

Step 5: Incorporate Activity Structures

We suggest that you incorporate a variety of activity structures, including partner, independent, small-group, and whole-class work. Because it's important for students to work closely with the ideas in the text, it is essential that students work with a pencil in hand. The texts in this book can be photocopied as needed, so you might make copies available to those students who want to jot down ideas, underline portions, and mark the text in various other ways. Sticky notes also work well.

ARE THESE IDEAS RELEVANT TO INFORMATIONAL TEXTS?

Many of the ideas described above are also relevant to informational texts. Specifically Steps 3, 4, and 5 work just as well as they do for narrative texts, but Steps 1 and 2 need revision for use with informational texts. Notice that we combine Steps 1 and 2 below because there are fewer language possibilities in informational text for close reading than there are in narratives, so we don't devote a separate section to language for these texts. However, when there is language with which to take advantage for close reading, we do include that.

Steps 1 and 2: Reread the Text and Think about the Content[2]

Reread the text, paying close attention to the content and whether the content is presented clearly. Mark places that are particularly unusual, important, or confusing and that you'd like to reinforce. Think about one or two of the following questions while rereading—or ask yourself some of the questions below and search for them in the text.

- In history, is there a chronology for which we could reinforce the sequence by developing a time line?
- In science, is there a process for which the steps could be diagrammed?
- If the main idea had to be inferred, what clues led to the inference?
- Does the main idea need to be reinforced?

---

[2] Close reading was developed for literary pieces, and much attention is given to how the author uses language, for instance, to make his prose come alive, create a tone, or develop a mood. Sometimes there is interesting language in informational text that is worthy of close reading, but certainly not as much as for literature. Authors who write informational pieces want to be clear and accurate; they are not like literary authors who craft their language with metaphor, personification, etc. We have conceptualized close reading for informational text as a chance to emphasize what is most important. Just as a good student asks him- or herself, What should I know after I've worked with this material? What is important?—we ask, How can I make this content more memorable? This last question is something of a guiding idea for our informational close reading activities.

- How do the details support the main idea?
- Are there several main ideas? What are the most important? Why are they the most important?
- Are there theories? Is there evidence? How strong is the evidence?
- Are there words, phrases, or sentences that I particularly noticed? What is it that made me notice?
- Are there places in the text that are confusing and need to be reconsidered and unpacked?

Steps 3, 4, and 5

The directions in Steps 3, 4, and 5 for narratives are also relevant to informational text because they discuss general instructional issues (e.g., the importance of narrowing your list of content to what is most important, using a variety of activity structures, and identifying content that is worthy of close reading).

To restate what we have said earlier, some texts are not worthy of close reading. Don't try to find something that isn't there!

CHAPTER 8

Your Turn
for an Informational Article

This chapter provides the opportunity to develop a lesson for an informational article, "Pythons Invade the Florida Everglades" (Readworks, 2013). We follow the same steps as in Chapter 7. If you have not read Chapter 7, it is important to read it first because we explain our purpose for developing the *Your Turn* chapters and provide prompts for each of the steps, which are not repeated in this chapter.

STEP 1: READ THE TEXT CAREFULLY

Pythons Invade the Florida Everglades[1]

The Florida Everglades teem with life. Migratory and wading birds tiptoe through marshy grasslands. Orchids and ferns dot the hardwood forests. Alligators lounge in the shallows and on muddy riverbanks. Mangrove leaves rustle in the wind as the brackish water laps at their roots. All of this life is made possible by the presence of water. The Everglades are sometimes called the *River of Grass* (1947) after a book of the same name by author Marjory Stoneman Douglas. The phrase illustrates that the Everglades are basically a very wide and shallow river.

Tommy Owen, a tour guide in the Everglades National Park, was giving a tour of Florida's famous park wetlands to a group of tourists. He and the tourists were floating

---

[1]This text is appropriate for fourth and fifth grades. From ReadWorks (2013). Copyright 2013 by ReadWorks, Inc. All rights reserved. Used by permission.

in a boat through the shallow water that makes up the Everglades. One of the women in the boat he was steering saw a snake in the water. She got Tommy's attention and pointed the snake out to him. When Tommy saw the snake, he acted fast. He reached into the water and grabbed the animal by the head. He got a good grip and didn't let go. Tourists in the boat were worried when the snake wrapped itself around Tommy's arm. After several minutes, he got control of the animal and removed it from the water. The snake was a ten-foot-long Burmese python. It was a snake not native to Florida and, quite simply, it didn't belong there.

The Burmese python is native to tropical and subtropical zones in Southeast Asia. In their native habitat, Burmese pythons are nocturnal carnivores. When they live close to human habitations, pythons eat rats, mice, and rabbits that are attracted to human dwellings and farms. They can also eat small farm animals like chickens. When they live away from human habitations, pythons eat birds and small wild mammals. The python kills by constricting its body around its prey. Python eggs and hatchlings are a food source for other animals. In the wild, pythons grow to be on average 12 feet long.

In the United States the Burmese python is a popular pet. Docile and beautifully patterned in brown and gold diamond shapes, these snakes can be purchased at pet stores or reptile shows. Owners keep them in cages or tanks and feed them rats or mice. Most people buy pythons when the animals are small. Pythons can grow very quickly. For many pet owners, the pet pythons become too big to manage.

The first Burmese python was found in the Florida Everglades in 1979. It's presumed the animal was originally kept as a pet and then released by its owner. Starting in 1992—when it's thought that numerous Burmese pythons escaped pet stores and cages damaged in Hurricane Andrew—the numbers have grown at a faster rate.

The Burmese pythons that have been released in southern Florida have found a habitat they like in the Everglades. They are breeding in the Everglades and have reached numbers that designate them as an invasive species. Pythons are eating machines. They can eat anything from deer to bobcats, to raccoons to alligators. They especially enjoy dining on small mammals and birds. Studies have shown that since their appearance in the Everglades, the numbers of small mammals in the area are down significantly. Additionally, this population loss is not observed in areas where the python has not established itself.

Many agencies and individuals are trying to put a stop to the python invasion. The National Park Service has begun a program to study these animals in the Florida Everglades. Park Service scientists have implanted tracking devices into seventeen large pythons that were later re-released into the wild. They have provided scientists with information regarding python behavior.

In 2013 the Florida Fish and Wildlife Conservation program issued permits to hunt the snakes within state wildlife-managed areas of the Everglades. Sixty-eight animals were captured.

In the meantime, python records are still being broken.

In May of 2013 Jason Leon was driving in a rural area near Florida City when he spotted a python's head protruding from the brush. The man was a biologist, and was familiar with pythons. He approached the snake and pulled it out of the bush. The animal was bigger than he expected. After a struggle with the animal, Leon killed it. The python was 18 feet long and 128 pounds. Leon contacted the Florida Fish and Wildlife Conservation Commission, who agreed to pick up and examine the snake. The snake was found to be the largest ever in the state of Florida.

The state later issued a statement:

"Jason Leon's nighttime sighting and capture of a Burmese python of more than 18 feet in length is a notable accomplishment that set a Florida record. The Florida Wildlife Commission is grateful to him both for safely removing such a large Burmese python, and for reporting its capture."

Jot down anything you notice that may be difficult or confusing for your students. Consider those issues when you develop queries.

STEP 2: LIST IMPORTANT CONTENT

Below are two ideas from our list of important items. As we did in Chapter 7, we show them where we placed them on our list, but we remind you that rarely do two people use the same wording or have the same number of items.

3. People in the United States keep pythons as pets, but they get too big for people to manage.
6. People and agencies are trying to remove the pythons by allowing people to hunt them.

When your list is complete, compare it with ours:

1. Florida Everglades are beautiful marshy grasslands filled with lots of life.
2. Tourist guide finds a python, which doesn't belong in the Everglades.
3. People in the United States keep pythons as pets, but they get too big for people to manage.
4. Pythons have started to find their way to the Everglades.
5. Pythons are thriving in the Everglades.
6. People and agencies are trying to remove the pythons by allowing people to hunt them.
7. Agencies are having a hard time getting rid of them.
8. World record-sized python was found, proving that the pythons are really thriving in the Everglades.

STEP 3: DEVELOP QUERIES

Notice that the queries we develop here are directly related to the text segments we indicate in Step 4. This is a good example of planning the segmented text and queries at the same time. After you have developed your queries, compare them with ours, below.

Queries for "Pythons Invade the Florida Everglades"

1. **What did we learn in the first paragraph?**
   (The Florida Everglades are marshy grasslands filled with a lot of life.)

1a. **What picture of the Everglades is the author creating for the reader?**
   (It's a beautiful place with a lot going on.)

2. **What just happened in the second paragraph?**
   (While on a tourist trip, a guide discovered a Burmese python, a snake that didn't belong there.)

2a. **What does it mean that the snake didn't belong there?**
   (Florida is not its natural habitat. It lives in Southeast Asia.)

3. **What did we find out about the Burmese python in this section?**
   (People in the United States like to keep them as pets.)

3a. **How does that work out for them?**
   (Not so well. The pythons get so big the owners can't handle them.)

4. **What new information did we learn from what we just read?**
   (The pythons are making their way into the Everglades.)

5. **How's life going for the Everglade pythons?**
   (Pretty good. There is plenty for them to eat, and they are growing in numbers.)

5a. **What does it mean that they are an invasive species?**
   (They are "invading" the Everglades and are a problem because they are eating the small mammals.)

6. **How does this information connect with what we just discussed?**
   (People and agencies are trying to remove the pythons from the Everglades and return them to the wild.)

6a. **How are they trying to solve the problem?**
   (The Florida Fish and Wildlife Conservation program is giving permits to people to allow capturing the snakes.)

7. **What's the point of this article?**
   (Although agencies are trying to eliminate pythons, they still exist.)

7a. **The text states that this python was 18 feet long, which set a Florida record. What's the significance of this detail?**
   (Not only are the snakes still in Florida where they don't belong, they are thriving. This one was so big it set a record.)

STEP 4: SEGMENT THE TEXT

Segmented Text for "Pythons Invade the Florida Everglades"

The Florida Everglades teem with life. Migratory and wading birds tiptoe through marshy grasslands. Orchids and ferns dot the hardwood forests. Alligators lounge in the shallows and on muddy riverbanks. Mangrove leaves rustle in the wind as the brackish water laps at their roots. All of this life is made possible by the presence of water. The Everglades are sometimes called the *River of Grass* (1947) after a book of the same name by author Marjory Stoneman Douglas. The phrase illustrates that the Everglades are basically a very wide and shallow river. **1**

Tommy Owen, a tour guide in the Everglades National Park was giving a tour of Florida's famous park wetlands to a group of tourists. He and the tourists were floating in a boat through the shallow water that makes up the Everglades. One of the women in the boat he was steering saw a snake in the water. She got Tommy's attention and pointed the snake out to him. When Tommy saw the snake, he acted fast. He reached into the water and grabbed the animal by the head. He got a good grip and didn't let go. Tourists in the boat were worried when the snake wrapped itself around Tommy's arm. After several minutes, he got control of the animal and removed it from the water. The snake was a ten-foot-long Burmese python. It was a snake not native to Florida and, quite simply, it didn't belong there. **2**

The Burmese python is native to tropical and subtropical zones in Southeast Asia. In their native habitat, Burmese pythons are nocturnal carnivores. When they live close to human habitations, pythons eat rats, mice, and rabbits that are attracted to human dwellings and farms. They can also eat small farm animals like chickens. When they live away from human habitations, pythons eat birds and small wild mammals. The python kills by constricting its body around its prey. Python eggs and hatchlings are a food source for other animals. In the wild, pythons grow to be on average 12 feet long.

In the United States the Burmese python is a popular pet. Docile and beautifully patterned in brown and gold diamond shapes, these snakes can be purchased at pet stores or reptile shows. Owners keep them in cages or tanks and feed them rats or mice. Most people buy pythons when the animals are small. Pythons can grow very quickly. For many pet owners, the pet pythons become too big to manage. **3**

The first Burmese python was found in the Florida Everglades in 1979. It's presumed the animal was originally kept as a pet and then released by its owner. Starting in 1992—when it's thought that numerous Burmese pythons escaped pet stores and cages damaged in Hurricane Andrew—the numbers have grown at a faster rate. **4**

The Burmese pythons that have been released in southern Florida have found a habitat they like in the Everglades. They are breeding in the Everglades and have reached numbers that designate them as an invasive species. Pythons are eating machines. They can eat anything from deer to bobcats, to raccoons to alligators. They especially enjoy dining on small mammals and birds. Studies have shown that since their appearance in the Everglades, the numbers of small mammals in the area are down significantly. Additionally, this population loss is not observed in areas where the python has not established itself. **5**

Many agencies and individuals are trying to put a stop to the python invasion. The National Park Service has begun a program to study these animals in the Florida Everglades. Park Service scientists have implanted tracking devices into seventeen large pythons that were later re-released into the wild. They have provided scientists with information regarding python behavior.

In 2013 the Florida Fish and Wildlife Conservation program issued permits to hunt the snakes within state wildlife-managed areas of the Everglades. Sixty-eight animals were captured. **6**

In the meantime, python records are still being broken. In May of 2013 Jason Leon was driving in a rural area near Florida City when he spotted a python's head protruding from the brush. The man was a biologist, and was familiar with pythons. He approached the snake and pulled it out of the bush. The animal was bigger than he expected. After a struggle with the animal, Leon killed it. The python was 18 feet long and 128 pounds. Leon contacted the Florida Fish and Wildlife Conservation Commission, who agreed to pick up and examine the snake. The snake was found to be the largest ever in the state of Florida.

The state later issued a statement:

"Jason Leon's nighttime sighting and capture of a Burmese python of more than 18 feet in length is a notable accomplishment that set a Florida record. The Florida Wildlife Commission is grateful to him both for safely removing such a large Burmese python, and for reporting its capture." **7**

CLOSE READING ACTIVITIES FOR "PYTHONS INVADE THE FLORIDA EVERGLADES"

Descriptive Language

Imagery

In the first paragraph the author creates a vivid picture of the Florida Everglades through the use of imagery and personification. Have students close their eyes and imagine how the Everglades looks as you reread the first several lines:

"The Florida Everglades teem with life. Migratory and wading birds tiptoe through marshy grasslands. Orchids and ferns dot the hardwood forests. Alligators lounge in the shallows and on muddy riverbanks. Mangrove leaves rustle in the wind as the brackish water laps at their roots. All of this life is made possible by the presence of water."

Ask students what they saw when you read those lines and what ideas these pictures gave them of the Florida Everglades. (**The birds wading in the water and the alligators on the riverbanks. The flowers and the forest.)**

Personification

Tell students that one of the reasons the author was able to allow the reader to see the action was through the use of personification. Remind them that personification is when an author gives human-like qualities to something nonhuman.

- With a partner, have students reread the paragraph quoted above under *Imagery* and identify all the places where the author uses personification.
- Then, bring students together and have them discuss how each example may have helped them picture the Everglades. (**Could "see" birds tiptoeing through the grasslands, alligators lounging, flowers dotting, and water lapping.**)

Vocabulary

Word Choice

Tell students that the author's choice of words in the first paragraph contributed to providing readers with a clear picture of the Everglades. Draw attention to two words, *teem* and *brackish*. Reread the first several sentences again and ask students whether they can figure out from the sentences the meaning of the word *teem* (**an abundance of life**). Ask them how the use of *teem* instead of *filled* provides a better sense of the Everglades. (**It's not just filled with life. There is an abundance, way more than is needed.**) Next, reread the sentence with the word *brackish*: *Mangrove leaves rustle in the wind as the brackish water laps at their roots.* Students probably will be unfamiliar with the term, so tell them that *brackish* means salty, unpleasant tasting water. Then, reread the same sentence but eliminate the word *brackish*. Ask students how the sentence was different. What is added by the word *brackish*? (**It gives the water a characteristic different than, say, the clear fresh water in a running stream. It's salty and somewhat unpleasant, so the water lapping at the roots has a little "bite."**)

Author's Craft

Anecdote

Explain to students that an anecdote is a little story that is inserted into a text to provide a message or to support a point being made by the author.

Independently, have students reread the text and find the two anecdotes in the text. Then, with a partner, have students explain the role each anecdote plays in the text. You might want to have them create a chart similar to the one in Figure 8.1.

Theories

Tell students that, as is the case with most informational texts, this text includes theories.

• Have students review the text to find any theories mentioned in the text for why pythons made their way to the Everglades. (**Owners released their pets. Pythons escaped from pet stores during Hurricane Andrew.**) When the two theories are identified, ask students to look for any textual evidence that supports each theory. (**There is none, so the theory remains a theory; without evidence we cannot say it is a fact.**)

• Tell students to find any theories about what effect the pythons are having on the Everglade animal population. (**Decrease in small animals.**)

• Ask students to find any evidence that supports that theory. (**Studies have shown that since the pythons' first appearance in the Everglades, the number of small animals in the area has decreased significantly. Additionally, the population loss is not observed in areas where the pythons have not established themselves.**)

Review the theories and evidence together as a class. Draw attention to the idea that there is no textual evidence for how pythons made their way into the

Anecdote	Role
The story of Tommy Owen, the tour guide who found the snake.	Contrasts the first paragraph where the author sets up the Everglades as beautiful and full *of life* with the idea that the Everglades is a place that is home to a large, dangerous python.
The story of Jason Leon, who found the largest snake ever in Florida.	Reinforces the idea that pythons do exist and are doing quite well, given the size of the one found. Also highlights the importance of notifying the authorities when such a snake is found.

FIGURE 8.1. Chart of anecdotes in "Pythons Invade the Florida Everglades."

Everglades. Ask students what kind of evidence would have been helpful to convince them that those theories are valid. **(Percentages from pet stores stating how many snakes they lost during Hurricane Andrew.)** Then discuss the textual support for the theory about the effect the pythons are having on the Everglades. Ask the students whether they think the evidence is valid, or if there is additional evidence that would have been helpful. **(Text says there are studies but doesn't give the name of the studies.)**

CHAPTER 9

Poetry
A Treasure Chest of Close Reading

The lesson examples we presented in the preceding chapters included texts from the two major text genres, narrative and expositon. In our narrative examples, we provided four subgenres: myths, folktales, mystery, and fantasy. The expository genre also includes several subgenres—text books, news articles, informative articles, and reports—but our expository examples have been informative articles. In this chapter, we introduce another genre, poetry.

Definitions of poetry virtually always mention that poems are written in meter and verse; include such characteristics as beauty, feelings, and imagination; and use literary techniques such as metaphor. The following definition of *poem* from *Oxford Dictionaries* seems both succinct and inclusive:

> A piece of writing that partakes of the nature of both speech and song that is nearly always rhythmical, usually metaphorical, and often exhibits such formal elements as meter, rhyme, and stanzaic structure. (*www.oxforddictionaries.com/ us/definition/american_english/poem*, 2015)

Nevertheless it was hard for us not to recall A. E. Housman's view about defining poetry: "I could no more define poetry than a terrier can define a rat." Although that nondefinition tells us a lot about what Housman thinks and feels about poetry, other poets have explained the meaning of poetry more directly, in par-ticular Samuel Taylor Coleridge: "Poetry: the best words in the best order." Edgar Allan Poe adds one more important feature: "Poetry is the rhythmical recreation of beauty in words."

We include poetry in this book because we want students to become familiar with the best words in the best order, and the beauty in words. We should also mention the intellectual benefits of reading poetry. Poems challenge us to figure out what may not be obvious, and they provide comforting connections between human universals and one's own experiences and emotions.

In this chapter we look at three very different poems that you can read with your students.[1] We begin with "The Ecchoing Green" by William Blake, a light joyful poem about elderly people watching children at play in a park. The second poem, "Advice to a Young Author" (1911), is by a well-known mystery author, Arthur Conan Doyle. And we couldn't resist including "Casey at the Bat" by Ernest Lawrence Thayer.

"THE ECCHOING GREEN" BY WILLIAM BLAKE

Read the title and the name of the poet. Tell students that William Blake was a famous artist and poet whose creative, imaginative poems weren't truly appreci-ated until after his death. Begin by reading the poem aloud to your students. Because the stanzas comprise five pairs of rhyming couplets, the poem lends itself to a consistent rhythm. Model that rhythm for your students and then have them join you while reading aloud the poem again.

After reading the poem twice, work with each stanza, supporting students to get the gist of the poem. There are two important matters to consider in this poem: (1) the use of metaphor (the day being described in the poem is a meta-phor for life), and (2) the significance of some of the poet's word choices.

---

[1]Quantitative measures do not lend themselves to providing complexity levels for poetry. Our view of these three poems is that "Advice to a Young Writer" is the most difficult because the metaphor is distant—comparing a ship to a writer's ideas and work—so we see it as appropriate for the seventh and eighth grades. We estimate "The Ecchoing Green" for the fourth and fifth grades. "Casey at the Bat" has a wide range, especially in areas where baseball is an important sport. We suggest that it might be appropriate from the third through the eighth grades. Some of our analyses of "Casey at the Bat" might need more scaffolding for earlier grades. Moreover, just reading the poem to younger students could be appropriate. Our grade levels are only suggestions. Teachers know better what their students can do, and they should have the last word on which poems are suitable for their own class.

The Ecchoing Green
by William Blake

The sun does arise,
And make happy the skies.
The merry bells ring
To welcome the Spring.
The sky-lark and thrush,
The birds of the bush,
Sing louder around,
To the bells' cheerful sound.
While our sports shall be seen
On the Ecchoing Green.

Old John, with white hair
Does laugh away care,
Sitting under the oak,
Among the old folk,
They laugh at our play,
And soon they all say.
'Such, such were the joys.
When we all girls & boys,
In our youth-time were seen,
On the Ecchoing Green.'

Till the little ones weary
No more can be merry
The sun does descend,
And our sports have an end:
Round the laps of their mothers,
Many sisters and brothers,
Like birds in their nest,
Are ready for rest;
And sport no more seen,
On the darkening Green.

Developing Queries

The first stanza is straightforward as it describes the happenings of spring. Students might not grasp that the Ecchoing Green is a green field where sports will be played, so you might need to draw attention to that point. Have the class read the first stanza aloud, and then ask the following query:

1. **What is the poet talking about in this first stanza?**
    (It's spring, and the sun is coming up. The birds are singing, and people are getting ready to play sports.)

1a. **What is the poet talking about with the term "Ecchoing Green?"**
    (It's the green field where they will play their sports.)

The second stanza is more challenging. The scene presents an elderly gentleman, John, and his companions as they watch the children play, but it also introduces the poem's metaphor. It is not a problem if students do not immediately recognize the metaphor at this point, as they will work with it in the first close reading task. However, some teachers have told us that at this point it is useful to tell students that the poem is a metaphor for life. Have the class read the second stanza aloud, and then ask:

2. **What's happening in this second stanza?**
    (An elderly man and his friends are watching the children play and remembering when they also enjoyed playing as children.)

The third stanza describes the ending of the day as the sun goes down and the sports come to an end. Again, students may not pick up on the metaphor that the day, like the lives of people, must eventually come to an end. Have the class read the third stanza aloud, and then ask:

3. **What is the poet talking about in this last stanza?**
    (The day is coming to an end as the sun goes down, so the children's games have ended.)

Close Reading Activities for "The Ecchoing Green"

Language

METAPHOR

If students have not mentioned the poem's metaphor, begin by reminding them that a metaphor, like a simile, compares two things, but without using *like* or *as*.

- Have students reread the poem with you and briefly discuss what is literally happening in the poem (**It's one full day in the spring where children begin playing games, and as the day ends, so do the games.**) Then, to support students toward analyses of the poem's metaphor, ask them what spring represents—not what the poet has said, but generally what spring represents. (**The idea of beginning of life—flowers bloom, trees grow leaves. . . .**) Reinforce the idea that spring represents the beginning of life, and that this poem is actually a metaphor for life.

- Have students work through the next two stanzas with a partner to continue to analyze the poem's metaphor. Have them find specific examples in the poem to support the idea that this playful day in spring is actually a metaphor for life. The entire cycle of each example may not be represented, but enough of each cycle is presented that students should be able to recognize how each reflects the metaphor for life:

  - **Each day: the rising and setting of the sun.**

  - **The seasons: spring is when plants and trees come to life and winter is when they die.**

  - **People's lives: they are born, grow old, and then die.**

Bring students together and have them share their examples.

- Now that students have unpacked each stanza and participated in a discussion, wrap up this part of the lesson by having students write a paragraph in which they describe, in their own words, the metaphor of the poem. Have them cite specific examples from the poem to support their ideas. You might want to suggest that they start their paragraphs with: *In "The Ecchoing Green," the poet William Blake compares what is happening on the green to life. The whole poem is a metaphor for life.* Then let students take over with examples from the poem that support the metaphor. We suggest that you provide the beginning, depending on students' experiences, as having models is a good way for students to learn.

WORD CHOICE

Ask students to describe an echo (**something that repeats a sound or voice**).

- Have students work in small groups to discuss how the title, "The Ecchoing Green," reflects the metaphor of the poem. Have them use the information that they found in the first activity to think about how those examples connect to an echo (**like an echo, these things repeat**).

- Bring students together and have them share what they discussed in their groups.

- Independently have students write a paragraph where they respond to the following prompt: The title of the poem is "The Ecchoing Green," and the last line of stanzas one and two conclude with "On the Ecchoing Green." However, the last line of the poem is "On the darkening Green." Based on the work you've done with this poem, write a paragraph in which you explain the role that the last line plays in the poem. (**It continues the metaphor; everything must eventually come to an end—the darkening of the day, the darkening of the seasons, and the darkness of the end of life**.) Remind students to cite evidence from the text to support your ideas.

"ADVICE TO A YOUNG AUTHOR"

Have students read the title and author of this poem, and ask if they know who the author is. If students don't know, tell them that the author wrote many great mystery stories about a detective named Sherlock Holmes. Ask why Arthur Conan Doyle would be a good person to give a young author advice. (**He was an outstanding author who wrote many great mystery stories.**)

Begin by reading the poem aloud as students follow along. With its consistent rhyming pattern, the poem lends itself well to a pleasant rhythm or beat. Model the beat for students, while emphasizing the lines that deliver the overall message, "Do your best and don't worry about anything else." When you have read the poem, ask students to join you and read the poem aloud again.

Advice to a Young Author
by Arthur Conan Doyle

1. Taking in.
   Cargo stored,
   All aboard,
   Think about
   Giving out.
   Empty ship,
   Useless trip!

2. Never strain
   Weary brain,
   Hardly fit,
   Wait a bit!
   After rest
   Comes the best.

3. Sitting still,
   Let it fill;
   Never press;
   Nerve stress
   Always shows.
   Nature knows.

4. Critics kind,
   Never mind!
   Critics flatter,
   No matter!
   Critics curse,
   None the worse.
   Critics blame,
   All the same!
   Do your best.
   Hang the rest!

Developing Queries

After the two readings of the complete poem, it's time to work with each stanza. As always, first we look for the gist—what the stanza is about. Language and stylistic devices are part and parcel of poetry, so sometimes we can't leave close reading language activities until after the gist is established. We spell out how to proceed carefully below; we just want to give you a heads-up that the lessons for poetry are designed in light of the major role that language plays in poetry.

The first stanza is confusing, and many students probably won't recognize the metaphor. Don't spend time working with the idea that this is a metaphor, as students will discuss metaphors during close reading. At this stage, you just want them to recognize the point that, if there's nothing on a ship, taking a trip on it would be a barren journey. Have the class read the first stanza aloud, and then ask the following query:

1. **What is the poet talking about in this first stanza?**
   (First, you start by bringing everything into a ship, but if the ship is empty, then there's no point in taking the trip, and your efforts loading the ship are wasted.)

The second stanza is more straightforward with the notion that "if it's not working right now, wait a bit and it will come to you." Have the class read the second stanza aloud, and then ask:

2. **What point is the poet making in the second stanza?**
   (It's not good to try to make something out of nothing. If something's not working, take a break because you usually do better after a rest.)

The third stanza isn't quite as straightforward as the second, but it still reinforces the point that one should not stress because it is obvious when one does.

3. *You read the stanza aloud and model its meaning, and then ask:* **What point is the poet making in this stanza?**
   (It's not good to force something and stress about it.)

The final stanza sums up the poet's point about writing: Don't worry about what others say, whether good or bad. You can only do your best and not worry about anything else.

4. **Have students read the last stanza independently, and call on some students to explain the meaning.**
   (Don't worry about what others think of your work, just do your best and forget about the rest.)

Close Reading Activities for "Advice to a Young Author"

Language

METAPHOR

As we have mentioned before, students generally have a harder time recognizing metaphor because, unlike a simile, metaphors do not have the signal words *like* and *as*, which make the comparison so obvious.

- Begin by having students reread the first stanza with you. Then unpack the stanza together, so they are able to appreciate the metaphor. Read the first three lines: *Taking in. Cargo stored, All aboard.* Ask students what the poet is talking about **(bringing goods onto something)**. Prompt as needed: "What words in those lines are cues that the something being talked about is a ship?" **(Cargo, all aboard.)** Discuss that *cargo* is goods being transported somewhere. *All aboard* signals that people have been asked to come aboard the ship because it's time to leave.

- At this point bring up the metaphor and tell students that the ship stands for a young writer. Remind students that a metaphor is a figure of speech in which something is compared to another thing, even though they are very different, but there is something about them that is similar. So far cargo and passengers are filling the ship, which means that the young writer is filling his mind with ideas.

- Move to the next two lines—*Think about Giving out*—and work with the meaning of those lines. **(Think about what you are giving out.)** What would a writer give out? **(Something he has written ideas about, what he is going to write about.)** Then finish with the last two lines, *Empty ship, Useless trip!* And ask students to explain the point here. **(All his ideas weren't good, so he's emptied his mind of those.)**

- Work with the class to unpack the points being made in the subsequent stanzas. The chart in Figure 9.1 is provided for your convenience, but you might want to work with the class to develop your own similar chart.

- How does the metaphor of the ship reflect what Doyle is saying about young writers?" **(If there isn't anything happening on the inside, then your efforts are wasted. Don't worry about what people say, just do your best.)**

Stanza	Explanation	
2. *Never strain* *Weary brain,* *Hardly fit,* *Wait a bit!* *After rest* *Comes the best.*	Lines 1–3:	Don't strain yourself because it's not good for you.
	Lines 4–6:	Take a break and then you'll do your best work.
3. *Sitting still,* *Let it fill;* *Never press;* *Nerve stress* *Always shows.* *Nature knows.*	Lines 1–2:	Just relax and let the ideas come to you.
	Lines 3–6:	Don't force things to happen because stressing about things is obvious.
4. *Critics kind,* *Never mind!* *Critics flatter,* *No matter!* *Critics curse,* *None the worse.* *Critics blame,* *All the same!* *Do your best.* *Hang the rest!*	Lines 1–8:	Doesn't matter if the critics say good things or bad things, don't pay attention to their words.
	Lines 9–10:	Just do your best and don't worry about anything else.

FIGURE 9.1. Chart of explanations of each stanza.

PUNCTUATION

Doyle uses the exclamation mark often throughout the poem, including four times in the last stanza. Have students analyze its role within the poem. Begin by rereading the poem with the students and having them underline each line that ends with an exclamation mark.

> Useless trip!
> Wait a bit!
> Never mind!
> No matter!
> All the same!
> Hang the rest!

Ask students whether they notice a pattern of when Doyle chooses to use the exclamation mark. (**They seem to be on lines that express a "don't worry, chill!" attitude.**) Ask students why those lines appear so often in the last stanza. (**That's where the poet reinforces the point of the poem. Don't try to force**

something to happen, and don't worry about what others say. Relax, do your best, and don't stress.)

Writing Activity

Independently, have students respond to the following prompt: Summarize in your own words what you consider to be Doyle's advice to young writers, and support your opinion with evidence from the poem.

"CASEY AT THE BAT"

"Casey at the Bat" is among the most well-known poems in American literature. We include it because of its importance, and because we wanted to include a poem that is better served by being read in its entirety *after* the gist has been discovered. The poem is a ballad and has the characteristics of a ballad, including the fact that it is meant to be sung. With its strong rhyme and meter, the poem's song-like feel comes across while it's being read. We suggest you draw students' attention to these features after the poem has been discussed. You don't want to spoil the ironic ending, so we suggest you hold off on reading the entire poem until students understand what happens when Casey has his turn at bat.

Read the title and the name of the poet. Tell students that "Casey at the Bat" is one of the most famous poems in American literature. Explain that this is a ballad and that after you have read through and discussed the poem, you will analyze it and discuss why it is a good representation of a ballad.

Casey at the Bat
A Ballad of the Republic, Sung in the Year 1888
Ernest Lawrence Thayer

The outlook wasn't brilliant for the Mudville nine that day;
The score stood four to two with but one inning more to play.
And then when Cooney died at first, and Barrows did the same,
A sickly silence fell upon the patrons of the game.

A straggling few got up to go in deep despair. The rest
Clung to that hope which springs eternal in the human breast;
They thought if only Casey could but get a whack at that—
We'd put up even money now with Casey at the bat.

But Flynn preceded Casey, as did also Jimmy Blake,
And the former was a lulu and the latter was a cake;
So upon that stricken multitude grim melancholy sat,
For there seemed but little chance of Casey's getting to the bat.

But Flynn let drive a single, to the wonderment of all,
And Blake, the much despised, tore the cover off the ball;
And when the dust had lifted, and men saw what had occurred,
There was Jimmy safe at second and Flynn a-hugging third.

Then from 5,000 throats and more there rose a lusty yell;
It rumbled through the valley, it rattled in the dell;
It knocked upon the mountain and recoiled upon the flat,
For Casey, mighty Casey, was advancing to the bat.

There was ease in Casey's manner as he stepped into his place;
There was pride in Casey's bearing and a smile on Casey's face.
And when, responding to the cheers, he lightly doffed his hat,
No stranger in the crowd could doubt 'twas Casey at the bat.

Ten thousand eyes were on him as he rubbed his hands with dirt;
Five thousand tongues applauded when he wiped them on his shirt.
Then while the writhing pitcher ground the ball into his hip,
Defiance gleamed in Casey's eye, a sneer curled Casey's lip.

And now the leather-covered sphere came hurtling through the air,
And Casey stood a-watching it in haughty grandeur there.
Close by the sturdy batsman the ball unheeded sped—
"That ain't my style," said Casey. "Strike one," the umpire said.

From the benches, black with people, there went up a muffled roar,
Like the beating of the storm-waves on a stern and distant shore.
"Kill him! Kill the umpire!" shouted someone on the stand;
And it's likely they'd have killed him had not Casey raised his hand.

With a smile of Christian charity great Casey's visage shone;
He stilled the rising tumult; he bade the game go on;
He signaled to the pitcher, and once more the spheroid flew;
But Casey still ignored it, and the umpire said, "Strike two."

"Fraud!" cried the maddened thousands, and echo answered fraud;
But one scornful look from Casey and the audience was awed.
They saw his face grow stern and cold, they saw his muscles strain,
And they knew that Casey wouldn't let that ball go by again.

The sneer is gone from Casey's lip, his teeth are clinched in hate;
He pounds with cruel violence his bat upon the plate.
And now the pitcher holds the ball, and now he lets it go,
And now the air is shattered by the force of Casey's blow.

Oh, somewhere in this favored land the sun is shining bright;
The band is playing somewhere, and somewhere hearts are light,
And somewhere men are laughing, and somewhere children shout;
But there is no joy in Mudville—mighty Casey has struck out.

Developing Queries

The first stanza is fairly straightforward, as it sets the stage for the baseball game's dramatic ending. Students familiar with baseball should be able to provide a description of what is happening. Read the first stanza aloud, and then ask:

1. **What is the poet talking about in this first stanza?**
   (They are playing a baseball game. Mudville is losing 4–2 in the last inning. The first two players made outs, so things aren't looking so good.)

The second stanza reinforces the gloom of the situation but introduces the people's hero, Casey. Read the second stanza aloud, and then ask:

2. **What did we find out in this stanza?**
   (Some of the people are leaving because they think there's no hope, but others are holding out hope that the player named Casey will have a turn at bat.)

The third stanza presents some challenging language, although the concept is quite simple. Again, students familiar with baseball should be able to figure out what is happening. Have the class read the stanza aloud, and then ask:

3. **How does what's happening in this stanza fit in with what we just talked about?**
   (Things still aren't looking very good. There are two batters ahead of Casey, and neither one of them is very good.)

The fourth stanza reflects a glimmer of hope for the Mudville team. Have the class read the fourth stanza aloud, and then ask:

4. **What just happened?**
   (The two guys who aren't very good got hits. Now, they have batters on second and third.)

The fifth and sixth stanzas continue the glimmer of hope for the Mudville team as Casey is at bat. It is here where we get our first glimpse of Casey's personality and what the fans think of him. Have the class read both stanzas aloud and ask,

5. **How are things looking for Mudville?**
   (Pretty good. Their hero is at bat.)

5a. **What's going on with the crowd?**
   (They are going crazy, standing and cheering.)

5b. **What do we learn about Casey?**
   (Given the situation, he is surprisingly confident and relaxed.)

The seventh and eighth stanzas continue to give the readers clues to Casey's personality as they describe the first strike. Have the class read both stanzas aloud and ask,

6. **What just happened?**
   (Casey took strike one.)

6a. **What more do we learn about Casey from the description in these two stanzas?**
   (He almost seems to be a bit cocky.)

The ninth stanza speaks to what the fans think of Casey and the power he holds over them. Have the class read the stanza aloud, and then ask:

7. **What is going on?**
   (The fans are having a fit and want to kill the umpire because he called a strike, but Casey motioned to them and they settled down.)

The tenth and eleventh stanzas replay what just happened, but this time with the second pitch. Have the class read both stanzas aloud, and then ask:

8. **Now, what happened?**
   (The umpire called a second strike, and the fans had a fit. Casey once again settled them down, this time with just a look.)

8a. **What does it mean that the fans knew Casey wouldn't let that ball go by again?**
   (No matter what the pitcher threw, Casey was going to swing.)

The twelfth and thirteenth stanzas reveal Casey's epic failure as he struck out. Have the class read both stanzas aloud, and then ask:

9. **How did things turn out?**
    (Not good. Casey struck out.)

Before going on to close reading, you should read the complete poem aloud with the class so that students can enjoy the clear and easy rhyme.

Close Reading Activities for "Casey at the Bat"
Content Analysis
BALLAD

Tell students that "Casey at the Bat" is a ballad, and that ballads share several characteristics, including that they are stories meant to be sung.

- Begin by having students reread the poem with you, and discuss what about the poem makes it sound like a song (the rhyming pattern creates a song-like melody).

  - Share with students some other common characteristics of ballads:

    ○ tell a story
    ○ simple language
    ○ third person
    ○ include dialogue
    ○ rhyming pattern ABAB (first and third lines rhyme and second and fourth lines rhyme), ABCB (second and fourth lines rhyme), or AABB (first and second lines rhyme and third and fourth lines rhyme)

- With a partner, have students work with the poem to identify which characteristics are evident in this poem. Have them underline the specific examples in the text to support their point.

  - Bring students together and share their responses. Together, recap the conclusion that the poem definitely tells a story, is written in the third person, includes dialogue, and has a rhyming pattern of AABB. There may be some debate about whether the poem uses simple language. Although the plot is simple, there are several places where it takes some work to figure out what Thayer is saying.

Language Analysis: Descriptive Language

Although the plot of the story is quite simple (fans couldn't wait for their hero to get a chance to save the day, but ironically, when he gets the chance to bat, he strikes out), the language the poet uses to get across that story is worthy of further analysis.

- Tell students that you are going to look closely at the language in several stanzas and discuss the meaning and the effect the poet's choices have on the reader and the poem.

- Reread the first stanza, drawing attention to the last two lines: *And then when Cooney died at first, and Barrows did the same, A sickly silence fell upon the patrons of the game.* Ask students why Thayer would describe a baseball game using such strong words as *died* and a *sickly silence*. (He is trying to get across the point that, to this crowd, getting a hit feels like a life-and-death situation, so the players who are getting outs are dying in the baseball world.)

- Divide the class into small groups and have each group analyze the following stanzas/lines and explain the role the strong and descriptive language plays in the poem:

  o Stanza 2: *The rest clung to the hope which springs eternal in the human breast.* (The feeling we get inside us when we are hopeful something good will happen.)

  o Stanza 3: *And the former was a lulu and the latter was a cake; So upon that stricken multitude grim melancholy sat.* (The next two batters are hopeless, and the descriptions reflect that idea; because the two batters are so bad, the feeling of gloom is still there.)

  o Stanza 7: *Five thousand tongues applauded when he wiped them on his shirt. Defiance gleamed in Casey's eye, a sneer curled Casey's lip.* (The fans are cheering Casey's every move, including wiping his hands on his shirt; Thayer seems to be hinting that Casey's confidence might be mixed with a bit of arrogance.)

  o Stanza 8: *And now the leather-covered sphere came hurtling through the air, And Casey stood a-watching it in haughty grandeur there.* (In simpler terms, the pitcher threw the ball across the plate; and Casey is beyond confident in his power; he is arrogant and thinks he can't be beaten.)

  o Stanza 10: *With a smile of Christian charity great Casey's visage shone; He stilled the rising tumult; he bade the game go on.* (All it took was a mere smile from Casey to calm down the crowd and its threats against the umpire.)

  o Stanza 12: *The sneer is gone from Casey's lip, his teeth are clinched in hate; He pounds with cruel violence his bat upon the plate.* (Casey's arrogance has turned to anger as he is determined to get a hit.)

- Bring the groups together and have them share their ideas. Ask students what effect the author's descriptive language had on them. Hopefully they will respond with something like the language gave readers a better understanding of Casey, the fans, and the situation. There could, of course, be some creative response to the effect on them of Thayer's language.

Content: Idolization of Sports Heroes

Today's students are quite familiar with the idea of idolization of sports heroes. It's easy to see that this poem fits well into that idea. So, to challenge the students, they are going to examine this poem from an additional aspect, Casey's overall attitude and how it relates to the idea of fan idolization.

- Begin by telling students that they are going to analyze the poem from two different angles related to the idea of fan idolization.
- First, they are going to work with a partner to find places in the poem that reflect what the fans think of Casey.
- Bring students together and chart the responses on a two-column chart. Figure 9.2 includes some examples of what the students might say. Students should conclude that Thayer's descriptions make it clear that the fans idolize Casey and think of him as their hero.
- Then, have students work with their same partner to read the poem again, this time finding places that describe Casey, his attitude, and his demeanor.
- Bring students together and chart their responses. Figure 9.3 shows some

Evidence/language	Explanation
Stanza 2: *They thought if only Casey . . . at the bat.*	The fans think that Casey is so good that if he had the chance to bat, they'd bet money he would get the needed hit.
Stanza 5: *Then from 5,000 throats . . . to the bat.*	The crowd is going wild because their hero is up at bat. They even refer to him as Casey, Mighty Casey.
Stanza 7: *Ten thousand eyes were on him . . . shirt.*	The fans are captivated by Casey's every move.
Stanza 9: *From the benches . . . on the stand;*	The fans are so angry that the umpire called a strike on their beloved Casey that they want to kill the umpire.
Stanza 11: *"Fraud!" cried . . . fraud;*	Again, the fans are furious that the umpire called a strike. There is no way Casey could be wrong.

FIGURE 9.2. Chart of fans' attitudes.

Evidence/language	Explanation
Stanza 6: *There was ease . . . doffed his hat.*	Casey appears to be calm and confident. He nods his hat to the fans showing his appreciation. So far, he seems like a pretty decent guy.
Stanza 7: *Then while the writhing pitcher . . . Casey's lip.*	While the pitcher is getting ready to throw the ball, Casey has a cocky attitude that seems to say, "Go ahead, I dare you to throw that ball."
Stanza 8: *And Casey stood . . . said Casey.*	Arrogant Casey doesn't bother swinging at the pitch because it wasn't his style.
Stanza 10: *With a smile . . . "Strike two."*	Casey has so much power not only over the game of baseball, but also the fans that he is able to quiet the angry crowd with a mere gesture and a smile.
Stanza 11: *But one scornful look . . . again.*	Again, all it took was a mere look from Casey to quiet the crowd, reinforcing the power he has. Fans also could tell that Casey wasn't going to take another strike. His ego wouldn't allow that to happen.
Stanza 12: *The sneer . . . the plate.*	Casey's arrogance has gotten the best of him, and he is angry about the situation and is determined to hit the next pitch.

FIGURE 9.3. Descriptions of Casey.

examples of what students might say. Students should reach the conclusion that Casey's confidence crossed the line to arrogance.

Follow-Up Writing Activity

Now that students have analyzed the poem looking closely at Casey and the fans separately, have them think more specifically about the relationship between the two by responding independently to the following prompt: "Describe the relationship between Casey and his fans. How is the way the fans treat Casey a reflection of his character? Cite specific examples from the poem to support your positions."

Singing the Ballad

Ballads were meant to be sung. "Casey at the Bat" can be sung to the music of "The Battle Hymn of the Republic." You can find the melody at *http:// specialneedsinmusic.com/audio_file_zip_downloads/folk_page_downloads/battle_ hymn_revised_09_0120.mp3.zip.*

Be aware that "The Battle Hymn of the Republic" has a chorus that is repeated after each verse. So, when singing "Casey at the Bat," wait till the chorus is over before singing the next stanza. It really is fun to do this! Students invariably enjoy it. They also learn more about this enduring poem.

CHAPTER 10

Younger Students
Last but Far from Least

We can't think of any teacher we know who isn't aware of the importance of early literacy activities for young children.[1] Probably the most highly recommended activity is reading aloud to children. Although this activity has been pursued in homes and schools for centuries, studies do not always show strong effects from reading aloud (see, e.g., Whitehurst et al., 1994).

Researchers, however, have provided consistent evidence about what makes reading aloud most effective. The strategies include keeping the focus of the discussion on major story ideas, and dealing with ideas as they are encountered. Those strategies are keys to literacy growth (Teale & Martinez, 1996) and stand in sharp contrast to initiating discussion after the entire story has been read.

Research also makes the point that the most valuable aspect of the read-aloud activity is that it gives children experience with *decontextualized* language. Decontextualized language, which is what we encounter in books, is not about the here-and-now. *Harry the Dirty Dog* (Zion, 1984) is not part of the actual context in which a group of children are listening to or reading the book. In contrast, *contextualized* language is about the here-and-now—children are in the same contexts in which the language is being spoken and heard. The most obvious contexts of contextualized language are at home, at school, and on the playground. But the language that is required to move ahead in school and life is the decontextualized language found in books and other forms of written language.

---

[1]The texts in this chapter are targeted to kindergarten through second grade. The stories can be read aloud or independently (when children are able to read) or as a combination of the two.

Two features that we have discussed in earlier chapters are just as relevant to younger children as they are to older students: (1) the value of interspersed reading and discussion, instead of waiting until the entire story has been read to initiate discussion; and (2) the importance of open queries instead of constrained questions. Research shows that it is not merely listening to book language, but the talk around it, that makes reading aloud valuable for future literacy. The lessons in this chapter, as well as all other chapters in this book, incorporate those important concepts.

"WHO HAS SEEN THE WIND?"

"Who Has Seen the Wind?" is a nursery rhyme written by Christina Rossetti for a collection of her nursery rhymes, *Sing-Song: A Nursery Rhyme Book* (1872). The poem is close to 150 years old and has been a popular favorite for all that time.

Begin by reading the poem aloud, and then have students join you as you reread it. Model for them the rhythm of the poem and emphasize the question at the beginning of each stanza.

Who Has Seen the Wind?
by Christina Rossetti

Who has seen the wind?
Neither I nor you
But when the leaves hang trembling,
The wind is passing through.

Who has seen the wind?
Neither you nor I:
But when the trees bow down their heads,
The wind is passing by.

Developing Queries

1. **What did we learn in the first stanza?**
   (Neither of us has seen the wind, but we know it's there when we see the leaves hanging down.)

2. **How does the second stanza add to what we learned in the first stanza?**
   (We still can't see the wind, but we still know it's there. This time we know it's there because the tree branches bow down to it.)

Close Reading Activities for "Who Has Seen the Wind?"

Language

PERSONIFICATION

Tell students that you are going to look at a literary element called *personification*. Explain that personification is when an author gives human-like traits to something that is nonhuman. Explain to them that using personification brings that object to life and portrays a more vivid picture of the object. Share the following example with them: *The fire roared through the forest and swallowed everything in its path.*

• What words did the author include in that sentence that only people and animals can do? **(swallowed, roared)** Reinforce the idea that the author used personification when he described the fire as *roaring* and *swallowing*. Ask, "How did your use of personification give them a better sense of the fire?" **(Roaring made it seem like it was really strong, like a lion, and saying that it swallowed everything made it seem like it was really huge.)**

• Have students reread the poem and identify places where the poet uses personification and explain how they are examples of personification.

• Bring students together and have them share their examples and explain them. You might want to place the information in a chart similar to the one below and explain how the author of "Who Has Seen the Wind?" uses personification to bring the leaves and trees to life.

Example	What does the example reveal?
But when the leaves hang trembling	This gives the wind power. The leaves are so afraid of it that they are trembling.
But when the trees bow down their heads	Usually when someone bows down to someone or something, they are showing respect for that person or thing. So, the trees are showing the wind respect.

Using a Poet's Language for a Model

Students tend to lack confidence when writing original poems and have difficulty using stylistic devices. One way to support students is to have them play with the language in others' poems. Rossetti's poem is a perfect place to begin that work because the two examples of personification are so clear and the meanings are rather obvious.

- Begin by reviewing the two things that the examples of personification in this poem revealed. **(The leaves were afraid and the trees showed respect.)** Make the point that because fear and respect are things leaves and trees can't really feel, the author was using personification.

- Tell the class that you and they are going to play with the language in the poem to create their own examples of personification using the same two lines from the poem. Tell them to think about other *person-like* traits or *person-like* feelings the poet could have given to the leaves or the trees. You might begin by suggesting that the trees could have been angry at the wind. Then model for them how you might change the line to reflect that the trees were angry rather than respectful. **(But when the trees give a snarling look, the wind is passing by.)** Ask students how that line reflects that the trees were angry, and why it is an example of personification.

- Have students brainstorm with partners about how else the leaves and trees could have felt about the wind. Then instruct them to play with the two lines to create their own examples of personification and place them in the first column on a chart similar to the one above.[2] Once students are finished, have them exchange their examples with another pair of students. Tell the second pair to explain *what the examples reveal* in the second column.

- Bring students together and have them share examples. Conclude the activity by having students share what they learned about personification and why authors/poets use this particular literary technique.

- Ask whether any student or pairs of students would like to read the poem aloud, using expression that fits the poem. Give students opportunities to read the poem to the class.

"THE MUSICIANS OF BREMEN"

"The Musicians of Bremen" is an old story from the Brothers Grimm that has been retold by many others. Students may be familiar with a bright-colored trade book version, but hearing it again, without pictures, is useful.

---

[2] If you are working with a kindergarten class and writing as much as required is too big a challenge, the students can tell you what to write and you and the class can develop a class chart.

The Musicians of Bremen
(Retold by Theo Arvenitis, from the Brothers Grimm)

Once upon a time, an old donkey was badly treated by his master. Tired of such unkindness, he decided to run away. He thought he had a pretty good braying voice, so when he heard that Bremen Town was looking for singers he thought he might be accepted.

As he went along the road, the donkey met a skinny dog, covered with sores. "Come with me. If you have a good bark, you'll find a job with the band too. Just wait and see!"

A little later, a stray cat, no longer able to catch mice, joined them and the trio trotted hopefully on towards the town. As they passed a farmyard, they stopped to admire an elderly rooster who was crowing to the skies. "You sing well," they told him. "What are you so happy about?" "Happy?" muttered the rooster with tears in his eyes. "They want to put me in the pot and make broth of me. I'm singing as hard as I can today, for tomorrow I'll be gone." But the donkey told him, "Run away with us. With a voice like yours, you'll be famous in Bremen!" Now there were four of them.

The way was long, night fell, and very frightened, the four creatures found themselves in a thick forest. They scarcely knew whether to press on or to hide in some caves and rest. Suddenly, in the distance they saw a light amongst the trees. It came from a little cottage and they crept up to the window. The donkey placed his front hoofs on the window ledge. Anxious to see, the dog jumped on the donkey's back, the cat climbed onto the dog and the rooster flew on top of the cat to watch what was going on inside.

Now, the cottage was the hideaway of a gang of bandits who were busily celebrating their latest robbery. The hungry donkey and his friends became excited when they saw the food on the table. Upset by the jittery crew on his back, the donkey stuck his head through the window. Then his three companions toppled on to the lamp. The light went out and the room rang with the braying of the donkey, the barking of the dog, and the snarling of the cat. The rooster screeched along with the others.

Taken completely by surprise, the terrified bandits fled screaming: "The Devil! The Devil!" And their abandoned meal ended up in the four friends' stomachs.

Later, however, just as the donkey and his companions were dropping off to sleep, one of the bandits crept back to the now quiet house. He went in to find out what had taken place. The bandit opened the door, and with his pistol in his hand, he stepped trembling towards the fire. However, mistaking the glow of the cat's eyes for burning coals, the bandit dropped a candle next to the cat. Instantly the furious cat sank its claws into the bandit's face. The man fell backwards on to the dog, dropping his gun, which went off. The dog's sharp teeth sank into his leg. When the donkey saw the bandit at the door, he gave a tremendous kick, sending the man flying right through the doorway. The rooster greeted the bandit's action with a grim crowing sound.

"Run!" screamed the bandit. "Run! A horrible witch in there scratched my face. A demon bit me on the leg. A monster beat me with a stick! And . . ." But the other bandits were no longer listening. They had taken to their heels and fled. And so the donkey, the dog, the cat and the rooster took over the house without any trouble. And with the money left behind by the bandits, they always had food on the table, and lived happy and contented for many years.

Segments and Queries

The formatting used below for "The Musicians of Bremen" shows the segments in the left column and the corresponding queries in the right column. We use the same format for the information article "Dolphins Are Special" that follows next in this chapter, and this will be the format that we use throughout the lessons in Part Two of the book. Both "The Musicians of Bremen" and "Dolphins Are Special" are offered here as completed lessons, so we have formatted them for your convenience. Conducting completed lessons is a very useful learning device. For example, you can see what goes well, what needs to be tinkered with, whether something needs to be omitted, or whether there needs to be more of a particular strategy.

Text segments	Queries/targeted responses
Once upon a time, an old donkey was badly treated by his master. Tired of such unkindness, he decided to run away. He thought he had a pretty good braying voice, so when he heard that Bremen Town was looking for singers he thought he might be accepted. **1**	1. **What happened in the first paragraph of our story?** (A donkey was badly treated, so the donkey ran away to try to join the Bremen band.)
As he went along the road, the donkey met a skinny dog, covered with sores. "Come with me. If you have a good bark, you'll find a job with the band too. Just wait and see!" A little later, a stray cat, no longer able to catch mice, joined them and the trio trotted hopefully on towards the town. As they passed a farmyard, they stopped to admire an elderly rooster who was crowing to the skies. "You sing well," they told him. "What are you so happy about?" "Happy?" muttered the rooster with tears in his eyes. "They want to put me in the pot and make broth of me. I'm singing as hard as I can today, for tomorrow I'll be gone." But the donkey told him, "Run away with us. With a voice like yours, you'll be famous in Bremen!" Now there were four of them. **2**	2. **What's going on as the donkey goes along the road?** (He met a dog, a cat, and a rooster and invited them to come along.) 2a. **What did you learn about these animals?** (They all had different problems. The dog was skinny and covered with sores; the cat couldn't catch mice any longer; and the rooster was about to be dinner. But together they were heading to Bremen to be famous singers.)
The way was long, night fell, and very frightened, the four creatures found themselves in a thick forest. They scarcely knew whether to press on or to hide in some caves and rest. **3**	3. **Now, what's the problem?** (They are in a dark forest, and they are scared.)

Suddenly, in the distance they saw a light amongst the trees. It came from a little cottage and they crept up to the window. The donkey placed his front hoofs on the window ledge. Anxious to see, the dog jumped on the donkey's back, the cat climbed onto the dog and the rooster flew on top of the cat to watch what was going on inside. **4**

Now, the cottage was the hideaway of a gang of bandits who were busily celebrating their latest robbery. The hungry donkey and his friends became excited when they saw the food on the table. Upset by the jittery crew on his back, the donkey stuck his head through the window. Then his three companions toppled on to the lamp. The light went out and the room rang with the braying of the donkey, the barking of the dog, and the snarling of the cat. The rooster screeched along with the others.

Taken completely by surprise, the terrified bandits fled screaming: "The Devil! The Devil!" And their abandoned meal ended up in the four friends' stomachs. **5**

Later, however, just as the donkey and his companions were dropping off to sleep, one of the bandits crept back to the now quiet house. He went in to find out what had taken place. The bandit opened the door, and with his pistol in his hand, he stepped trembling towards the fire. However, mistaking the glow of the cat's eyes for burning coals, the bandit dropped a candle next to the cat. Instantly the furious cat sank its claws into the bandit's face. The man fell backwards on to the dog, dropping his gun, which went off. The dog's sharp teeth sank into his leg. When the donkey saw the bandit at the door, he gave a tremendous kick, sending the man flying right through the doorway. The rooster greeted the bandit's action with a grim crowing sound. **6**

"Run!" screamed the bandit. "Run! A horrible witch in there scratched my face. A demon bit me on the leg. A monster beat me with a stick! And . . ." But the other bandits were

4. **What are the animals up to now?**
   (They found a cottage and wanted to peek in the window.)

4a. **Describe the scene.**
   (The donkey was on the ground, and the other animals were on top of him, one on top of another. It must have been pretty funny.)

5. **What was going on in the cottage?**
   (A gang of bandits were counting their money.)

5a. **What happened with the animals?**
   (The animals got excited and caused quite a scene. The dog, cat, and rooster fell off the donkey's back and were making a lot of noise.)

5b. **What did the bandits think about the animals?**
   (They thought the animals were the devil, so they ran away.)

6. **What was one of the bandits up to?**
   (He came back to the house to try to see what had taken place.)

6a. **How did that work out for him?**
   (Not good. He thought the cat's eyes were burning coals, and he knocked over a candle that hit the cat. The cat clawed him, the dog bit him, the donkey kicked him, and the rooster crowed. What a scene!)

7. **Now, what did the bandit think about what happened to him?**
   (He thought the cat was a witch, the dog a demon, and the donkey

no longer listening. They had taken to their heels and fled. And so the donkey, the dog, the cat and the rooster took over the house without any trouble. And with the money left behind by the bandits, they always had food on the table, and lived happy and contented for many years. **7**

a monster. So, he ran away from the cottage.)

7a. **How did things turn out for the four animal friends?**
(Great. They lived happily together for many years, using the bandits' money to buy food.)

Close Reading Activities for "The Musicians of Bremen"

Younger students sometimes have trouble summarizing a story because they tend to focus on a particular event or character, or even a random detail that they liked, so it's important to work with them so they are able to see how the characters and events of a story all work together.

Summarizing the Text

- Begin by telling students that you are going to work together to provide a summary of the story. Explain to them that a summary includes the important ideas in a story. Tell them it should include the main characters, what happened in the story, and only the important details.

- Tell students you are going to reread the story again, and this time you want them to listen for three things: the main characters, what happens in the story, and the important details. (If you are teaching this story with kindergarteners, you might divide the class into three groups and have each group focus on just one of those elements. If you are reading this story with second graders, you might have them mark these things on their copies as you are reading aloud.)

- After reading the story, you might want to chart the information they found as you were reading. After charting or sharing the information, tell students they can use the information on the chart to help develop a summary. Offer them the first sentence in the summary on the next page and ask what the next sentence might be. If there is difficulty, ask the students: What's the first thing that happened when the donkey was on the road? If they tell you about each animal the donkey met, remind them that this is a summary and help them put the information about each animal in one sentence. Depending on how the students are doing, you may want to call on a student to suggest what they should talk about next. Using such scaffolding, develop the rest of the summary as a group, or ask a student to pick it up at some place and finish the summary independently.

A Summary

A master was mistreating his donkey, so the donkey decided to run away. Along the way, he ran into other animals with problems and invited them to join him on his journey. They ended up in a dark forest where they found a cottage and saw a group of bandits counting their money. The bandits thought the animals were the devil, so they ran away. One bandit came back but the cat clawed him, the dog bit him, and the donkey kicked him. The bandit thought the cat was a witch, the dog a demon, and the donkey a monster, so he ran away again. The animals moved into the cottage and lived there happily for many years.

Analysis: Recognizing How Things Change in a Story

• Now students should have a solid understanding of what happened in the story. Next have them work with a partner to discuss how things changed for the animals from the beginning of the story to the end. Tell them to think about what was happening in the beginning of the story and what happened at the end of the story. If you charted the information, encourage them to use the chart for support. (For first and second grade, have students write a sentence or two that describes how things have changed for the characters. For kindergarten, have them share a sentence or two, orally, with their partners.)

• Bring students together and have them share how things have changed. **(In the beginning of the story, the animals had it pretty rough because they had problems and were no longer wanted, but now they have friends and a wonderful place to live.)**

Structure: Noticing a Pattern

• Often, stories include a pattern, and recognizing that pattern can help support comprehension. When readers recognize a pattern, they are better able to piece together the events in the story.

• Reread the beginning of the story again and then have students work with a partner to talk about what was similar about what was happening with the animals.

• Bring students together and chart their responses on a three-column chart. In the first column, place the name of the animal; in the second column chart the animal's problem; and in the third column, chart the solution to the animal's problem. Then, ask students if they notice anything about the chart. **(There is a pattern. The animals all had different problems, but they all had the same solution—go to Bremen.)**

Analysis: Appreciating Descriptive Language

It's never too early to have readers take a closer look at how authors use words to get across a point or to paint a picture for readers. There are two sections in this story that we think are perfect for introducing or (for those students already familiar with) reinforcing the idea of descriptive language.

- Begin by asking students to close their eyes, and then reread the following section: *However, mistaking the glow of the cat's eyes for burning coals, the bandit dropped a candle next to the cat. Instantly the furious cat sank its claws into the bandit's face. The man fell backwards on to the dog, dropping his gun, which went off. The dog's sharp teeth sank into his leg. When the donkey saw the bandit at the door, he gave a tremendous kick, sending the man flying right through the doorway. The rooster greeted the bandit's action with a grim crowing sound.*

- Have students share what they saw when the author was describing this scene. Then ask them to share which specific words the author used to give them such vivid images and to explain how these images influenced their thinking. You might begin by offering a place that allowed you to "see" exactly what was happening in the text and how it made you feel as a reader. **(Comparing the glow of the cat's eyes to burning coals really allowed me to see the cat's dark eyes with red or orange glowing from them. It painted a pretty scary picture for me.)**

- Next have students work with a partner to analyze the remaining sections; this provides students with the opportunity to work with descriptive language. Tell the partners to read each sentence, identify specific words that let them "see" what was happening in the text, and explain how those words made them feel or think.

> Paragraph 4. *Anxious to see, the dog jumped on the donkey's back, the cat climbed onto the dog and the rooster flew on top of the cat to watch what was going on inside.*
>
> Paragraph 5. *Now, the cottage was the hideaway of a gang of bandits who were busily celebrating their latest robbery.*
>
> Paragraph 5. *The hungry donkey and his friends became excited when they saw the food on the table. Upset by the jittery crew on his back, the donkey stuck his head through the window.*
>
> Paragraph 5. *Then his three companions toppled on to the lamp. The light went out and the room rang with the braying of the donkey, the barking of the dog, and the snarling of the cat. The rooster screeched along with the others.*

- Conclude the activity by having students discuss what they learned about descriptive language, how it influences the reader, and the role it played in this particular text.

"DOLPHINS ARE SPECIAL"

Dolphins Are Special
by Rita Carboni

Recently, a young girl visited a zoo aquarium and stopped to do some flips in front of a window. A dolphin was swimming on the other side of the window and stopped to watch the girl's performance. The dolphin loved it! The girl kept flipping, and the dolphin kept nodding its head. It seemed to be saying, "Do more flips, please." Scientists explain that humans and dolphins have interacted for years, and this is just another example of that special bond.

One possible reason humans and dolphins may have a special bond is because dolphins are really smart. One study showed that bottlenose dolphins are able to recognize themselves in a mirror. This surprised researchers who thought animals weren't able to recognize themselves. Another study showed that some dolphins use sea sponges as tools. The researchers from the study think this shows that dolphins are able to problem solve, a sure sign of intelligence. Because dolphins are so intelligent, they are able to communicate with people.

Another reason humans may have a special bond with dolphins is because dolphins are entertaining. People love watching dolphins dive down into the water and then jump high in the air. Some dolphins can leap as high as thirty feet in the air. Other dolphins can be trained to do hard tricks. Some dolphins can jump through hoops. Some can play basketball, and others can even paint pictures. People enjoy seeing all of the different things dolphins can do, and dolphins enjoy entertaining people. After watching a dolphin show, one man commented that he was convinced that the dolphins gave the fans a big smile after they finished their performances.

Another reason dolphins share a bond with humans is because they can be helpful, just like people. A British man was in the ocean for an eight-hour swim. The water was freezing, and he didn't think he was going to make it. Then, things got even worse. A shark began to swim near him. It kept swimming next to him and would not leave. The swimmer was very scared and thought the shark was going to attack him, but then a group of dolphins came to his rescue. They stayed by his side and protected him as he continued swimming. The dolphins looked at the man as if to say, "Don't worry, we'll stay with you until you are safe." The man said the dolphins saved his life.

Dolphins also have been known to help other animals. In New Zealand, a group of whales got caught in a terrible storm. The storm washed the whales onto the shore. People tried to get the whales back in the water, but nothing they did worked. Finally, the people got the whales back in the water, but the whales were confused. They didn't know which way to swim. A group of dolphins saw what was happening and hurried to help. It seemed as if the dolphins were actually worried about the whales and didn't want to see them die. They swam next to the whales and guided them back to sea. The dolphins saved the whales!

For years, people told stories about how dolphins saved drowning sailors from the rough waters of the sea. People are now beginning to believe those stories. Today, there are plenty of examples of how dolphins came to the rescue. Dolphins are not only helpful, but they are intelligent and entertaining. It is no wonder that people have a special bond with such special creatures.

Segments and Queries

Text segments	Queries/targeted responses
Recently, a young girl visited a zoo aquarium and stopped to do some flips in front of a window. A dolphin was swimming on the other side of the window and stopped to watch the girl's performance. The dolphin loved it! The girl kept flipping, and the dolphin kept nodding its head. It seemed to be saying, "Do more flips, please." Scientists explain that humans and dolphins have interacted for years, and this is just another example of that special bond. **1**	1. **What did we learn in the first paragraph?** (A girl was doing flips in front of a dolphin, and the dolphin really liked it.) 1a. **What did we learn from the scientists?** (Scientists say that people and dolphins have always interacted with each other.) 1b. **So, how does the scientist's comment connect with what we learned in this first paragraph?** (It's an example of this interaction [or special bond] that people have with dolphins.)
One possible reason humans and dolphins may have a special bond is because dolphins are really smart. One study showed that bottlenose dolphins are able to recognize themselves in a mirror. This surprised researchers who thought animals weren't able to recognize themselves. Another study showed that some dolphins use sea sponges as tools. The researchers from the study think this shows that dolphins are able to problem solve, a sure sign of intelligence. Because dolphins are so intelligent, they are able to communicate with people. **2**	2. **What did we learn about dolphins in this paragraph?** (That they are really smart and are even able to communicate with people.)
Another reason humans may have a special bond with dolphins is because dolphins are entertaining. People love watching dolphins dive down into the water and then jump high in the air. Some dolphins can leap as high as thirty feet in the air. Other dolphins can be trained to	3. **Now, what did we find out in this paragraph?** (Not only are dolphins smart, but also they are entertaining.)

do hard tricks. Some dolphins can jump through hoops. Some can play basketball, and others can even paint pictures. People enjoy seeing all of the different things dolphins can do, and dolphins enjoy entertaining people. After watching a dolphin show, one man commented that he was convinced that the dolphins gave the fans a big smile after they finished their performances. **3**

Another reason dolphins share a bond with humans is because they can be helpful, just like people. A British man was in the ocean for an eight-hour swim. The water was freezing, and he didn't think he was going to make it. Then, things got even worse. A shark began to swim near him. It kept swimming next to him and would not leave. The swimmer was very scared and thought the shark was going to attack him, but then a group of dolphins came to his rescue. They stayed by his side and protected him as he continued swimming. The dolphins looked at the man as if to say, "Don't worry, we'll stay with you until you are safe." The man said the dolphins saved his life. **4**

4. **What's the main idea in this paragraph?**
   (Like people, dolphins are very helpful. They even saved a swimmer from sharks.)

Dolphins also have been known to help other animals. In New Zealand, a group of whales got caught in a terrible storm. The storm washed the whales onto the shore. People tried to get the whales back in the water, but nothing they did worked. Finally, the people got the whales back in the water, but the whales were confused. They didn't know which way to swim. A group of dolphins saw what was happening and hurried to help. It seemed as if the dolphins were actually worried about the whales and didn't want to see them die. They swam next to the whales and guided them back to sea. The dolphins saved the whales! **5**

5. **How does the information in this paragraph connect to what we just talked about?**
   (Dolphins not only help people, but they also have helped other animals.)

For years, people told stories about how dolphins saved drowning sailors from the rough waters of the sea. People are now beginning to believe those stories. Today, there are plenty of examples of how dolphins came to the rescue. Dolphins are not only helpful, but they are intelligent and entertaining. It is no wonder that people have a special bond with such special creatures. **6**

6. **What final point is the author making in this section?**
   (That people and dolphins really do share a special bond.)

Close Reading Activities for "Dolphins Are Special"

Main Ideas and Supporting Details

As we have mentioned, students often have difficulty differentiating the main idea from supporting details, especially with informational texts. This becomes even more of a challenge with younger students because they tend to latch onto their favorite detail, and miss the big picture.

- As a class, discuss the main idea of the text. (**People and dolphins share a special bond.**) If students struggle to identify the main idea, reread the first paragraph together, drawing attention to the last line.

- Then have students work with a partner to list the details that support the main idea and provide an explanation for how their examples connect to the main idea. It might be helpful for students to work with a chart similar to the one in Figure 10.1.

- If you are working with nonreaders, reread the text to the class and have students raise their hands when they hear a detail that supports the main idea. Chart the student's response and ask students to explain how that example connects to the main idea.

- Have students restate the main idea of the text and then explain what they learned about main ideas and supporting details. Have several students share how this lesson will help them in the future when they read other texts.

Language Analysis

The author in this text uses language that suggests what a dolphin might be thinking. By doing so, it influences the reader to feel a certain way or think a certain way about these animals.

- Begin by reading aloud the first paragraph. Draw attention to the following line: *The dolphin loved it! The girl kept flipping, and the dolphin kept nodding its head. It seemed to be saying, "Do more flips, please."*

- Ask students what those lines let them know. (**The dolphin was having so much fun watching the girl flip, it wanted her to do more.**)

- Explain that the author was letting the reader in on the dolphin's thoughts. Since dolphins don't speak, the author was speaking for him.

| Main idea: People and dolphins share a special bond. ||
Detail	Explanation/connection to main idea
Bottlenose dolphins recognize themselves in the mirror. Dolphins use sea sponges as tools.	Dolphins are really smart like people. In fact, they are so smart they are able to communicate with people. Their intelligence and ability to communicate allow them to have a special bond with people.
Dolphins are entertaining: They can leap as high as 30 feet, jump through hula hoops, play basketball, and paint pictures.	People love to watch dolphins and their amazing tricks, and dolphins love entertaining the people.
A dolphin saved a swimmer from sharks.	Dolphins have been known to help people, so it seems that they care about people.
A group of dolphins helped save a group of whales.	Like most people, this example shows that dolphins are helpful and caring.

FIGURE 10.1. Chart of main ideas in "Dolphins Are Special."

• Have students work with a partner and go through the text to find other places that might be the dolphins' thoughts. Have them cite the example and what the example reveals about the dolphin's thoughts.

• Again, if you are working with nonreaders, reread the text to the class and have students raise their hands when they hear a place where the author lets the dolphin's thoughts be known. Have them share what that example revealed about the dolphin's thoughts.

• Bring students together and share their examples. You might want to chart students' responses once you bring them together (see Figure 10.2).

Example	Lets us know . . .
The dolphin loved it! . . . It seemed to be saying, "Do more flips, please."	The dolphin was having so much fun watching the girl flip, it wanted her to do more.
After watching a dolphin show, one man commented that he was convinced that the dolphins gave the fans a big smile after they finished their performances.	The dolphins were letting the people know that they enjoyed performing for the people as much as the people enjoyed watching them perform.
The dolphins looked at the man as if to say, "Don't worry, we'll stay with you until you are safe."	The dolphins seem to really care about the man and aren't going to leave him until he is safe.
It seemed as if the dolphins were actually worried about the whales and didn't want to see them die.	Again, this seems like the dolphins were actually worried about the whales and they wanted to make sure they would be okay.

FIGURE 10.2. Text examples that revealed the dolphins' thoughts.

Frequently Asked Questions

We have gathered many of the following questions from acquaintances of ours who work in schools—teachers, administrators, curriculum folks—where currently there is much talk about the Common Core and associated issues. Other questions came from educators we mention in the Acknowledgments, who read the manuscript and offered feedback. Some questions, especially ones about comprehension, arose during our earlier work but remain relevant to matters in this book. We look forward to additional questions from those who read and use our ideas presented in this book.

1. **Although most recommendations indicate that close reading should be done with a short piece of text (a paragraph or two), you use complete texts. Can you explain why?**

Good question. The main purpose of our book is to help scaffold teachers' understanding and implementation of surface or gist comprehension and close reading. A key to doing so is to provide them with many features and activities appropriate for engaging in close reading in the context of authentic texts. So we consider whole texts as potential grist for close reading and choose paragraphs, sentences, and words from that text that are good grist for close reading. At this point we are not focusing on either the students or teacher doing a close reading of a complete short text. Our purpose is to support teachers in providing students with the kinds of features that a close reading might reveal. We do this because we want teachers to have many features of language to which they can bring attention, and many activities for engaging students with those features. When teachers are first starting to plan close reading—and perhaps even after they are more skilled—we envision them thumbing through our close reading lessons for ideas about what features and activities they could use and to stimulate additional ideas for the text they are planning.

2. Do I have to do multiple reads? Why can't I tackle it all during the first read?

We were believers in doing multiple reads even before the present recommendations that students engage in multiple reads. Like many others, we have had the experience of seeing a movie for the second time and noticing things that went by the wayside the first time. The experience of reading a text for the second time offers the reader opportunities to notice new and interesting features. An apt incident was when my (Isabel's) son, Mark, moved to a new school for fifth grade. In the new school, the fifth graders used the same basal series that Mark had used in fourth grade. His original school was kind of "nongraded" and used a fifth-grade basal in fourth grade. When Mark told me during the first week of school that he would be reading the same book, I asked him if he wanted me to talk with his teachers. He did not want that! Well, the outcome is that Mark was not held back in his reading achievement by reading the basal texts the second time; indeed his achievement went up by close to 2 years. More importantly, he ended up liking his "second read" and occasionally mentioned something new he had noticed. For example, he became interested in the myths, which had not been the case during his "first read," and pursued that interest out of school. Perhaps the reason is that he noticed some things about myths that had not really registered the first time. Multiple reads are useful across skill levels. For struggling readers, some familiarization with the decoding issues might free them up to comprehend more or better. For skilled readers, like Mark, it is likely that they will understand some things that they passed by, and perhaps even notice authors' language. We do think students need to be taught to notice authors' language, and second reads are the ideal places to draw student's attention to it. Thus we attempt in close reading to point to aspects of language, with the goal of having students eventually notice details of language themselves.

3. I want to plan a close reading lesson. What type of text should I use?

If the lesson you are planning is your first attempt to engage with your students in close reading, we suggest you identify some models of lessons for specific texts and use them before you develop your own. We have many models in this book; in fact, instructional models for specific texts are at the core of this book. On the Internet, *www.achieve.org* is a website that publishes lessons that have been vetted. But if you want to give it a try yourself, let us offer some suggestions:

- To start with, we suggest you use a literary text, as the language is usually richer than in an informational text.[1]
- Identify a complex text (see Chapter 5). It might be a stand-alone text, or it might come from a longer piece, say, a novel the class is reading. For instance, the target of your lesson could be the next chapter to be read. It is likely the chapter will be longer than we recommend for a first try, which is no more than 700 words, so you might consider using an excerpt from that chapter.
- Develop queries and segment the text (see Chapter 4).
- Develop close reading activities. See Chapter 5 and the last section of Chapter 7, and review some of our close reading activities, including those for the texts in Part Two.
- Use your queries and segments and engage in interspersed reading.
- Use the close reading activities you have developed and engage the class in close reading.

4. What suggestions do you have for my struggling readers?

Often struggling readers have decoding and fluency problems, and it is not unlikely that those are the root cause of comprehension problems. But frequently those students can comprehend what they hear. When using interspersed reading and discussing, asking students to read a section aloud helps to provide the struggling students with the content. Moreover, when you ask the group to read a section silently and then discuss that section, the struggling reader will learn from

---

[1] Yet, one of the top three most language-rich texts in our book is an informational piece, John F. Kennedy's *Inaugural Address* (1961). In general, speeches that hold a place in our culture are language-rich.

the interspersed discussion what the section is about that he or she had trouble getting through. This provides the struggling reader with the content that he or she would have missed during silent reading, and thus he or she can go to the next section knowledgeable about what has preceded it.

5. Are queries text-based?

Absolutely. As we discussed at the beginning of Chapter 3, the queries in our earlier QtA work were 85–90% text-based, but we did also fold in some analytic language-focused questions. We did so because we wanted some attention paid to those matters, and at that time reading instruction rarely talked about subsequent reads. Now, with multiple reads, we have moved those more language-analytic queries to the second read and enlarged their presence in text lessons.

6. Is it really possible to do a close read as a kindergarten teacher?

Without a doubt. It's quite remarkable what young children can do with some prompting and scaffolding. For instance, recall the difference in the kinds of responses students gave to constrained queries compared to open queries (see Chapter 3, Figures 3.1 and 3.2). When teachers changed their queries from constrained to open and worked with students, they eventually enlarged their responses from a single word to full ideas.[2] This was all part of the first read.

Similarly, young students can also engage in close reading activities in early grades. For an example of what very young children can do, consider the poem "Who Has Seen the Wind?" by Christina Rossetti. The poet uses personification— she gives human qualities to things that are nonhuman, such as the wind causing the leaves to "hang trembling" and "the trees bow down their heads." Bringing children's attention to this device and identifying it as *personification* may encourage students to pay attention to authors' techniques. Personification is just one of a myriad of language analyses that young children can be brought along to understand. Certainly alliteration, similes, and mood are other good candidates. Why start so early? Think of the attention students could pay to language if from an early age they were made aware of some of the techniques, devices,

---

[2]Initially children had difficulty developing full responses, in contrast to the customary responses of a word or two. But with teacher prompting and scaffolding they learned, and full responses became the norm. We mention this because we've learned to be very cautious about assuming what students can't do at first blush.

tricks, word play, and the like that authors use. All of this enables us to reach our definition of close reading, which includes "keen attention to the fine details of language and structure for the purpose of appreciating an author's craft."

Think of the repetition and patterns found in literature. In "The Musicians of Bremen," as the donkey travels the road to Bremen, he meets three animals, each of whom has been mistreated, each of whom is alone, and each of whom the donkey invites to come along to Bremen. Why not point that out—or better yet, asks students what *they* notice about the content, what is the same about the animals, and so on. Consider Shel Silverstein's wonderful *The Giving Tree* (1964, 1992), which begs to be read again and again. On later reads, why not ask children to notice the first word on most of the pages (*and*). Then have them notice the first word on some of the other pages (*but*). What happens on the *and* pages? (The boy plays in and around the tree.) What happens on the *but* pages? (Something changes.)

Although we are not inclined to think that direct teaching of vocabulary falls legitimately under close reading, we mention it here for two reasons. First, vocabulary is so necessary for proficient reading that it probably doesn't matter under which topic it is taught, as long as it is given the attention that it needs. And second, trade books are superb sources of vocabulary. Consider some examples of the fairly sophisticated words that can be found in trade books for kindergarten and first grade: *scour*, *examine*, and *extraordinary* from *Socrates* (Bogaerts & Bogaerts, 1992); *speck* and *sprucing* from *Mrs. Potter's Pig* (Root, 1996); and *delicate*, *morsel*, and *remarkable* from *Doctor De Soto* (Steig, 1982).

In "Text Talk" (Beck & McKeown, 2001), an approach to read-alouds, several words from the story are brought forward and discussed after the story is read. If a word is not essential for comprehension, we strongly favor bringing that word up after reading. One reason is that the story context can be used in the instructional routine.[3]

7. Is there a reason why the shorter stories in your book have about the same number of queries as the longer stories? Is there a range of about a dozen queries that is optimal?

We are so glad you asked these questions! The answer to the first question is *yes, there is a reason*. The answer to the second question is *no, there is not an optimal*

---

[3] We have long been involved in developing direct instruction for vocabulary. For a variety of instructional approaches and strategies, see our most recent publication, *Bringing Words to Life, Second Edition* (Beck, McKeown, & Kucan, 2013).

number of queries. The text is what should determine how many queries seem appropriate. The reason we include about the same number of queries for both a long and a short text is due to differences in the nature of the texts. We use several texts that were adapted from longer stories, and these adapted versions are shorter than the originals. For example, the version of "The Lady, or the Tiger?" in our book is 716 words long, which is only about 35% the length of the original story. Our adapted version is similar to how that story has been presented in several middle school anthologies.[4]

In contrast to this shortened version of "The Lady, or the Tiger?," we use Edgar Allan Poe's original story "The Tell-Tale Heart," which is over 2,000 words long. Yet for gist comprehension during the first read, the two stories had almost the same number of queries: 13 for "The Lady" and 14 for the Poe story. How can that be?

When texts are shortened, what is usually omitted are details, lengthy dialogue, and elaborated language. What is left are the bare bones of a story, which is gist material. In order to develop a coherent representation, the dense gist content is what is queried. But the original "Tell-Tale Heart" of over 2,000 words has details, dialogue, and richly elaborated language. The gist material is only a portion of Poe's story. His abundant remarkable language is taken up in close reading. Just compare the amount, and the kind, of close reading we were able to provide for this story as compared to "The Lady, or the Tiger?"

---

[4]We used several adapted texts because we wanted teachers to have experience with different kinds of text materials.

PART TWO

Text Lessons for Comprehension and Close Reading

Does an Elephant Never Forget?

by Rita Carboni

Grade Level: 3–4

Introduction: This article deals with the extent to which elephants do have the remarkable memories attributed to them. The article reports research that indicates that elephants recognize the bones of their former herd mates. Carboni also points to how their amazing memories have helped them survive in the wild. In one example, those herds who had older matriarchs who had lived through drought before remember the way to get to places where there was water and food. In contrast those elephants who had younger matriarchs who had never experienced a drought did not know where to lead their herd. The article also tells of a heart-warming incident in which two elephants that had been together for a few months and then separated for 22 years recognized each other and immediately attempted to get through their cages to get to one another.

Does an Elephant Never Forget?
by Rita Carboni

Have you ever heard the saying "an elephant never forgets" and wondered how true that statement really is? Well, it is true, sort of. Although it is impossible for elephants to remember everything, there is some truth to the old proverb. Researchers have spent years studying memories of elephants and have concluded that elephants really do have exceptional memories.

Researchers have conducted a number of studies to see how much elephants can remember. One study found that elephants can recognize and remember as many as 30 of their fellow elephants. In another experiment researchers showed elephants a number of different objects. The elephants gave the strongest reaction to the bones of their relatives. Researchers concluded that they were able to recognize them.

In addition to using their memories to recognize other elephants, elephants use their amazing memories to help them survive in the wild. In one study, researchers followed three different herds of elephants during a terrible drought. The older matriarchs who had lived through droughts before remembered other places where they could get food and water. They led their herds to those sources. The herd with the younger matriarch who hadn't lived through a drought had no idea where they could get food or water. So, she kept her herd in the same spot, and the herd suffered the consequences. Sixteen of the 81 babies born to the three herds died that year. Ten of them were from the herd with the younger matriarch. Researchers concluded that the older matriarchs remembered the food and water sources from a drought that happened over thirty years prior to this drought. They also remembered the routes to reach the food and water.

Ian Douglas-Hamilton, a zoologist who is an authority on pachyderms, supports the idea that elephants have exceptional memories. He developed a special friendship with one of the elephants and often took walks with her in the wild. He left the park and did not return for four years. When he did return, his elephant "friend" greeted him immediately. They began their strolls again just like old friends.

One of the most heart-warming stories that support the theory that an elephant never forgets is the story of Jenny and Shirley. Shirley was an elephant in her twenties who had been performing with the Carson and Barnes Circus. One day, a young elephant named Jenny joined the circus. The two elephants bonded, and Shirley became like a mother to Jenny. The elephants performed together only for a few months before being sent to separate zoos. Twenty-two years later, the two elephants were reunited at an elephant sanctuary. Immediately, the two elephants tried to get as close to one another as they could. They were banging on the gate and roaring loudly. They were so anxious to be next to each other, they even bent the metal bars when they tried to climb through the gate. Workers opened the gate, and the two elephants were together again. Shirley again took on the role of mother to Jenny, and the two remained inseparable until Jenny's death ten years later.

It is common knowledge that elephants have the largest brain of all mammals. Adult brains can weigh as much as 10.5 pounds and researchers believe that is why elephants have such good memories.

Elephants use these big brains to help them remember old friends and animals that are enemies. They also use their exceptional memory skills to remember locations of food and water and the routes to take them there. All of these memories help elephants to survive in the wild.

SEGMENTED TEXT AND QUERIES

Text segments	Queries/targeted responses
Have you ever heard the saying "an elephant never forgets" and wondered how true that statement really is? Well, it is true, sort of. Although it is impossible for elephants to remember everything, there is some truth to the old proverb. Researchers have spent years studying memories of elephants and have concluded that elephants really do have exceptional memories. **1**	1. **What did we find out in this first paragraph?** (Elephants have really good memories.)
Researchers have conducted a number of studies to see how much elephants can remember. One study found that elephants can recognize and remember as many as 30 of their fellow elephants. In another experiment researchers showed elephants a number of different objects. The elephants gave the strongest reaction to the bones of their relatives. Researchers concluded that they were able to recognize them. **2**	2. **How does the information in this second paragraph connect with what we just talked about?** (It provides support for the idea that an elephant never forgets.)
In addition to using their memories to recognize other elephants, elephants use their amazing memories to help them survive in the wild. In one study, researchers followed three different herds of elephants during a terrible drought. The older matriarchs who had lived through droughts before remembered other places where they could get food and water. They led their herds to those sources. The herd with the younger matriarch who hadn't lived through a drought had no idea where they could get food or water. So, she kept her herd in the same spot, and the herd suffered the consequences. Sixteen of the 81 babies born to the three herds died that year. Ten of them were from the herd with the younger matriarch. Researchers concluded that the older matriarchs remembered the food and water sources from a drought that happened over thirty years prior to this drought. They also remembered the routes to reach the food and water. **3**	3. **What's the big idea in this paragraph?** (It's a good thing that elephants have such exceptional memories. Their memories help them survive in the wild.)
Ian Douglas-Hamilton, a zoologist who is an authority on pachyderms, supports the idea that elephants have exceptional memories. He developed a special friendship with one of the elephants and often took walks with her in the wild. He left the park and did not return for four years. When he did return, his elephant "friend" greeted him immediately. They began their strolls again just like old friends. **4**	4. **What did we learn in this section?** (Elephants don't just remember other elephants and things in the wild. They also remember people.)

One of the most heart-warming stories that support the theory that an elephant never forgets is the story of Jenny and Shirley. Shirley was an elephant in her twenties who had been performing with the Carson and Barnes Circus. One day, a young elephant named Jenny joined the circus. The two elephants bonded, and Shirley became like a mother to Jenny. The elephants performed together only for a few months before being sent to separate zoos. Twenty-two years later, the two elephants were reunited at an elephant sanctuary. Immediately, the two elephants tried to get as close to one another as they could. They were banging on the gate and roaring loudly. They were so anxious to be next to each other, they even bent the metal bars when they tried to climb through the gate. Workers opened the gate, and the two elephants were together again. Shirley again took on the role of mother to Jenny, and the two remained inseparable until Jenny's death ten years later. **5**

5. **How does the information in this section add to what we already discussed?**
(Elephants' memories really are exceptional. Jenny and Shirley were only with each other for a few months, and it was a very long time ago, but they remembered each other and did everything they could to be together.)

It is common knowledge that elephants have the largest brain of all mammals. Adult brains can weigh as much as 10.5 pounds and researchers believe that is why elephants have such good memories. Elephants use these big brains to help them remember old friends and animals that are enemies. They also use their exceptional memory skills to remember locations of food and water and the routes to take them there. All of these memories help elephants survive in the wild. **6**

6. **What new information did we learn in this paragraph?**
(An elephant's exceptional memory might be because it has a really large brain.)

6a. **How does the author end this article?**
(By summarizing the important point that elephants use their exceptional memories to remember old friends and to help them survive in the wild.)

CLOSE READING

Content: Summarization

Summarizing a text can be challenging for young readers. Often, they latch onto an interesting detail and talk only about that point. Or, even more often, they will include every detail in the text. It is important for these young readers to be able to identify the main idea in a text, find the significant details that support that idea, and then provide a summary that pulls that information together.

• Begin by asking students to share their thoughts on the main idea of the text. The following questions might be helpful in providing support: What did the author talk about throughout the entire text? What was the topic you learned about? What idea do all the important details support?

• Have students write down one sentence that they believe is the main idea of the text. For younger students have them share their idea with a partner. Once students have their ideas, have them share with the class.

• Students should agree that the main idea of the text is that elephants have really good memories.

• Next, have students work with a partner to identify all the places in the text that support the idea that elephants have really good memories. (They can remember other elephants and people; they can recognize bones of relatives; they can remember food and water sources; they can remember routes to get to the sources.) Chart their responses.

• To conclude the activity, have students review the information on the chart and think about what they shared when discussing the main idea and important details. Then, have them write a paragraph summarizing the text (for younger students, have them share orally).

Vocabulary: Word Meaning from Context

• Have students go to the third paragraph, second sentence, and read the next three sentences aloud:

> The older matriarchs who had lived through droughts before remembered other places where they could get food and water. They led their herds to those sources. The herd with the younger matriarch who hadn't lived through a drought had no idea where they could get food or water.

• Underline the words that appear two times in those sentences (*matriarch, drought*) and tell students that you are going to work to figure out what those words mean by looking closely at the language of the text.

• Ask students, "What does matriarch mean?" **(The female head of a herd of elephants.)** Prompt as needed: What did the older matriarchs in the first sentence do? **(Go to places where there was food and water.)** What did the last sentence tell you about the younger matriarch? **(She didn't know where they**

could get food or water.) Why are the matriarchs the ones that need to find food and water? **(They are the leaders of the herd.)** What do you think matriarchs are, male or female? Prompt as needed: If I tell you that *patriarch* is a male leader, what is a matriarch? **(A female leader.)**

- Explain to students that together you used the clues in the story to figure out the meaning of the word *matriarch*. Then, tell students they are going to do the same kind of work to figure out the meaning of the word *drought*. (With older students, consider having them do the work with a partner. With younger students, continue working together.)

- Read the two sentences again and ask students: What does *drought* mean? Prompt as needed: What did the older matriarchs in the first sentence do? **(Remember other places where they could get food and water.)** Why did they have to remember where to get food and water? **(Because of the drought.)** So what does drought mean? **(A place where there is no food or water.)** Conclude by explaining that a drought is when a place doesn't have rain for so long that it dries up the land and destroys the crops, so there is little food and water.

Li Ju and the Magic Tapestry
(an Old Chinese Folktale)

Grade Level: 3–4

Synopsis: Long ago in China there lived a woman, who was an exceptional weaver, and her three sons. The woman was able to support her family by selling her tapestries. One day she started a very large tapestry and worked on it for months and months. Since she didn't sell any tapestries during this time, the family became very poor. The two older brothers wanted her to sell the new tapestry.

One day a whirling wind came through the windows and blew the tapestry away. The distraught woman sent her eldest son to find the tapestry. He encountered an old woman, who had magical powers. The woman told the eldest brother that the fairies had taken the tapestry and would return it if he asked them. But to get to where the fairies lived, several very dangerous challenges had to be accomplished. The son was reluctant, and the old woman offered him a bag of gold, which he accepted and then went on his way. The widow sent her second son, but he also encountered the old woman and took her offer of the gold. The youngest son did not take the gold, achieved several dangerous challenges, found the fairies, returned the tapestry, and married the beautiful fairy.

Li Ju and the Magic Tapestry
(an Old Chinese Folktale)

A long time ago a widow lived in a small house near a forest in China. She made her living by weaving tapestry. Her tapestries brought the highest prices, and she was able to raise her three sons—Li Mo, Li Tu, and Li Ju—on the gold people paid for her work.

One day she began to weave a picture of a fine house with flower gardens, trees, and green fields. She worked on it month after month. Her eldest son, Li Mo, and her middle son, Li Tu, wanted the gold they could get for the tapestry and tried to make her stop working on the tapestry. To get food for the family, the youngest son, Li Ju, became a woodcutter. He earned just enough to buy rice for them all. His brothers complained that he made only enough to keep them alive.

But the old woman stayed at her loom, working by sunlight and candlelight. After a year, the old woman nearly finished. She said "A few more days will complete my tapestry." "Mother, it's beautiful," said Li Ju, gazing at the grand house that stood in a garden of rainbow-colored flowers. The next morning, the widow wove the likeness of herself and the image of Li Ju into the tapestry scene.

Suddenly Li Mo bustled into the room and cried, "Aren't you done yet? Hurry and finish so we can sell this." His mother replied, "This tapestry is a picture of everything I hold dear in my dreams and in my life. All my children should be in it, but I haven't had time to put you there. "What does it matter?" asked Li Mo. Li Tu added, "We want the gold this will bring."

Suddenly a wind blew in through the window, ripped the tapestry from its frame, and whirled it out the window. They all ran after it, but it floated away. The woman fainted. When she could speak again, she told her eldest son, "Li Mo, go and find my tapestry, or I will die."

Grumbling, Li Mo set out and traveled east. After a month he came to a mountain pass, where he found a stone hut with a stone horse standing in front of it. A white-haired woman leaned out of a window and asked, "Where are you going, young man?" Li Mo told her what happened. "That tapestry was taken by the fairies of Sun Mountain," said the old woman. "They love beautiful things, but they will return it, if you ask.

"However, it is very difficult to get there. First you have to cut your finger and place ten drops of blood on my stone horse so he can move. Then you must ride him through the flame mountains. There you must not make a sound. And if you show any fear, you will be burned to ashes. Then you must cross a sea filled with ice and hit by terrible winds. But if you complain or even shiver, you will turn to ice and sink to the bottom of the sea."

Li Mo hesitated, thinking of blood and fire and ice. The woman laughed and said, "If this frightens you, take this gold instead." And she held out a bag filled with gold coins. Li Mo grabbed it and ran away to the city to spend it on himself.

The widow grew more sickly. When Li Mo didn't come back, she said to her middle son, "Li Tu, bring back my tapestry or I will die." With much complaining, Li Tu set out. After a month's journey he met the woman in the stone hut. But when she told him the things he would have to do to get the tapestry, he, too, took the gold she offered and hurried off.

The old mother grew thin as a reed. Finally, her youngest son, Li Ju, said, "Let me go and search for the tapestry." It took him only half a month to reach the hut with the stone horse in front. The white-haired woman told him what he had to do, then offered Li Ju her gold. But he answered, "No, I must fetch my mother's tapestry." So he followed the old woman's instructions and ten drops of blood fell on the stone horse. It came to life, eager to begin their journey. Li Ju jumped on its back and they galloped away. Soon they came to the flaming mountains and the icy sea. Though the heat of the mountains blistered Li Ju's face, he let himself show no fear. When they came to the icy sea, Li Ju did not allow himself the tiniest shiver.

On the farthest shore, they came to Sun Mountain. Beautiful fairies stared at the human who had risked such dangers to reach them. The most beautiful one of all, dressed in red, greeted Li Ju. When he told her why he had come, she said, "We will return the tapestry to you. Rest, and I will bring you the tapestry in the morning." But the red-robed fairy had fallen in love with the young man. She spent the night weaving a picture of herself and part of her magic into the tapestry.

The next morning Li Ju took the folded tapestry, galloped night and day to where his mother lay. "Mother! Mother!" he cried, "I've brought your tapestry back!" He pinned it to the wall and she raised herself up out of her bed. The cloth began to grow and grow, until it covered the whole wall. And soon it became a landscape into which mother and son could step.

Together they walked toward a magnificent house. And, waiting at the front door was the beautiful fairy. As it happened, Li Ju married the beautiful fairy, and the three of them—mother, son, wife—lived very happily together.

SEGMENTED TEXT AND QUERIES

Text segments	Queries/targeted responses
A long time ago a widow lived in a small house near a forest in China. She made her living by weaving tapestry. Her tapestries brought the highest prices, and she was able to raise her three sons—Li Mo, Li Tu, and Li Ju—on the gold people paid for her work. **1**	1. **What did we find out in this first paragraph?** (A widow was able to support herself and her three sons by selling her beautiful tapestries.)
One day she began to weave a picture of a fine house with flower gardens, trees, and green fields. She worked on it month after month. Her eldest son, Li Mo, and her middle son, Li Tu, wanted the gold they could get for the tapestry and tried to make her stop working on the tapestry. To get food for the family, the youngest son, Li Ju, became a woodcutter. He earned just enough to buy rice for them all. His brothers complained that he made only enough to keep them alive. **2**	2. **What's going on with the family?** (The mother was taking too long to finish the tapestry, so the youngest son got a job.) 2a. **What do the older brothers think of the situation?** (They complained that the youngest isn't making enough money.)
But the old woman stayed at her loom, working by sunlight and candlelight. After a year, the old woman nearly finished. She said, "A few more days will complete my tapestry." "Mother, it's beautiful," said Li Ju, gazing at the grand house that stood in a garden of rainbow-colored flowers. The next morning, the widow wove the likeness of herself and the image of Li Ju into the tapestry scene. Suddenly Li Mo bustled into the room and cried, "Aren't you done yet? Hurry and finish so we can sell this." His mother replied, "This tapestry is a picture of everything I hold dear in my dreams and in my life. All my children should be in it, but I haven't had time to put you there. "What does it matter?" asked Li Mo. Li Tu added, "We want the gold this will bring." **3**	3. **How are things coming along with the tapestry?** (It was almost finished, but first she wanted to place an image of all her sons in the tapestry.) 3a. **What does Li Mo think of this idea?** (He thinks it's a waste of time. He wants her to sell it now to get the gold.)
Suddenly a wind blew in through the window, ripped the tapestry from its frame, and whirled it out the window. They all ran after it, but it floated away. The woman fainted. When she could speak again, she told her eldest son, "Li Mo, go and find my tapestry, or I will die." **4**	4. **What just happened?** (The tapestry blew out the window, and the widow told Li Mo if he doesn't find it, she will die.)

Grumbling, Li Mo set out and traveled east. After a month he came to a mountain pass, where he found a stone hut with a stone horse standing in front of it. A white-haired woman leaned out of a window and asked, "Where are you going, young man?" Li Mo told her what happened. "That tapestry was taken by the fairies of Sun Mountain," said the old woman. "They love beautiful things, but they will return it, if you ask.

"However, it is very difficult to get there. First you have to cut your finger and place ten drops of blood on my stone horse so he can move. Then you must ride him through the flame mountains. There you must not make a sound. And if you show any fear, you will be burned to ashes. Then you must cross a sea filled with ice and hit by terrible winds. But if you complain or even shiver, you will turn to ice and sink to the bottom of the sea."

Li Mo hesitated, thinking of blood and fire and ice. The woman laughed and said, "If this frightens you, take this gold instead." And she held out a bag filled with gold coins. Li Mo grabbed it and ran away to the city to spend it on himself. **5**

The widow grew more sickly. When Li Mo didn't come back, she said to her middle son, "Li Tu, bring back my tapestry or I will die." With much complaining, Li Tu set out. After a month's journey he met the woman in the stone hut. But when she told him the things he would have to do to get the tapestry, he, too, took the gold she offered and hurried off. **6**

The old mother grew thin as a reed. Finally, her youngest son, Li Ju, said, "Let me go and search for the tapestry." It took him only half a month to reach the hut with the stone horse in front. The white-haired woman told him what he had to do, then offered Li Ju her gold. But he answered, "No, I must fetch my mother's tapestry." So he followed the old woman's instructions and ten drops of blood fell on the stone horse. It came to life, eager to begin their journey. Li Ju jumped on its back and they galloped away. Soon they came to the

5. **What's going on with Li Mo's trip?**
   (An old woman told Li Mo that fairies took the tapestry. If he wants it back, he has to cut his finger, ride a stone horse through flaming mountains without a word and showing no fear, and cross a sea filled with ice and terrible winds without shivering. Or, he can forget the tapestry in exchange for some gold.)

5a. **What does Li Mo think about the deal?**
   (He takes the gold.)

6. **What did we find out here?**
   (The widow is getting worse, so she sends out her middle son to get the tapestry.)

6a. **How did that turn out?**
   (He took the same deal as his brother and left with the gold.)

7. **What's happening here?**
   (The widow has gotten sicker. Her youngest son volunteers to go and search for the tapestry. He meets the same woman but unlike his brothers, he agrees to attempt the necessary tasks in order to retrieve the tapestry.)

7a. **How is the trip going so far?**
   (Although it is challenging, Li Ju is determined to accomplish all the tasks and is staying strong.)

flaming mountains and the icy sea. Though the heat of the mountains blistered Li Ju's face, he let himself show no fear. When they came to the icy mountain, Li Ju did not allow himself the tiniest shiver. **7**

On the farthest shore, they came to Sun Mountain. Beautiful fairies stared at the human who had risked such dangers to reach them. The most beautiful one of all, dressed in red, greeted Li Ju. When he told her why he had come, she said, "We will return the tapestry to you. Rest, and I will bring you the tapestry in the morning." But the red-robed fairy had fallen in love with the young man. She spent the night weaving a picture of herself and part of her magic into the tapestry. **8**

8. What's going on now?
(Li Ju accomplished all the tasks, so the fairies agreed to give him the tapestry the next morning.)

8a. How are things going with the fairies?
(One fairy fell in love with Li Ju and wove a picture of herself and part of her magic into the tapestry.)

Since it's not explicitly known why the fairy would weave herself into the tapestry, maybe make a comment such as, "Hmmm, she wove a picture of herself and part of her magic into the tapestry. I wonder what she's up to."

The next morning Li Ju took the folded tapestry, galloped night and day to where his mother lay. "Mother! Mother!" he cried, "I've brought your tapestry back!" He pinned it to the wall and she raised herself up out of her bed. The cloth began to grow and grow, until it covered the whole wall. And soon it became a landscape into which mother and son could step.

Together they walked toward a magnificent house. And, waiting at the front door was the beautiful fairy. As it happened, Li Ju married the beautiful fairy, and the three of them— mother, son, and wife—lived very happily together. **9**

9. How did things turn out for Li Ju and his mother?
(Great. They stepped into the tapestry toward a beautiful house where the fairy was waiting. Li Ju married the fairy, and they all lived happily ever after.)

CLOSE READING

Language: Symbolism

Explain to students that *symbolism* is a literary technique in which one thing is used to represent something else. Remind them that sometimes it is difficult to understand what the item is representing, so it's important to read the text again and think about the deeper meaning of the item.

- Tell students that the tapestry in the text is more than just a piece of cloth that the widow weaves in order to make money. She even says, "This tapestry is a picture of everything I hold dear in my dreams and in my life." Have students find that sentence in the fourth paragraph, and read it aloud. Ask students if that description is the whole meaning of the tapestry, or if it represents something else to the story and the other characters. Before students answer, ask them to think about the word *dreams*: "Dreams don't always refer to something you do when you are asleep. What else can dreams mean?" **(Dreams can be what you hope for.)** "What do we know about what the widow has woven into her tapestry so far? Part of the answer is in the second paragraph. Find it and let's read it aloud." **(A picture of a fine house with flower gardens, trees, and green fields.)** "The rest of what she wove is described in the third paragraph. Go to the third paragraph and find what else the widow had woven into her tapestry. Raise your hand when you find it." Call on a student to read it aloud. (**. . . The likeness of herself and the image of Li Ju into the tapestry scene.)** What does the tapestry represent? **(It represents their future. Since she and Li Ju are the only two in the tapestry—until the fairy adds herself—they are the two who will step into the future together.)**

- Tell students that you are going to name some objects that are symbols in the story and ask them to identify what they might represent. Have students work in small groups to read through the text and explain what each object represents. You might place their ideas on a chart similar to the one that follows. Remind them to use what they've learned about the characters and the events in the story to figure out what each object represents.

Item	What it symbolizes and explanation
Gold—This is an excellent example because in this story gold represents greed, but in other stories it represents riches. This is a great opportunity to reinforce the idea that the same object can symbolize different things depending on the story.	Greed—the selfish sons are willing to let their mother die for the sake of their own wealth.
The color red	Love—the fairy who becomes Li Ju's wife is "dressed in red" and "red-robed."
Drops of blood	Commitment to their mother—In order to get the tapestry, the first thing they must do is give up a piece of themselves (drops of blood) in order to make the horse move.

Genre Study: Folktale

- Discuss with students common characteristics frequently found in folktales:
    - Handed down from generation to generation via storytelling
    - Element of magic
    - Overcome near impossible tasks
    - Teach a moral or lesson
    - Patterns
    - Stereotypical characters (good, evil, jealous . . .)
    - Setting not part of reality
    - Characters live "happily ever after"

- Have students work with a partner, and using the characteristics above identify places in the text that are representative of common elements in folktales.

- Independently, have students choose one of the elements they found with their partner and write a paragraph in which they explain how this particular element represents a folktale.

- Bring students together and have them discuss their findings and their paragraphs. You might want to chart their responses on a table similar to the following:

Characteristic	Example from text
Element of magic	Fairy weaves her magic into the tapestry. The stone horse comes to life. The tapestry comes to life.
Setting not part of reality	Li Ju rides through flame mountains and goes across a sea filled with ice.
Patterns	Each son goes to the old woman and is given the same deal.
Overcome close-to-impossible tasks	Li Ju's journey through the close-to-impossible tasks.
Teaches a moral or lesson	Greed will get you nowhere, but love and respect will get you everywhere.
Stereotypical characters	Two sons are evil, and one son is good.

- Conclude the activity by having students write a short paragraph in which they explain how engaging in identifying characteristics of a folktale should be of help to them when they read stories in the future. (It would be helpful to students if they made the point that they will recognize these characteristics and understand that they are reading a folktale).

Literary Techniques

Explain to students that authors use various literary techniques to give readers a more vivid image of characters and events in a story. Tell them you are going to talk about two of these techniques, *personification* and *simile*.

- Explain that personification is a technique in which an author gives human qualities to nonhuman things. To help students understand the concept, write the following example on the board:

    > After an exhausting day of work, the elderly woman collapsed into the chair. The armrests of the chair wrapped around and held her closely while she napped.

- Ask, "What thing did the author give human qualities to?" (**The armrests of the chair.**) "How did the author give the armrests human qualities?" (**By saying that they wrapped around the woman and held her closely; arm rests can't actually do that.**) "What's the name of the literary technique that authors use when they give human qualities to nonhuman things?" (**Personification.**)

- Tell students that a simile is when an author compares two things using the words *like* and *as*. If students are unsure of how to recognize a simile, give them the following example: *She is as busy as a bee.* Explain that a bee is typically very busy and constantly moving, so to say that someone is as busy as a bee means that they are full of energy and always doing something. Give them the following example using *like*: *Life is like a box of chocolates. You never know what you are going to get.* Ask students to explain the simile. (**Whenever you choose a piece of candy, you don't know what kind of chocolate it will be, and with life, you never know what is going to happen.**)

- Have students work with a partner to reread the text and find the example of personification and the example of a simile. Have them explain how the author used each device.

    - **Personification.** *Suddenly a wind blew in through the window, ripped the tapestry from its frame, and whirled it out the window. They all pursued it, but it swirled away into the distance.* (The author makes the wind sound like a person by saying it pulled the tapestry from its frame.)
    - **Simile.** *The old mother grew thin as a reed.* (The mother was so thin that she looked like a reed, which is a very thin plant.)

- Conclude the activity by having students independently respond to the following question: How did the author's use of personification and simile give you a more vivid picture of what was being described?

Vocabulary: Character Traits

Not all texts are filled with rich vocabulary words; however, all texts and characters can be described using rich words. Because the characters in this text are quite different, this is the perfect story for students to work with Tier Two words, as they can come up with a variety of words to describe the characters in the story.

- Begin by telling students that you are going to work with character traits, a character's attitude, or the way he or she acts.

- Tell students that the word you thought of that describes the mother is *devoted*. Explain that you chose that word because *devoted* means very loving and loyal and you feel that word best describes the relationship the mother had with her three sons. Explain that the part of the story that made you think of that word was when the mother didn't want to sell her tapestry before she wove all three of her sons into the picture because "This tapestry is a picture of everything I hold dear in my dreams and in my life. All my children should be in it, but I haven't had time to put you there." Tell them that example shows how important her children were to her and how much she loved them.

- Next, have students work in small groups to discuss each character in the story. Have them talk about the characters' attitudes, behaviors, and what they did in the story. You might have them create a chart similar to the one below.

Character	Actions/attitude
Mother	Loves her sons. Weaves beautiful tapestries.
Li Ju	Youngest son Loves his mother. Would do anything for her, including going on the trip and facing the challenges.
Li Mo	Eldest son Takes the gold instead of facing the challenges to retrieve his mother's tapestry. Complains that there isn't enough money. Tries to get his mother to sell tapestry so they can get money. Speaks to his mother in a rude manner.

Li Tu	Middle son
	Takes the gold instead of facing the challenges and retrieving his mother's tapestry.
	Complains that there isn't enough money.
	Tries to get his mother to sell tapestry so they can get money.

- Have students work with a partner to choose words that describe each character on the chart. Have them think about the following question: Based on the information listed on the chart, what words describe each of the characters (*resourceful, adamant, determined, selfish, greedy, disrespectful*)?

- Finally, have students independently write a paragraph where they choose a word that describes one of the characters in the story and have them explain why that word reflects that particular character. Have them cite specific examples from the text to support their word and description of the character.

Arachne, the Spinner
(a Greek Myth)

Retold by Theo Arvanitis

Grade Level: 5–6

Synopsis: Arachne, an excellent weaver, boasted that she was a better weaver than Athena, a goddess. Arachne was even so bold as to say that if Athena challenged her to a contest, she would participate. Athena was very angry, but agreed to the contest. Athena wove a gorgeous tapestry showing the gods and goddesses doing good deeds for the people. Arachne wove a spectacular tapestry that made fun of the gods and goddesses. It showed them behaving badly. When Athena saw it she became even angrier. She was forced to admit that Arachne's work was flawless, but the disrespectful choice of subject made her finally lose her temper, and she turned Arachne into a spider—allowing her to hang by a thread and continue to spin, as have all her descendants.

Lesson content	Page
Copy of text for duplication and distribution: *Arachne, the Spinner*	161
Segmented Text and Queries	163
Close Reading	165

Arachne, the Spinner
(a Greek Myth)

retold by Theo Arvanitis

A long time ago in ancient Greece, there lived a young spinner and weaver called Arachne. No spinner or weaver was more talented or gifted than Arachne. (Spinners spin materials like wool into thread, and weavers weave thread into cloth. Many people are both spinners and weavers.) Arachne wove all sorts of beautiful pictures into her cloth. Often the scenes were so lifelike that people felt they could almost touch and feel what was going on. Visitors travelled many miles to see her beautiful work. Not only were her finished products beautiful to look at, but just watching her weave was a sight to behold. Even the nymphs of the forest would stop their play and look on in wonder.

Arachne was rightly very proud of her work, but she was also very arrogant. So remarkable were her works that observers often commented that she must have been trained by Athena, the goddess of wisdom and crafts. Athena was also known for her ability to spin and weave beautiful pictures. Arachne was scornful of this. Why, she said, should she, with all her talent, be placed in an inferior place to the goddess? She would tell visitors that Athena, the goddess herself, could not produce work any better.

When news of Arachne's bold claim reached Athena she was very angry, but she decided to give the young woman a chance to redeem herself. So one day she disguised herself as an old peasant woman and went to visit Arachne. She gently warned her to be careful not to offend the gods by comparing her talents to those of an immortal. (A mortal is a person who dies, in contrast to the gods who are immortal and live forever.)

But Arachne told the old woman to save her breath. She boasted that she welcomed a contest with Athena, and, if she lost, would suffer whatever punishment the goddess decided. At this Athena revealed her true form. The visitors who had come to watch Arachne's weaving were very afraid, but Arachne stood her ground. She had made a claim, and she would prove it.

It was decided they would compete by each creating a tapestry. The two of them set up their looms in the same room and the contest began, the mortal Arachne at her loom and the goddess Athena at hers. They wove from early in the morning until it got too dark to see. The next day they compared what they had done.

Athena had woven a stunning cloth showing the gods and goddesses together on Mount Olympus doing good deeds for people. A beautiful scene had developed from the threads. Those witnessing the competition marveled at the work produced by the goddess. Arachne, however, had woven a cloth that made fun of the gods and goddesses. It showed them behaving very badly. Nevertheless, so exquisite was Arachne's work that the characters in the scene were lifelike.

When Athena saw it she was even angrier than she had been before. She was forced to admit that Arachne's work was flawless but the disrespectful choice of subject made her finally lose her temper. Athena destroyed Arachne's tapestry and loom. Then Athena touched Arachne's forehead, making sure that she felt guilt for her actions.

Arachne was ashamed. But the guilt was so overwhelming that it was far too deep for a mortal to bear. Realizing her folly Arachne was crushed with shame. Terrified and in turmoil she ran into a nearby wood and hanged herself from a tree.

Athena had not expected Arachne to take her own life and took pity on her.

Arachne, the Spinner *(page 2)*

Sprinkling Arachne with the juices of the aconite plant, Athena loosened the rope, which became a cobweb; then she said gently, "Spin if you wish to spin." At this Arachne slowly came back to life but not in human form. For as Athena spoke her words, Arachne's nose and ears disappeared, her arms and legs became long and slender and new legs grew beside them. Then her whole body shrank until she was just a tiny little spider.

For the rest of her life Arachne was to hang from a thread and to be a great weaver. And the descendants of Arachne still weave their magic webs all over the earth today.

SEGMENTED TEXT AND QUERIES

Segments	Queries/targeted responses

A long time ago in ancient Greece, there lived a young spinner and weaver called Arachne. No spinner or weaver was more talented or gifted than Arachne. (Spinners spin materials like wool into thread and weavers weave thread into cloth. Many people are both spinners and weavers.) Arachne wove all sorts of beautiful pictures into her cloth. Often the scenes were so lifelike that people felt they could almost touch and feel what was going on. Visitors travelled many miles to see her beautiful work. Not only were her finished products beautiful to look at, but just watching her weave was a sight to behold. Even the nymphs of the forest would stop their play and look on in wonder. **1**

1. **What did we learn in the first paragraph?**
   (Arachne was a talented spinner.)

1a. **What in the text helps you understand how talented Arachne was?**
   (Often the scenes were so lifelike that people felt they could almost touch and feel what was going on.)

Arachne was rightly very proud of her work but she was also very arrogant. So remarkable were her works that observers often commented that she must have been trained by Athena, the goddess of wisdom and crafts, also known for her ability to spin and weave beautiful pictures. Arachne was scornful of this. Why, she said, should she, with all her talent, be placed in an inferior place to the goddess? She would tell visitors that Athena, the goddess herself, could not produce work any better. **2**

2. **What else did we learn about Arachne?**
   (She is very proud and arrogant.)

2a. **Find the place in the text that shows Arachne's disrespect toward Athena.**
   (She would tell visitors that Athena, the goddess herself, could not produce work any better.)

When news of Arachne's bold claim reached Athena she was very angry, but she decided to give the young woman a chance to redeem herself. So one day she disguised herself as an old peasant woman and went to visit Arachne. She gently warned her to be careful not to offend the gods by comparing her talents to those of an immortal. (A mortal is a person who dies, in contrast to the gods who are immortal and live forever.) **3**

3. **What's going on here?**
   (Athena was very angry. Disguised as an old woman, she warned Arachne not to compare her talents with the gods, as gods are immortal.)

But Arachne told the old woman to save her breath. She boasted that she welcomed a contest with Athena, and, if she lost, would suffer whatever punishment the goddess

4. **How did Arachne react?**
   (She remained boastful and wanted a contest.)

decided. At this Athena revealed her true form. The visitors who had come to watch Arachne's weaving were very afraid, but Arachne stood her ground. She had made a claim, and she would prove it.

It was decided they would compete by each creating a tapestry. The two of them set up their looms in the same room and the contest began, the mortal Arachne at her loom and the goddess Athena at hers. They wove from early in the morning until it got too dark to see. The next day they compared what they had done. **4**

Athena had woven a stunning cloth showing the gods and goddesses together on Mount Olympus doing good deeds for people. A beautiful scene had developed from the threads. Those witnessing the competition marveled at the work produced by the goddess. Arachne, however, had woven a cloth that made fun of the gods and goddesses. It showed them behaving very badly. Nevertheless, so exquisite was the mortal's work that the characters in the scene were lifelike. **5**

When Athena saw it she was even angrier than she had been before. She was forced to admit that Arachne's work was flawless but the disrespectful choice of subject made her finally lose her temper. Athena destroyed Arachne's tapestry and loom. Then Athena touched Arachne's forehead, making sure that she felt guilt for her actions. **6**

Arachne was ashamed. But the guilt was so overwhelming that it was far too deep for a mortal to bear. Realizing her folly Arachne was crushed with shame. Terrified and in turmoil she ran into a nearby wood and hanged herself from a tree. **7**

4a. **What's the plan?**
(Athena and Arachne will each create a tapestry and they will be compared.)

5. **What did we find out about the tapestries?**
(Athena's shows gods doing good deeds. Arachne's shows the gods misbehaving.)

6. **What happened in this section?**
(Athena destroyed Arachne's tapestry and loom and touched Arachne's forehead, which made Arachne feel guilty.)

6a. **If students don't mention the result of Athena's touching Arachne, ask them: What did touching Arachne's forehead cause?**
(Arachne felt guilty for her actions.)

7. **What happened?**
(Arachne felt extreme guilt and hung herself from a tree.)

Athena had not expected Arachne to take her own life and took pity on her.

Sprinkling Arachne with the juices of the aconite plant, Athena loosened the rope, which became a cobweb; then she said gently, "Spin if you wish to spin." At this Arachne slowly came back to life but not in human form. For as Athena spoke her words, Arachne's nose and ears disappeared, her arms and legs became long and slender and new legs grew beside them. Then her whole body shrank until she was just a tiny little spider.

For the rest of her life Arachne was to hang from a thread and to be a great weaver and the descendants of Arachne still weave their magic webs all over the earth today. **8**

8. **What did we find out in the last section?**
   (She brought Arachne back to life and turned her into a spider.)

8a. **Why did Athena turn her into a spider rather than some other insect?**
   (As a spider she could continue to spin.)

8b. **Who are the *descendants* of Arachne?**
   (Spiders.)

CLOSE READING

Identify Characteristics of a Myth

Ask students what genre the story of Arachne is; if needed, tell them that the Arachne story is a myth. To review the characteristics of a myth, list the items below on a chart and discuss them. In the final activity below, students are asked to write an original myth, so knowing the characteristics of a myth will be helpful to them. Be sure to make the point that every myth does not have each of the characteristics. A myth often:

- Involves supernatural beings or events.
- Teaches a moral lesson.
- Involves nature.
- Involves magic.
- Transforms a character into something else.
- Includes characters that are often gods/goddesses.
- Includes gods/goddesses who frequently appear in disguises.
- Often have a hero.

After reviewing the list, have students read the text independently (or, if needed, read the text aloud yourself and have students follow along). Then, as they reread the text, tell them to label each characteristic that is commonly found in a myth (e.g., magic, goddess) in the margins as they find it. Next, bring the class together and discuss the students' findings. Creating a chart like the one below during the discussion works well. In the first column, write the content that students underlined. In the second column, write the characteristic of a myth that this reflects.

Text example	Characteristic
Athena	goddess
Athena disguises herself as a peasant woman.	Gods/goddesses often use disguises.
Athena touches Arachne's forehead.	use of magic
Athena turns Arachne into a spider.	Arachne is transformed into something else.

Identify the Moral of the Story

After discussing each characteristic listed on the chart, tell students they are going to focus on another characteristic, the moral of the story. Have students work with a partner to discuss what they believe is the moral of the story. With their partners, ask them to locate textual support for their opinions. Students will likely reach the conclusion that "one should not be boastful." However, students might also suggest that "one should not disrespect the gods." Remind them that it is important to find textual support for their ideas.

Character Analysis

The two main characters, Arachne and Athena, are worthy of a closer analysis. While working with a partner, have students read through the text again and find places that describe each of the characters, or places that talk about events/ actions that reflect the personality or character of each. Have them underline with a pencil the words, phrases, and actions that describe Arachne. Then, with a different colored pen or pencil, have them underline the places that describe Athena. Help the students develop a chart like the one on the next page. Students can draw the chart, or you can give them an empty chart. In either case, it's best to make the chart horizontal, with fairly wide cells, so there is enough space for students to write.

Arachne	Athena
No spinner or weaver was more talented or gifted.	Athena was angry with Arachne.
Proud	Wanted to give Arachne a chance to redeem herself.
Arrogant	Gave Arachne a warning.
Thought her work was better than Athena's.	Wove a stunning tapestry showing good deeds of the gods.
Boasted that she welcomed a contest with Athena.	Destroyed Arachne's work.
Wove an exquisite tapestry showing the gods and goddesses unfavorably.	Took pity on Arachne.
Ashamed and guilty	Turned Arachne into a spider so she could continue to weave.
Hanged herself.	
Ended up as a spider.	

After students have completed their charts, have the class discuss their findings. Then ask what the information on the chart reveals about each of the characters. What does the information tell us about their personalities?

Writing Activity

• Tell students that they will be working in groups to write an original myth. Since an important characteristic of a myth is that it teaches a lesson, discuss some possible lessons their myth might teach, for example, look before you leap, be tolerant of differences, a bird in the hand is worth two in the bush, honesty is the best policy, don't brag, be kind.

• Write each moral discussed on the board. Be sure to ask students what other lessons their myth might tell, and add them to the list.

• Make a list of features of a story that have to be included. Write the first feature on the board. Then add a feature one at a time and discuss that feature with students:

- ○ "What lesson will our myth teach?"
- ○ "Who will be the characters?"
- ○ "Where is the setting?"
- ○ "What is the plot?"
- ○ "How does the myth start?"
- ○ "How does the myth end?"
- ○ "What happens between the beginning and the end?"

- Divide the class into groups of three to four and have them work together to write a myth that includes some of its main characteristics. Have each group choose a leader who will keep the group going and following the rules of collaboration. Choose a recorder who will write ideas with which there is some agreement. Perhaps students can outline what needs to be included in a myth: characters, setting, plot—beginning, middle, and end—and lesson. Come to consensus about each. Then students can choose, or get assigned randomly, a part of the myth for them to write. Arrange so that students can come together at various times and incorporate their parts, by changing, adding, deleting, etc. You may find another way to have a group work together on a writing task.

- When their narratives are complete, have groups exchange their stories and then underline the characteristics of myths that they recognize in their peers' stories. If these characteristics are not represented, ask students to revise their myths.

- Finally, attend to revising, editing, spelling, and punctuation.

Tribute to a Dog

by George Graham Vest

Grade Level: 5–6

Introduction: George Graham Vest was a U.S. senator from Missouri from 1879 to 1903 and became one of the leading orators and debaters of his time. This delightful speech is from an earlier period in his life when he practiced law in a small Missouri town. It was given in court while representing a man who sued another for the killing of his dog. During the trial, Vest ignored the testimony, and when his turn came to present a summation to the jury, he made the following speech and won the case.

As you go through Vest's arguments about the negative relationships people have with people, try to help students understand that the negative characterization of these relationships is being presented as a tongue-in-cheek attempt to emphasize the value of the relationships between people and dogs. Vest is trying to convince a jury about the huge loss experienced by a man who owned a dog that was killed by another man.

Lesson content	Page
Copy of text for duplication and distribution: *Tribute to a Dog*	170
Segmented Text and Queries	171
Close Reading	172

Tribute to a Dog

by George Graham Vest

Gentlemen of the Jury: The best friend a man has in the world may turn against him and become his enemy. His son or daughter that he has reared with loving care may prove ungrateful. Those who are nearest and dearest to us, those whom we trust with our happiness and our good name may become traitors to their faith. The money that a man has, he may lose. It flies away from him, perhaps when he needs it most. A man's reputation may be sacrificed in a moment of ill-considered action. The people who are prone to fall on their knees to do us honor when success is with us, may be the first to throw the stone of malice when failure settles its cloud upon our heads.

The one absolutely unselfish friend that man can have in this selfish world, the one that never deserts him, the one that never proves ungrateful or treacherous is his dog. A man's dog stands by him in prosperity and in poverty, in health and in sickness. He will sleep on the cold ground, where the wintry winds blow and the snow drives fiercely, if only he may be near his master's side. He will kiss the hand that has no food to offer. He will lick the wounds and sores that come in encounters with the roughness of the world. He guards the sleep of his pauper master as if he were a prince. When all other friends desert, he remains. When riches take wings, and reputation falls to pieces, he is as constant in his love as the sun in its journey through the heavens.

If fortune drives the master forth, an outcast in the world, friendless and homeless, the faithful dog asks no higher privilege than that of accompanying him, to guard him against danger, to fight against his enemies. And when the last scene of all comes, and death takes his master in its embrace and his body is laid away in the cold ground, no matter if all other friends pursue their way, there by the graveside will the noble dog be found, his head between his paws, his eyes sad, but open in alert watchfulness, faithful and true even in death.

SEGMENTED TEXT AND QUERIES

Text segments	Queries/targeted responses
Gentlemen of the Jury: The best friend a man has in the world may turn against him and become his enemy. His son or daughter that he has reared with loving care may prove ungrateful. Those who are nearest and dearest to us, those whom we trust with our happiness and our good name may become traitors to their faith. **1**	1. **What point is the writer making in these first few lines?** (We really can't trust people, even family members. They can all turn against us.)
The money that a man has, he may lose. It flies away from him, perhaps when he needs it most. A man's reputation may be sacrificed in a moment of ill-considered action. The people who are prone to fall on their knees to do us honor when success is with us, may be the first to throw the stone of malice when failure settles its cloud upon our heads. **2**	2. **How does the rest of this paragraph connect with what we just talked about?** (It's not just people that we can lose. We can also lose things like money, success, and our reputation.) 2a. **According to the writer, how do people respond to such failures?** (The ones that are our supporters when things are going well will turn against us when things turn bad.)
The one absolutely unselfish friend that man can have in this selfish world, the one that never deserts him, the one that never proves ungrateful or treacherous is his dog. A man's dog stands by him in prosperity and in poverty, in health and in sickness. He will sleep on the cold ground, where the wintry winds blow and the snow drives fiercely, if only he may be near his master's side. He will kiss the hand that has no food to offer. He will lick the wounds and sores that come in encounters with the roughness of the world. He guards the sleep of his pauper master as if he were a prince. When all other friends desert, he remains. When riches take wings, and reputation falls to pieces, he is as constant in his love as the sun in its journey through the heavens. **3**	3. **What point is the writer making in this section?** (The only one that you can truly trust is a dog because a dog will stick by you no matter how bad things are.)
If fortune drives the master forth, an outcast in the world, friendless and homeless, the faithful dog asks no higher privilege than that of accompanying him, to guard him against danger, to fight against	4. **How does this section connect with what we just read?** (The dog will be faithful, no matter how bad things are, and will be there for you even in death.)

is enemies. And when the last scene of all comes, and death takes his master in its embrace and his body is laid away in the cold ground, no matter if all other friends pursue their way, there by the graveside will the noble dog be found, his head between his paws, his eyes sad, but open in alert watchfulness, faithful and true even in death. **4**

CLOSE READING

Language Analysis

- Begin by telling students that this text is filled with challenging, yet lovely, descriptive language, so it is important to unpack the meaning of several of these challenging sentences.

- Have students find the last sentence in the first paragraph, and then read it aloud with the class: *The people who are prone to fall on their knees to do us honor when success is with us, may be the first to throw the stone of malice when failure settles its cloud upon our heads.* Tell students that first they are going to look at the first part of the sentence and read it aloud. *The people who are prone to fall on their knees to do us honor when success is with us*, and ask students what is being talked about in just that first part. (**When things are going well, people honor us.**) Ask them why the writer would have people falling to their knees. (**Dropping to your knees is considered a sign of respect and honor. Students might reference this as something they do in their religion.**) Summarize what the students have concluded about the first part of the sentence. (**When things are going well, people honor us so much that some drop to their knees.**) Then read the second part of the sentence: *may be the first to throw the stone of malice when failure settles its cloud upon our heads.* Ask students how this second part fits in with what they've concluded about the first part. (**The same people that honor us when we are doing well are the first to turn against us when things go bad.**)

- Have students work with a partner to write a paraphrase of the original sentence. Remind them that paraphrase means to say what someone else said in your own words. Bring the class together, and ask several students to share their paraphrases. If their paraphrases are not adequate, develop a class paraphrase.

- Tell students you are going to analyze another sentence, this time from the second paragraph. Read the following line: *He will lick the wounds and sores that come in encounters with the roughness of the world*. Explain that the author is using a metaphor here, and ask them what a metaphor is. (**A metaphor is something that represents or is symbolic of something else.**) Ask them how the author is using a metaphor with that sentence. (**The dog isn't literally licking wounds and sores from his owner. He is making him feel better when he encounters the cruelty of the world.**)

- Another line worthy of further analysis is the following: *When riches take wings, and reputation falls to pieces, he is as constant in his love as the sun in its journey through the heavens.* Ask students to explain what the writer is saying in the sentence. (**When you lose money and your reputation, the dog will still be there, lovingly, to support you.**) Then ask students if they recognize the technique the author uses to make this point. (**Simile.**) If students don't recognize that this is a simile, remind them that a simile is a comparison of two things using *like* or *as*. Ask the students to explain the simile. (**Like the sun and its never-changing position in the universe, the dog's love is never changing.**)

Content

- The purpose of this speech is to compare the relationship people have with their dogs to the relationship people have with other people. Begin that analysis by having students reread the speech independently and underline the places that they feel best describe the relationship people have with dogs, and put a star next to the places that best describe the relationship people have with other people.

- Have students work with a partner to compare notes and narrow their choices to the two best representations for each relationship. Have them discuss why they believe these are the best representations of the author's thoughts.

- Bring students together and chart their responses as in the following example.

Relationship with People

Example	Explanation
The best friend a man has in the world may turn against him and become his enemy.	This sums it up pretty strongly—people can't even trust their best friends.
His son or daughter that he has reared with loving care may prove ungrateful.	This is another really strong statement as it essentially says even your own family members may turn against you.

Relationship with Dogs

Example	Explanation
He will sleep on the cold ground, where the wintry winds blow and the snow drives fiercely, if only he may be near his master's side.	The image is so strong that it makes the relationship clear. Instead of the dog searching for shelter, he will brave the elements to be near his master.
And when the last scene of all comes, and death takes his master in its embrace and his body is laid away in the cold ground, no matter if all other friends pursue their way, there by the graveside will the noble dog be found, his head between his paws, his eyes sad, but open in alert watchfulness, faithful and true even in death.	This emphasizes what Vest is saying about the relationship man has with his dog— even in death, the dog will be faithful.

- Conclude the analysis by asking students to write an essay about why Vest's characterization of people-to-people relationships is overstated, given that many of these relationships are actually kind and loving. Suggest that students start their essays with something like the following: *George Vest's description of people-to-people relationships is not the way many human relationships are.* Then ask students to explain what Vest says about people-to-people relationships and to compare his views with their own. Tell students to cite specific examples from the text to support Vest's view and specific examples from their own lives to support their own views.

The Lady, or the Tiger?

by Frank Stockton
(retold by Shirley Hazlett)

Grade Level: 5–6

Synopsis: A backward king decided that guilt or innocence should be determined by chance. When he discovered that his daughter was having a relationship with a commoner, he set a date for a trial to which all the kingdom came. The trial was to be held in the arena where two doors that looked exactly the same had been constructed. The accused was required to open one of the doors. Behind one door there was a tiger, and behind another there was a beautiful woman. If he opened the door behind which there was a tiger, he would be declared guilty, the tiger would attack him, and he would be killed. If he opened the door behind which there was the beautiful lady, he would be declared innocent and would marry the lady. At the end of the story, the author leaves it to the reader to decide which door the accused opened.

Lesson content	Page
Copy of text for duplication and distribution: *The Lady, or the Tiger?*	176
Segmented Text and Queries	178
Close Reading	181
For duplication and distribution: Copy of page *The Author Talks about the Question*	184

The Lady, or the Tiger?

by Frank Stockton
(retold by Shirley Hazlett)

Long ago, in the very olden time, there lived a powerful king. Some of his ideas were progressive, but others caused people to suffer. One of the king's ideas was a public arena as an agent of poetic justice. Crime was punished, or innocence was decided, by the result of chance. When a person was accused of a crime, his future would be judged in the public arena.

All the people would gather in the arena. The king sat high up on his ceremonial chair. He gave a sign. A door under him opened. The accused person stepped out into the arena. Directly opposite the king were two doors. They were side by side, exactly alike. The person on trial had to walk directly to these doors and open one of them. He could open whichever door he pleased.

If the accused man opened one door, out came a hungry tiger, the fiercest in the land. The tiger immediately jumped on him and tore him to pieces as punishment for his guilt. But, if the accused opened the other door, there came forth from it a woman, chosen especially for the person. To this lady he was immediately married, in honor of his innocence. It was not a problem that he might already have a wife and family, or that he might have chosen to marry another woman. The king permitted nothing to interfere with his great method of punishment and reward.

This was the king's method of carrying out justice. Its fairness appeared perfect. The accused person could not know which door was hiding the lady. He opened either as he pleased, without knowing whether, in the next minute, he was to be killed or married. This method was a popular one. When the people gathered together on one of the great trial days, they never knew whether they would see a bloody killing or a happy ending. So everyone was always interested. And the thinking part of the community would bring no charge of unfairness against this plan. Did not the accused person have the whole matter in his own hands?

The king had a beautiful daughter who was like him in many ways. He loved her above all humanity. The princess secretly loved a young man who was the best-looking and bravest in the land. But he was a commoner, not part of an important family.

One day, the king discovered the relationship between his daughter and the young man. The man was immediately put in prison. A day was set for his trial in the king's public arena. This, of course, was an especially important event. Never before had a common subject been brave enough to love the daughter of the king.

The king knew that the young man would be punished, even if he opened the right door. And the king would take pleasure in watching the series of events, which would judge whether or not the man had done wrong in loving the princess.

The day of the trial arrived. From far and near the people gathered in the arena and outside its walls. The king and his advisers were in their places, opposite the two doors. All was ready. The sign was given. The door under the king opened and the accused entered the arena. As the young man entered the public arena, his eyes were fixed on the princess, who sat to the right of her father.

From the day it was decided that the sentence of her young man should be decided in the arena, she had thought of nothing but this event. The princess had more power, influence and force of character than anyone who had ever before been interested in such a case. She had done what no other person had done. She had possessed herself of the secret of the doors. She knew behind which door stood the tiger, and behind which waited the lady. Gold, and the power of a woman's will, had brought the secret to the princess.

She also knew who the lady was. The lady was one of the loveliest in the kingdom. Now and then the princess had seen her looking at and talking to the young man. The princess hated the woman behind that silent door. She hated her with all the intensity of the blood passed to her through long lines of cruel ancestors.

The young man turned to look at the princess. His eye met hers as she sat there, paler and whiter than anyone in the large ocean of tense faces around her. He saw that she knew behind which door waited the tiger and behind which stood the lady. He had expected her to know it. The only hope for the young man was based on the success of the princess in discovering this mystery. When he looked at her, he saw that she had been successful, as he knew she would succeed.

Then his quick and tense look asked the question: "Which?" It was as clear to the princess as if he shouted it from where he stood. There was no time to be lost. The princess raised her hand, and made a short, quick movement toward the right. No one but her young man saw it. Every eye but his was fixed on the man in the arena. He turned, and with a firm and quick step he walked across the empty space. Every heart stopped beating. Every breath was held. Every eye was fixed upon that man. He went to the door on the right and opened it.

Now, the point of the story is this: Did the tiger come out of that door, or did the lady?

SEGMENTED TEXT AND QUERIES

Text segments	Queries/targeted responses
Long ago, in the very olden time, there lived a powerful king. Some of his ideas were progressive. But others caused people to suffer. One of the king's ideas was a public arena as an agent of poetic justice. Crime was punished, or innocence was decided, by the result of chance. When a person was accused of a crime, his future would be judged in the public arena. **1**	1. **What did we learn in this first paragraph?** (King determined guilt or innocence by chance.) 1a. **What does it mean that he determined guilt or innocence "by chance"?** (If something happens by chance it means it can't be predicted.)
All the people would gather in this building. The king sat high up on his ceremonial chair. He gave a sign. A door under him opened. The accused person stepped out into the arena. Directly opposite the king were two doors. They were side by side, exactly alike. The person on trial had to walk directly to these doors and open one of them. He could open whichever door he pleased. **2**	2. **What did we learn about the arena?** (There were two doors that were exactly alike.) 2a. **How does the accused fit into this scene?** (He has to open one of the doors.)
If the accused opened one door, out came a hungry tiger, the fiercest in the land. The tiger immediately jumped on him and tore him to pieces as punishment for his guilt. But if the accused opened the other door, there came forth from it a woman, chosen especially for the person. To this lady he was immediately married, in honor of his innocence. It was not a problem that he might already have a wife and family, or that he might have chosen to marry another woman. The king permitted nothing to interfere with his great method of punishment and reward. **3**	3. **How does this new information connect to what we already learned?** (There was a lady behind one and a tiger behind the other.) 3a. **What is the significance of what is behind each door?** (If he opened the door behind which there was a tiger, he would be declared guilty and be attacked. If he opened the door behind which there was a lady, he would be declared innocent and would marry the lady.)
This was the king's method of carrying out justice. Its fairness appeared perfect. The accused person could not know which door was hiding the lady. He opened either as he pleased, without knowing whether,	4. **What did the people think of the king's method?** (It was popular with the people.) 4a. **What words and sentences in the story let you know that?**

in the next minute, he was to be killed or married. Sometimes the fierce animal came out of one door. Sometimes it came out of the other. This method was a popular one. When the people gathered together on one of the great trial days, they never knew whether they would see a bloody killing or a happy ending. So everyone was always interested. And the thinking part of the community would bring no charge of unfairness against this plan. Did not the accused person have the whole matter in his own hands? **4**

(The method was a popular one. . . . everyone was always interested. The thinking part of the community would bring no charge of unfairness against this plan.)

The king had a beautiful daughter who was like him in many ways. He loved her above all humanity. The princess secretly loved a young man who was the best-looking and bravest in the land. But he was a commoner, not part of an important family. One day, the king discovered the relationship between his daughter and the young man. The man was immediately put in prison. A day was set for his trial in the king's public arena. This, of course, was an especially important event. Never before had a common subject been brave enough to love the daughter of the king.

The king knew that the young man would be punished, even if he opened the right door. And the king would take pleasure in watching the series of events, which would judge whether or not the man had done wrong in loving the princess. **5**

5. **What did we learn here?**
   (The king found out his daughter was having a relationship with a young man who was a commoner, so he ordered a trial for the young man.)

The day of the trial arrived. From far and near the people gathered in the arena and outside its walls. The king and his advisers were in their places, opposite the two doors. All was ready. The sign was given. The door under the king opened and the accused entered the arena. As the young man entered the public arena, his eyes were fixed on the princess, who sat to the right of her father. **6**

6. **What did we read here?**
   (It's the day of the trial and everyone is coming in to see what happens.)

6a. **What does it mean that the young man's eyes were fixed on the princess?**
   (He stared at her and didn't take his eyes off her.)

From the day it was decided that the sentence of the accused should be decided in the arena, the princess had thought of nothing but this event. She had more power, influence and force of character than anyone who had ever before been interested in such a case. She had done what no other person had done. She had possessed herself of the secret of the doors. She knew behind which door stood the tiger, and behind which waited the lady. Gold, and the power of a woman's will, had brought the secret to the princess.

She also knew who the lady was. The lady was one of the loveliest in the kingdom. Now and then the princess had seen her looking at and talking to the young man. The princess hated the woman behind that silent door. She hated her with all the intensity of the blood passed to her through long lines of cruel ancestors. **7**

The young man turned to look at the princess. His eyes met hers as she sat there, paler and whiter than anyone in the large ocean of tense faces around her. He saw that she knew behind which door waited the tiger and behind which stood the lady. He had expected her to know it. The only hope for the young man was based on the success of the princess in discovering this mystery. When he looked at her, he saw that she had been successful, as he knew she would succeed. **8**

Then his quick and tense look asked the question: "Which?" It was as clear to the princess as if he shouted it from where he stood. **9**

7. **What did we find out here?**
   (The princess knows what is behind each door.)

7a. **How did the princess feel about the lady behind the door?**
   (She hated her.)

8. **What's going on between the princess and the accused?**
   (The accused could tell from the expression on her face that she had found out what was behind each door.)

9. **How does this information connect with what we just talked about?**
   (Because the accused knew that the princess had the answer, he looked at her in a way that asked "which.")

9a. **Did the princess understand the young man's question?** (Yes.) **How do you know?**
   (In the text it said, "It was as clear to her as if he shouted it from where he stood.")

There was no time to be lost. The princess raised her hand, and made a short, quick movement toward the right. No one but the young man saw it. Every eye but his was fixed on the accused in the arena. He turned, and with a firm and quick step he walked across the empty space. Every heart stopped beating. Every breath was held. Every eye was fixed upon that man. He went to the door on the right and opened it. Now, the point of the story is this: Did the tiger come out of that door, or did the lady? **10**

10. **So, what happened?**
(The accused chose the door on the right.)

10a. **Why?**
(The princess signaled him.)

10b. **How do you know that the princess signaled him?**
(In the text it said, "The princess raised her hand, and made a short quick movement toward the right.")

Note: When students finish the story, they probably will be annoyed that they were left to answer the question, "What was behind the door on the right?" To respond to the question have them do a quick write-in response to the question: "What do you think was behind the door on the right? Briefly explain why you think so." Tell students that they will have another opportunity to think about the question. Make sure students keep their quick-write responses.

CLOSE READING

Language

Sometimes a reader knows the meaning of individual words in a phrase or sentence but finds them collectively challenging. For the sentences below, have students locate each sentence in the text and read it aloud. Then ask what they think the sentence means. Prompts are provided as needed.

- **Paragraph 1.** What does *"Some of [the king's] ideas were progressive. But others caused people to suffer?"* mean? (**Some of the king's ideas were modern or forward-thinking, but others hurt people.**) Prompt as needed: "**How many kinds of ideas does the king have?**" (**Two.**) "Which idea was mean—the first or second?" (**The second.**) "What does the word *but* at the beginning of the second sentence tell you?" (**The second idea would not be like the first idea.**) "So what might *Some of the king's ideas were progressive* mean?" (**Forward-thinking, good.**) Students are likely to say that progressive ideas are "good" and "not mean." Tell them that they are close, and that *progressive* means forward-looking, which is a good way to look at the world.

- **Paragraph 1.** "What does *One of the king's ideas was a public arena as an agent of poetic justice* mean?" **(The arena is the agent or thing that delivers the reward or punishment the accused has coming to them.)** Prompt as needed: To get at the meaning of *agent*, ask students whether they've ever heard of a real estate agent, or a basketball player's agent. Discuss what those agents do and establish two important meanings of *agent*: (1) somebody who represents other people or things, like an apartment management agent, or (2) somebody that delivers something, like a customer service agent who delivers a refund on faulty merchandise.

"What does *poetic justice* mean?" **(You get what you deserve.)**

Prompt as needed: Suppose someone took bananas from the cafeteria, dropped peels on the floor and laughed as people slipped and fell. Poetic justice would be served if that person went back into the cafeteria to get more bananas, but slipped on a peel that had fallen out of the trash can.

Discuss the following question: Based on what we've learned about the phrase, how is the arena an agent of poetic justice?

- **Paragraph 4.** "What does *And the thinking part of the community would bring no charge of unfairness against [the king's] plan* mean? **(The educated members of the community would not accuse the king of unfairness.)**

Ask students who "the thinking members of the community" are.

Prompt as needed: Tell students to suggest some characteristics of someone who is a thinking person. Responses such as intelligent, educated, or smart are likely.

What does *bring no charge* mean? **(Not accuse someone.)**

Prompt as needed: "What does it mean when someone is charged with a crime?" Responses that suggested *accuse* are likely.

Tell students to use the information they have discussed and paraphrase the original sentence. If needed remind them that to paraphrase is to say something in your own words that still communicates the meaning of the original sentence. Since students have already dealt with comprehension of the story in their first read, tell them to include why the people would not bring any charge of unfairness to the king. **(The intelligent members of the community would not accuse the king of unfairness because they were afraid they would be punished.)**

- **Paragraph 7.** "What does *The king knew that the young man would be punished even if he opened the right door* mean?" **(The young man would have to** marry and live with the lady who was behind the door all his life, but he loved the princess.)

Prompt as needed: How did the young man feel about the princess? (**He loved her.**) With that in mind, what might the king know? (**The young man would be unhappy because he would not be able to marry the princess.**)

- **Paragraph 9.** "What does *Gold, and the power of a woman's will, had brought the secret to the princess* mean?" (**The princess's determination and the ability to give people gold (or to pay people) for information had enabled her to find out what was behind each door.**)

Prompt as needed: "What is a person's will?" (**Their determination, their persistence.**) "What is a person's will power?" (**The strength of their determination.**)

Prompt as needed: "What is gold?" (**A precious metal.**)

"With that information, what does the sentence mean?" (**The princess's determination and the ability to give people gold (or to pay people) for information had enabled her to find out what was behind each door.**)

AUTHOR'S ADDITIONAL COMMENTS

Tell students that the author had some additional thoughts about the question regarding who came out of the door. Pass out the following page and have students read it independently.

STUDENTS' FINAL RESPONSE

Tell students to read their first response to the question. In light of the new information, have them write a new response in which they state their opinion. Remind them to:

- Introduce their claim and acknowledge what the other claim is.
- Support whichever position they take in their essay with logical reasoning and text evidence. That evidence can come from the original story as well as from the author's discussion of the question.
- Provide a concluding statement that supports the argument presented.

The Author Talks about the Question "Which Came out of the Open Door— the Lady, or the Tiger?"

The more we think about this question, the harder it is to answer. It involves a study of the human heart. Think of it not as if the decision of the question depended upon yourself, but as if it depended upon that hot-blooded princess, her soul at a white heat under the fires of sadness and jealousy. She had lost him, but who should have him? How often, in her waking hours and in her dreams, had she started in wild terror, and covered her face with her hands? She thought of the young man opening the door on the other side of which waited the sharp teeth of the tiger!

But how much oftener had she seen him open the other door? How had she ground her teeth, and torn her hair, when she had seen his happy face as he opened the door of the lady! How her soul had burned in pain when she had seen him run to meet that woman, with her look of victory. When she had seen the two of them get married. And when she had seen them walk away together upon their path of flowers, followed by the happy shouts of the crowd, in which her one sad cry was lost!

Would it not be better for him to die quickly, and go to wait for her in that blessed place of the future? And yet, that tiger, those cries, that blood! Her decision had been shown quickly. But it had been made after days and nights of thought. She had known she would be asked. And she had decided what she would answer. And she had moved her hand to the right.

The question of her decision is one not to be lightly considered. And it is not for me to set myself up as the one person able to answer it. And so I leave it with all of you:

Which came out of the open door—the lady, or the tiger?

The Hound of the Baskervilles
Chapter 1: Mr. Sherlock Holmes

by Arthur Conan Doyle

Grade Level: 7–8

Introduction: At breakfast, Sherlock Holmes and Dr. Watson notice that their visitor from the night before had left behind a walking stick. The walking stick is inscribed: "To James Mortimer, M.R.C.S., from his friends of the C.C.H." With that information they begin making deductions about who the owner of the stick is and what his occupation is. They do so by using Holmes's methods of observing several details about the object and then making inferences from those details. Watson offers some ideas, which Holmes finds impressive, even though Watson's ideas are wrong.

Explain to students that Sherlock Holmes is a very famous fictional detective and that the material they are going to read is the first chapter of a book, *The Hound of the Baskervilles*, in which Holmes solves a complicated mystery. Tell them they may want to get the book from the library. The language is somewhat formal and old-fashioned, and as such we recommend the use of discussion interspersed with reading for the first read.

The Hound of the Baskervilles
Chapter 1: Mr. Sherlock Holmes

by Sir Arthur Conan Doyle

Mr. Sherlock Holmes, who was usually very late in the mornings, save upon those not infrequent occasions when he was up all night, was seated at the breakfast table. I stood upon the hearth-rug and picked up the stick which our visitor had left behind him the night before. It was a fine, thick piece of wood, bulbous-headed, of the sort which is known as a "Penang lawyer." Just under the head was a broad silver band nearly an inch across. "To James Mortimer, M.R.C.S., from his friends of the C.C.H.," was engraved upon it, with the date "1884." It was just such a stick as the old-fashioned family practitioner used to carry— dignified, solid, and reassuring.

"Well, Watson, what do you make of it?"

Holmes was sitting with his back to me, and I had given him no sign of my occupation.

"How did you know what I was doing? I believe you have eyes in the back of your head."

"I have, at least, a well-polished, silver-plated coffee-pot in front of me," said he. "But, tell me, Watson, what do you make of our visitor's stick? Since we have been so unfortunate as to miss him and have no notion of his errand, this accidental souvenir becomes of importance. Let me hear you reconstruct the man by an examination of it."

"I think," said I, following as far as I could the methods of my companion, "that Dr. Mortimer is a successful, elderly medical man, well-esteemed since those who know him give him this mark of their appreciation."

"Good!" said Holmes. "Excellent!"

"I think also that the probability is in favor of his being a country practitioner who does a great deal of his visiting on foot."

"Why so?"

"Because this stick, though originally a very handsome one, has been so knocked about that I can hardly imagine a town practitioner carrying it. The thick-iron ferrule is worn down, so it is evident that he has done a great amount of walking with it."

"Perfectly sound!" said Holmes.

"And then again, there is the 'friends of the C.C.H.' I should guess that to be the local hunt to whose members he has possibly given some surgical assistance, and which has made him a small presentation in return."

"Really, Watson, you excel yourself," said Holmes, pushing back his chair and lighting a cigarette. "I am bound to say that in all the accounts which you have been so good as to give of my own small achievements you have habitually underrated your own abilities. It may be that you are not yourself luminous, but you are a conductor of light. Some people without possessing genius have a remarkable power of stimulating it. I confess, my dear fellow, that I am very much in your debt."

He had never said as much before, and I must admit that his words gave me keen pleasure, for I had often been piqued by his indifference to my admiration and to the attempts which I had made to give publicity to his methods. I was proud, too, to think that I had so far mastered his system as to apply it in a way which earned his approval. He now took the stick from my hands and examined it for a few minutes with his naked eyes. Then with an expression of interest he laid down his cigarette, and carrying the cane to the window, he looked over it again with a convex lens.

"Interesting, though elementary," said he as he returned to his favorite corner of the settee. "There are certainly one or two indications upon the stick. It gives us the basis for several deductions."

"Has anything escaped me?" I asked with some self-importance. "I trust that there is nothing of consequence which I have overlooked?"

"I am afraid, my dear Watson, that most of your conclusions were erroneous. When I said that you stimulated me I meant, to be frank, that in noting your fallacies I was occasionally guided towards the truth. Not that you are entirely wrong in this instance. The man is certainly a country practitioner. And he walks a good deal."

SEGMENTED TEXT AND QUERIES

Text segments	Queries/targeted responses

Text segments

Mr. Sherlock Holmes, who was usually very late in the mornings, save upon those not infrequent occasions when he was up all night, was seated at the breakfast table. I stood upon the hearth-rug and picked up the stick which our visitor had left behind him the night before. It was a fine, thick piece of wood, bulbous-headed, of the sort which is known as a "Penang lawyer." Just under the head was a broad silver band nearly an inch across. "To James Mortimer, M.R.C.S., from his friends of the C.C.H.," was engraved upon it, with the date "1884." It was just such a stick as the old-fashioned family practitioner used to carry—dignified, solid, and reassuring. **1**

"Well, Watson, what do you make of it?"

Holmes was sitting with his back to me, and I had given him no sign of my occupation.

"How did you know what I was doing? I believe you have eyes in the back of your head."

"I have, at least, a well-polished, silver-plated coffee-pot in front of me," said he. "But, tell me, Watson, what do you make of our visitor's stick? Since we have been so unfortunate as to miss him and have no notion of his errand, this accidental souvenir becomes of importance. Let me hear you reconstruct the man by an examination of it." **2**

"I think," said I, following as far as I could the methods of my companion, "that Dr. Mortimer is a successful, elderly medical man, well-esteemed since those who know him give him this mark of their appreciation."

"Good!" said Holmes. "Excellent!"

"I think also that the probability is in favor of his being a country practitioner who does a great deal of his visiting on foot."

Queries/targeted responses

1. **What did we learn in the first paragraph?**
   (Two people realize that the man who visited them the night before left his walking stick behind.)

2. **This part is a little tricky. What's going on here?**
   (Two men, Holmes and Watson, are having a conversation about the visitor and the walking stick that he left behind.)

2a. **What do we learn about these two men from their conversation?**
   (Watson thinks Holmes is pretty clever because he knew what Watson was up to, but it was simply because Holmes saw his reflection in the coffee pot. Holmes is curious about what Watson thinks he's learned about their visitor just by examining his walking stick.)

3. **What do we learn from this conversation?**
   (Watson gives his analysis of Dr. Mortimer, their visitor.)

3a. **What does Holmes think of Watson's analysis?**
   (He seems to be impressed with Watson's analytical skills.)

"Why so?"

"Because this stick, though originally a very handsome one has been so knocked about that I can hardly imagine a town practitioner carrying it. The thick-iron ferrule is worn down, so it is evident that he has done a great amount of walking with it."

"Perfectly sound!" said Holmes.

"And then again, there is the 'friends of the C.C.H.' I should guess that to be the Something Hunt, the local hunt to whose members he has possibly given some surgical assistance, and which has made him a small presentation in return." **3**

"Really, Watson, you excel yourself," said Holmes, pushing back his chair and lighting a cigarette. "I am bound to say that in all the accounts which you have been so good as to give of my own small achievements you have habitually underrated your own abilities. It may be that you are not yourself luminous, but you are a conductor of light. Some people without possessing genius have a remarkable power of stimulating it. I confess, my dear fellow, that I am very much in your debt." **4**

4. **What is Holmes saying here?**
(He tells Watson that although Watson himself may not be a genius, he is able to spark brilliance in others.)

He had never said as much before, and I must admit that his words gave me keen pleasure, for I had often been piqued by his indifference to my admiration and to the attempts which I had made to give publicity to his methods. I was proud, too, to think that I had so far mastered his system as to apply it in a way which earned his approval. He now took the stick from my hands and examined it for a few minutes with his naked eyes. Then with an expression of interest he laid down his cigarette, and carrying the cane to the window, he looked over it again with a convex lens. **5**

5. **What do we learn from Watson's thoughts?**
(He was happy with what Holmes said about him, and was glad that he finally earned his approval.)

"Interesting, though elementary," said he as he returned to his favorite corner of the settee. "There are certainly one or two indications upon the stick. It gives us the basis for several deductions."

"Has anything escaped me?" I asked with some self-importance. "I trust that there is nothing of consequence which I have overlooked?"

"I am afraid, my dear Watson, that most of your conclusions were erroneous. When I said that you stimulated me I meant, to be frank, that

6. **What final point is Holmes making?**
(Most of what Watson said was wrong, but his comments helped Holmes reach the correct conclusions about Dr. Mortimer.)

in noting your fallacies I was occasionally guided towards the truth. Not that you are entirely wrong in this instance. The man is certainly a country practitioner. And he walks a good deal." **6**

CLOSE READING

Language

Explain that Sir Arthur Conan Doyle writes in a very formal and, to some extent, old-fashioned way. Begin by rereading the following paragraph with your students:

> "Really, Watson, you excel yourself," said Holmes, pushing back his chair and lighting a cigarette. "I am bound to say that in all the accounts which you have been so good as to give of my own small achievements you have habitually underrated your own abilities. It may be that you are not yourself luminous, but you are a conductor of light. Some people without possessing genius have a remarkable power of stimulating it. I confess, my dear fellow, that I am very much in your debt."

Note: Some of the examples below were used in more elaborate ways in Chapter 5 as support to students when unpacking sentences. You may want to review them, or you can use the shorter version that follows.

- "What does this sentence mean?: *It may be that you are not yourself luminous, but you are a conductor of light.*" (**Watson himself might not be brilliant, but he brings out the brilliance in others.**)

  Prompt as needed: If students have difficulty, tell them that *luminous* is related to *illuminate*. Ask what it means if someone says that she "illuminated the dark room." (**Turned a dark room light.**) Ask what a conductor is. (**Leader of an orchestra, the person who collects tickets and manages the passengers on a train.**) Now ask students the initial question again.

- With a partner, have students underline the rest of the words and phrases Holmes uses to describe Watson. Ask them to explain what Holmes means with each description of Watson. You might ask students to place this information on a table similar to the one on the next page. When students have finished, bring them together to discuss what they found. Or you could develop a chart as a group.

Example	Explanation
Segment 4: Really, Watson, you excel yourself, . . .	You've done even better than you usually do.
Segment 4: . . . you have habitually underrated your own abilities.	You don't give yourself enough credit.
Segment 4: Some people without possessing genius have a remarkable power of stimulating it.	Some people who are not geniuses themselves are able to prompt it in others.

Writing Activity

Using the information on your table and what we have discussed, ask students to do a quick write explaining what the author means by the last line of the paragraph: *I confess, my dear fellow, that I am very much in your debt.*

Content: The Dynamic between Holmes and Watson

Tell students that you are going to take a closer look at the relationship between Holmes and Watson by having them reread the text and focus on the passages that speak to how Holmes and Watson feel about and treat each other.

- Ask students to reread the text independently and mark places that give the reader an idea of what Holmes thinks of Watson and what Watson thinks of Holmes, and how they interact with each other. Then, in small groups of three to four, have them share what they found and discuss why the examples they have marked represent their relationship. Have each group create a table similar to the following:

Example	Explanation
Segment 2: "Well, Watson, what do you make of it?" . . . "I have, at least, a well-polished, silver-plated coffee-pot in front of me," said he.	Watson is surprised that Holmes knew what he was up to and he seems to be impressed with Holmes.
Segment 2: "Let me hear you reconstruct the man by an examination of it."	Holmes challenges Watson to give a description of the visitor. He's seeing what kind of an analytical mind Watson has.

Segment 3: "I think," said I, following as far as I could the methods of my companion, . . .

Watson is trying to think like Holmes. Again, he is impressed with Holmes and his intelligence.

Segment 3: "Good!" said Holmes. "Excellent!"

"Perfectly sound!" said Holmes.

"Really, Watson, you excel yourself," said Holmes.

Holmes is praising Watson for his analysis. Do you think there is a tone of sarcasm?

Segment 4: "I am bound to say that in all the accounts which you have been so good as to give of my own small achievements . . . that I am very much in your debt."

First Holmes acknowledges that Watson's comments to others about Holmes are generous. Second, he thanks Watson for the kind comments he has made about Holmes.

Segment 4: He had never said as much before, and I must admit that his words gave me keen pleasure, . . .

I was proud, too, to think that I had so far mastered his system as to apply it in a way which earned his approval.

Watson is pleased with Holmes's compliment. Proud that he is learning Holmes's system for identifying clues and coming to a conclusion.

Segment 6: "Interesting, though elementary," said he . . .

Holmes uses the expression often. He is telling Watson that his analysis is simple or basic.

Segment 6: "Has anything escaped me?" I asked with some self-importance. "I trust that there is nothing of consequence which I have overlooked?"

It seems that Watson is still trying to impress Holmes with his intelligence.

Segment 6: "When I said that you stimulated me I meant, to be frank, that in noting your fallacies I was occasionally guided towards the truth."

Here, Holmes tells Watson that his fallacies (mistakes) help Holmes reach the truth about their visitor.

• Bring the class together and have them share what they marked. As students provide examples, remind them to explain what their examples show about the relationship between Holmes and Watson.

Vocabulary

Have students work with a partner to figure out the meaning of the underlined words below. If they ask for a hint, provide the italicized information after each item. If they can't figure out the meaning of a word, ask them to look it up in a dictionary. If they think they know, tell them to be sure to check the meanings with a dictionary. Bring the students together and discuss their findings. Then with the students develop a class definition.

- Interesting but <u>elementary</u>. (*Think about the difference between an elementary school and a high school.*)
- With that information they begin making <u>deductions</u> about who the owner of the stick is and what his occupation is. (*They are looking at the stick for clues to the occupation of the person who left the stick.*)
- I am afraid, my dear Watson, that most of your conclusions were <u>erroneous</u>. (*What word do you know that starts like erroneous?*)

Writing Activity

Have students choose two words, one word that describes Holmes and one that describes Watson. Tell them to use the information from the charts and their discussions to help them think of words. Or, if you think students could use more support, have the class volunteer different words that they think are applicable to each character. Then have them explain in writing how each word reflects each of the men, by introducing the topic, organizing the ideas, and comparing and contrasting the two characters. Remind students to cite specific examples from the text to support their ideas, and provide a concluding sentence.

The Tell-Tale Heart

by Edgar Allan Poe

Grade Level: 7–8+

Introduction: Edgar Allan Poe was a master of the gothic tale, which is pervaded by a dark and foreboding atmosphere. The narrator, who speaks directly to readers, starts by informing us that he is very nervous—but not mad. He then tells us how he murdered an old man, all the while insisting that he is clever, not crazy. The police, who come because noise has been heard in the area, are not aware of the crime. But the narrator's guilty conscious (he hears the beating heart of the dead man) makes him confess, as he believes the police also hear the beating heart and they are mocking him by not saying that they hear it.

We do not recommend that the teacher or students read the entire text through on the first read. The ending is dramatic, and its impact would be reduced if the ending were known. We have included many close reading activities for this story because there are so many possibilities. There is no need to do all of them; just choose the ones you want to do. This should be the case for all of our lessons.

Lesson content	Page
Copy of text for duplication and distribution: *The Tell-Tale Heart*	195
Segmented Text and Queries	198
Close Reading	202

The Tell-Tale Heart

by Edgar Allan Poe

A TRUE!—nervous—very, very dreadfully nervous I had been and am; but why will you say that I am mad? The disease had sharpened my senses—not destroyed—not dulled them. Above all was the sense of hearing acute. I heard all things in the heaven and in the earth. I heard many things in hell. How, then, am I mad? Hearken! and observe how healthily—how calmly I can tell you the whole story.

It is impossible to say how first the idea entered my brain; but once conceived, it haunted me day and night. Object there was none. Passion there was none. I loved the old man. He had never wronged me. He had never given me insult. For his gold I had no desire. I think it was his eye! yes, it was this! He had the eye of a vulture—a pale blue eye, with a film over it. Whenever it fell upon me, my blood ran cold; and so by degrees—very gradually—I made up my mind to take the life of the old man, and thus rid myself of the eye forever.

Now this is the point. You fancy me mad. Madmen know nothing. But you should have seen me. You should have seen how wisely I proceeded—with what caution—with what foresight—with what dissimulation I went to work! I was never kinder to the old man than during the whole week before I killed him. And every night, about midnight, I turned the latch of his door and opened it—oh so gently! And then, when I had made an opening sufficient for my head, I put in a dark lantern, all closed, closed, that no light shone out, and then I thrust in my head. Oh, you would have laughed to see how cunningly I thrust it in! I moved it slowly—very, very slowly, so that I might not disturb the old man's sleep. It took me an hour to place my whole head within the opening so far that I could see him as he lay upon his bed. Ha! Would a madman have been so wise as this? And then, when my head was well in the room, I undid the lantern cautiously—oh, so cautiously—cautiously (for the hinges creaked)—I undid it just so much that a single thin ray fell upon the vulture eye. And this I did for seven long nights—every night just at midnight—but I found the eye always closed; and so it was impossible to do the work; for it was not the old man who vexed me, but his Evil Eye. And every morning, when the day broke, I went boldly into the chamber, and spoke courageously to him, calling him by name in a hearty tone, and inquiring how he has passed the night. So you see he would have been a very profound old man, indeed, to suspect that every night, just at twelve, I looked in upon him while he slept.

Upon the eighth night I was more than usually cautious in opening the door. A watch's minute hand moves more quickly than did mine. **B** Never before that night had I felt the extent of my own powers—of my sagacity. I could scarcely contain my feelings of triumph. To think that there I was, opening the door, little by little, and he not even to dream of my secret deeds or thoughts. I fairly chuckled at the idea; and perhaps he heard me; for he moved on the bed suddenly, as if startled. Now you may think that I drew back—but no. His room was as black as pitch with the thick darkness, (for the shutters were close fastened, through fear of robbers), and so I knew that he could not see the opening of the door, and I kept pushing it on steadily, steadily.

I had my head in, and was about to open the lantern, when my thumb slipped upon the tin fastening, and the old man sprang up in bed, crying out—"Who's there?" I kept quite still and said nothing. For a whole hour I did not move a muscle, and in the meantime I did

---

The letters will be used later when we engage in close reading.

not hear him lie down. He was still sitting up in the bed listening;—just as I have done, night after night, hearkening to the deathwatches in the wall.

Presently I heard a slight groan, and I knew it was the groan of mortal terror. **C** It was not a groan of pain or of grief—oh, no!—it was the low stifled sound that arises from the bottom of the soul when overcharged with awe. I knew the sound well. Many a night, just at midnight, when all the world slept, it has welled up from my own bosom, deepening, with its dreadful echo, the terrors that distracted me. I say I knew it well. I knew what the old man felt, and pitied him, although I chuckled at heart. I knew that he had been lying awake ever since the first slight noise, when he had turned in the bed. His fears had been ever since growing upon him. He had been trying to fancy them causeless, but could not. He had been saying to himself—"It is nothing but the wind in the chimney—it is only a mouse crossing the floor," or "It is merely a cricket which has made a single chirp." Yes, he had been trying to comfort himself with these suppositions: but he had found all in vain. All in vain; because Death, in approaching him had stalked with his black shadow before him, and enveloped the victim. **D** And it was the mournful influence of the unperceived shadow that caused him to feel—although he neither saw nor heard—to feel the presence of my head within the room.

When I had waited a long time, very patiently, without hearing him lie down, I resolved to open a little—a very, very little crevice in the lantern. So I opened it—you cannot imagine how stealthily, stealthily—until, at length a simple dim ray, like the thread of the spider, shot from out the crevice and fell full upon the vulture eye. It was open—wide, wide open—and I grew furious as I gazed upon it. I saw it with perfect distinctness—all a dull blue, with a hideous veil over it that chilled the very marrow in my bones; but I could see nothing else of the old man's face or person: for I had directed the ray as if by instinct, precisely upon the damned spot.

And have I not told you that what you mistake for madness is but over-acuteness of the sense?—now, I say, there came to my ears a low, dull, quick sound, such as a watch makes when enveloped in cotton. I knew that sound well, too. It was the beating of the old man's heart. It increased my fury, as the beating of a drum stimulates the soldier into courage.

But even yet I refrained and kept still. I scarcely breathed. I held the lantern motionless. I tried how steadily I could maintain the ray upon the eye. Meantime the hellish tattoo of the heart increased. It grew quicker and quicker, and louder and louder every instant. The old man's terror must have been extreme! It grew louder, I say, louder every moment!—do you mark me well I have told you that I am nervous: so I am. And now at the dead hour of the night, amid the dreadful silence of that old house, so strange a noise as this excited me to uncontrollable terror. Yet, for some minutes longer I refrained and stood still. But the beating grew louder, louder! I thought the heart must burst. And now a new anxiety seized me—the sound would be heard by a neighbor! The old man's hour had come! With a loud yell, I threw open the lantern and leaped into the room. He shrieked once—once only. In an instant I dragged him to the floor, and pulled the heavy bed over him. I then smiled gaily, to find the deed so far done. But, for many minutes, the heart beat on with a muffled sound. This, however, did not vex me; it would not be heard through the wall. At length it ceased. The old man was dead. I removed the bed and examined the corpse. Yes, he was stone, stone dead. I placed my hand upon the heart and held it there many minutes. There was no pulsation. He was stone dead. His eye would trouble me no more.

E If still you think me mad, you will think so no longer when I describe the wise precautions I took for the concealment of the body. The night waned, and I worked hastily, but in silence. First of all I dismembered the corpse. I cut off the head and the arms and the legs.

I then took up three planks from the flooring of the chamber, and deposited all between the scantlings. I then replaced the boards so cleverly, so cunningly, that no human eye—not even his—could have detected anything wrong. There was nothing to wash out—no stain of any kind—no blood-spot whatever. I had been too wary for that. A tub had caught all—ha! ha!

When I had made an end of these labors, it was four o'clock—still dark as midnight. As the bell sounded the hour, there came a knocking at the street door. I went down to open it with a light heart,—for what had I now to fear? There entered three men, who introduced themselves, with perfect suavity, as officers of the police. A shriek had been heard by a neighbor during the night; suspicion of foul play had been aroused; information had been lodged at the police office, and they (the officers) had been deputed to search the premises.

I smiled,—for what had I to fear? I bade the gentlemen welcome. The shriek, I said, was my own in a dream. The old man, I mentioned, was absent in the country. I took my visitors all over the house. I bade them search—search well. I led them, at length, to his chamber. I showed them his treasures, secure, undisturbed. In the enthusiasm of my confidence, I brought chairs into the room, and desired them here to rest from their fatigues, while I myself, in the wild audacity of my perfect triumph, placed my own seat upon the very spot beneath which reposed the corpse of the victim.

F The officers were satisfied. My manner had convinced them. I was singularly at ease. They sat, and while I answered cheerily, they chatted of familiar things. But, ere long, I felt myself getting pale and wished them gone. My head ached, and I fancied a ringing in my ears: but still they sat and still chatted. The ringing became more distinct:—It continued and became more distinct: I talked more freely to get rid of the feeling: but it continued and gained definiteness—until, at length, I found that the noise was not within my ears. No doubt I now grew very pale;—but I talked more fluently, and with a heightened voice. Yet the sound increased—and what could I do? It was a low, dull, quick sound—much such a sound as a watch makes when enveloped in cotton. I gasped for breath—and yet the officers heard it not. I talked more quickly—more vehemently; but the noise steadily increased. I arose and argued about trifles, in a high key and with violent gesticulations; but the noise steadily increased.

Why would they not be gone? I paced the floor to and fro with heavy strides, as if excited to fury by the observations of the men—but the noise steadily increased. Oh God! what could I do? I foamed—I raved—I swore! I swung the chair upon which I had been sitting, and grated it upon the boards, but the noise arose over all and continually increased. It grew louder—louder—louder! And still the men chatted pleasantly, and smiled. Was it possible they heard not? Almighty God!—no, no! They heard!—they suspected!—they knew!—they were making a mockery of my horror!—this I thought, and this I think. But anything was better than this agony! Anything was more tolerable than this derision! I could bear those hypocritical smiles no longer! I felt that I must scream or die! and now—again!— hark! louder! louder! louder! louder!

"Villains!" I shrieked, "dissemble no more! I admit the deed!—tear up the planks here, here!—It is the beating of his hideous heart!"

SEGMENTED TEXT AND QUERIES

Text Segments	Queries/targeted responses
TRUE!—nervous—very, very dreadfully nervous I had been and am; but why will you say that I am mad? The disease had sharpened my senses—not destroyed—not dulled them. Above all was the sense of hearing acute. I heard all things in the heaven and in the earth. I heard many things in hell. How, then, am I mad? Hearken! and observe how healthily—how calmly I can tell you the whole story. **1**	1. **What did we learn about the narrator?** (The narrator explains that he isn't "mad." He just has a disease that has sharpened his senses.)
It is impossible to say how first the idea entered my brain; but once conceived, it haunted me day and night. Object there was none. Passion there was none. I loved the old man. He had never wronged me. He had never given me insult. For his gold I had no desire. I think it was his eye! yes, it was this! He had the eye of a vulture—a pale blue eye, with a film over it. Whenever it fell upon me, my blood ran cold; and so by degrees—very gradually—I made up my mind to take the life of the old man, and thus rid myself of the eye forever. **2**	2. **What is the narrator up to?** (He is going to kill the old man whom he claims to love because he hates his eye.)
Now this is the point. You fancy me mad. Madmen know nothing. But you should have seen me. You should have seen how wisely I proceeded—with what caution— with what foresight—with what dissimulation I went to work! I was never kinder to the old man than during the whole week before I killed him. And every night, about midnight, I turned the latch of his door and opened it—oh so gently! And then, when I had made an opening sufficient for my head, I put in a dark lantern, all closed, closed, that no light shone out, and then I thrust in my head. Oh, you would have laughed to see how cunningly I thrust it in! I moved it slowly—very, very slowly, so that I might not disturb the old man's sleep. It took me an hour to place my whole head within the opening so far that I could see him as he lay upon his bed. Ha! would a madman have been so wise as this? And then, when my head was well in the room, I undid the lantern cautiously—oh, so cautiously— cautiously (for the hinges creaked)—I undid it just so much that a single thin ray fell upon the vulture eye. And this I did for seven long nights—every night just at midnight—but I found the eye always closed; and so it was impossible to do the work; for it was not the old man who vexed me, but his Evil Eye. And every morning, when the day broke, I went	3. **What's happening in this section?** (Each night the narrator creeps into the old man's room and shines a single ray of light from a lantern into the old man's eye.) 3a. **Why doesn't he kill the old man the first night?** (Because the eye is not open; it is the eye that he hates.)

boldly into the chamber, and spoke courageously to him, calling him by name in a hearty tone, and inquiring how he has passed the night. So you see he would have been a very profound old man, indeed, to suspect that every night, just at twelve, I looked in upon him while he slept. **3**

Upon the eighth night I was more than usually cautious in opening the door. A watch's minute hand moves more quickly than did mine. Never before that night had I felt the extent of my own powers—of my sagacity. I could scarcely contain my feelings of triumph. To think that there I was, opening the door, little by little, and he not even to dream of my secret deeds or thoughts. I fairly chuckled at the idea; and perhaps he heard me; for he moved on the bed suddenly, as if startled. Now you may think that I drew back—but no. His room was as black as pitch with the thick darkness, (for the shutters were close fastened, through fear of robbers), and so I knew that he could not see the opening of the door, and I kept pushing it on steadily, steadily.

I had my head in, and was about to open the lantern, when my thumb slipped upon the tin fastening, and the old man sprang up in bed, crying out—"Who's there?" I kept quite still and said nothing. For a whole hour I did not move a muscle, and in the meantime I did not hear him lie down. He was still sitting up in the bed listening;—just as I have done, night after night, hearkening to the death watches in the wall. **4**

Presently I heard a slight groan, and I knew it was the groan of mortal terror. It was not a groan of pain or of grief—oh, no!—it was the low stifled sound that arises from the bottom of the soul when overcharged with awe. I knew the sound well. Many a night, just at midnight, when all the world slept, it has welled up from my own bosom, deepening, with its dreadful echo, the terrors that distracted me. I say I knew it well. I knew what the old man felt, and pitied him, although I chuckled at heart. I knew that he had been lying awake ever since the first slight noise, when he had turned in the bed. His fears had been ever since growing upon him. He had been trying to fancy them causeless, but could not. He had been saying to himself—"It is nothing but the wind in the chimney—it is only a mouse crossing the floor," or "It is merely a cricket which has made a single chirp." Yes, he had been trying to comfort himself with these suppositions: but he had found all in vain. All in vain; because Death, in approaching

4. **What happened here?**
   (The old man woke up.)

5. **What happens on the eighth night?**
   (The man is really scared, and the narrator discovers that his eye is open.)

him had stalked with his black shadow before him, and enveloped the victim. And it was the mournful influence of the unperceived shadow that caused him to feel—although he neither saw nor heard—to feel the presence of my head within the room.

When I had waited a long time, very patiently, without hearing him lie down, I resolved to open a little—a very, very little crevice in the lantern. So I opened it—you cannot imagine how stealthily, stealthily—until, at length a simple dim ray, like the thread of the spider, shot from out the crevice and fell full upon the vulture eye. It was open—wide, wide open—and I grew furious as I gazed upon it. I saw it with perfect distinctness—all a dull blue, with a hideous veil over it that chilled the very marrow in my bones; but I could see nothing else of the old man's face or person: for I had directed the ray as if by instinct, precisely upon the damned spot. **5**

And have I not told you that what you mistake for madness is but over-acuteness of the sense?—now, I say, there came to my ears a low, dull, quick sound, such as a watch makes when enveloped in cotton. I knew that sound well, too. It was the beating of the old man's heart. It increased my fury, as the beating of a drum stimulates the soldier into courage.

But even yet I refrained and kept still. I scarcely breathed. I held the lantern motionless. I tried how steadily I could maintain the ray upon the eye. Meantime the hellish tattoo of the heart increased. It grew quicker and quicker, and louder and louder every instant. The old man's terror must have been extreme! It grew louder, I say, louder every moment!—do you mark me well I have told you that I am nervous: so I am. And now at the dead hour of the night, amid the dreadful silence of that old house, so strange a noise as this excited me to uncontrollable terror. Yet, for some minutes longer I refrained and stood still. But the beating grew louder, louder! I thought the heart must burst. And now a new anxiety seized me—the sound would be heard by a neighbor! The old man's hour had come! With a loud yell, I threw open the lantern and leaped into the room. He shrieked once—once only. In an instant I dragged him to the floor, and pulled the heavy bed over him. I then smiled gaily, to find the deed so far done. But, for many minutes, the heart beat on with a muffled sound. This, however, did not vex me; it would not be heard through the wall. At length it ceased. The old man was dead. I removed the bed and examined the corpse. Yes, he was stone, stone

6. **What did we just find out?**
   (He killed the old man.)

6a. **Now what's the problem?**
   (He hears the old man's beating heart.)

6b. **How does the narrator explain the sound of the beating heart?**
   (Because his senses have been strengthened so much that he is able to hear the old man's beating heart.)

dead. I placed my hand upon the heart and held it there many minutes. There was no pulsation. He was stone dead. His eye would trouble me no more. **6**

If still you think me mad, you will think so no longer when I describe the wise precautions I took for the concealment of the body. The night waned, and I worked hastily, but in silence. First of all I dismembered the corpse. I cut off the head and the arms and the legs.

I then took up three planks from the flooring of the chamber, and deposited all between the scantlings. I then replaced the boards so cleverly, so cunningly, that no human eye—not even his—could have detected anything wrong. There was nothing to wash out—no stain of any kind—no blood-spot whatever. I had been too wary for that. A tub had caught all—ha! ha! **7**

When I had made an end of these labors, it was four o'clock—still dark as midnight. As the bell sounded the hour, there came a knocking at the street door. I went down to open it with a light heart,—for what had I now to fear? There entered three men, who introduced themselves, with perfect suavity, as officers of the police. A shriek had been heard by a neighbor during the night; suspicion of foul play had been aroused; information had been lodged at the police office, and they (the officers) had been deputed to search the premises.

I smiled,—for what had I to fear? I bade the gentlemen welcome. The shriek, I said, was my own in a dream. The old man, I mentioned, was absent in the country. I took my visitors all over the house. I bade them search—search well. I led them, at length, to his chamber. I showed them his treasures, secure, undisturbed. In the enthusiasm of my confidence, I brought chairs into the room, and desired them here to rest from their fatigues, while I myself, in the wild audacity of my perfect triumph, placed my own seat upon the very spot beneath which reposed the corpse of the victim. **8**

7. **What's the narrator up to now?**
   (He dismembers the body and hides the parts underneath the floor planks.)

7a. **How do those actions connect with his argument?**
   (He claims his actions support his argument that he is clever and not mad. He thinks it took wisdom to conceal the body in such a manner. Most people, however, will feel that his actions support the argument that he is insane.)

8. **Now what's the problem?**
   (The police show up.)

8a. **Why did the narrator take the police to sit on the spot where the old man was buried?**
   (He was so confident of his plan that he was sure the police would not discover the body.)

The officers were satisfied. My manner had convinced them. I was singularly at ease. They sat, and while I answered cheerily, they chatted of familiar things. But, ere long, I felt myself getting pale and wished them gone. My head ached, and I fancied a ringing in my ears: but still they sat and still chatted. The ringing became more distinct:—It continued and became more distinct: I talked more freely to get rid of the feeling: but it continued and gained definiteness—until, at length, I found that the noise was not within my ears. No doubt I now grew very pale;—but I talked more fluently, and with a heightened voice. Yet the sound increased—and what could I do? It was a low, dull, quick sound—much such a sound as a watch makes when enveloped in cotton. I gasped for breath—and yet the officers heard it not. I talked more quickly—more vehemently; but the noise steadily increased. I arose and argued about trifles, in a high key and with violent gesticulations; but the noise steadily increased.

Why would they not be gone? I paced the floor to and fro with heavy strides, as if excited to fury by the observations of the men—but the noise steadily increased. Oh God! what could I do? I foamed—I raved—I swore! I swung the chair upon which I had been sitting, and grated it upon the boards, but the noise arose over all and continually increased. It grew louder—louder—louder! And still the men chatted pleasantly, and smiled. Was it possible they heard not? Almighty God!—no, no! They heard!—they suspected!—they knew!—they were making a mockery of my horror!—this I thought, and this I think. But anything was better than this agony! Anything was more tolerable than this derision! I could bear those hypocritical smiles no longer! I felt that I must scream or die! and now—again!—hark! louder! louder! louder! louder!

"Villains!" I shrieked, "dissemble no more! I admit the deed!—tear up the planks! here, here!—It is the beating of his hideous heart!" **9**

9. **At the beginning of this passage, the narrator was confident that he committed the perfect crime. How did that thought play out?**

(He confessed to the crime because he could no longer stand the sound of the old man's beating heart. He was convinced that the police also heard the sound and were making a mockery of his agony.)

CLOSE READING

Language Analysis

"The Tell-Tale Heart" is so full of challenging, figurative language that the possibilities for close reading are huge. Although we limited ourselves, we still could not resist including a number of close reading activities. As in any classroom decision, the teacher needs to choose which activities may be most useful to her students. Additionally, even if you are going to limit the number of close reading activities for this story, we think you will find it useful to read through them all. They could well provide ideas for close readings of other texts.

- Explain to students that Edgar Allan Poe is well known as a master of the mysterious and the gothic tale, and explain that his challenging, figurative language sets the tone and mood for his stories. It is his use of language that enhances the mysterious, creepy, gruesome mood being created in "The Tell-Tale Heart." In this close reading section, students examine some of the remarkable language Poe uses that makes this story a literary classic.

- To keep the narrator's problem and his plan well in mind, ask students to read the first two paragraphs of **section A** independently and be prepared to tell what the narrator's issues are in the first paragraph (h**e argues that he is not mad, rather that he is clever and wise**) and what his plan is in the second paragraph (t**o kill the old man**). **Note:** *These issues were covered in the previous gist comprehension section, so you might want to skip this activity if you think your students don't need the recap.*

- Next, read the third paragraph of **section A** and have students read along with you. When you finish reading, ask students to find the sentence *You should have seen how wisely I proceeded with what caution—with what foresight—with what dissimulation.* Discuss how the sentence helps us "see" how slowly and carefully the narrator visits the old man's room each night. (Mention that *dissimulation* means dishonesty.) Have students find phrases in the paragraph that describe how slowly and carefully the narrator goes to the old man's room. Tell them to put a little check at the beginning of each phrase or sentence that they find.

> ✓ *I proceeded—with what caution—with what foresight—with what dissimulation*
>
> ✓ *I turned the latch of his door and opened it—oh so gently!*
>
> ✓ *I put in a dark lantern, all closed, closed, that no light shone out,*
>
> ✓ *I moved it slowly—very, very slowly,*
>
> ✓ *It took me an hour to place my whole head within the opening*
>
> ✓ *I undid the lantern cautiously—oh, so cautiously—cautiously*
>
> ✓ *I undid it just so much that a single thin ray fell upon the vulture eye*

- Bring the class together and discuss the phrases that students identified. The phrases above seem the most obvious. However, deal with other instances that the students think make them see what happens when the narrator visits the old man each night. Be sure that students explain what it is that each phrase lets them see in the scene. You might ask several students to act out a phrase/sentence.

- Then ask: What is the connection between the narrator's slow and deliberate actions and his argument that he is not mad? (**The narrator would want readers to recognize that someone who is mad would not be so careful in his planning.**)

  - Write the following sentences on the board:

    ○ *Death, in approaching him had stalked with his black shadow before him, and enveloped the victim.*

    ○ *Death, in approaching had followed him with his black shadow before him, and surrounded the victim.*

- Together read the sentences aloud. Tell students that both sentences have the same meaning. Then ask them which sentence is stronger and more intense and why. (Students should mention the differences between *stalked* and *enveloped* and *followed* and *surrounded*.)

- Conclude the activity by asking students to close their eyes and try to picture death as it stalked and enveloped the victim. Have them share the images.

- To continue work with figurative language, have students examine **section D**. Have students work with a partner and find examples of figurative language and then have them discuss the impact Poe's choice of words had on the story and the reader.

- The first two paragraphs of **section E** also are quite powerful as they describe how "cleverly" he concealed the body. Although the details are gruesome, the language is worthy of discussion. Have the students read the two paragraphs independently. Then ask: What is the connection between the specific details of how he concealed the body and the story's ongoing argument? Cite specific examples from the text to support your ideas. (**The narrator continues to convince us of how clever he is. He gives a play-by-play description of the steps he took to conceal the body and suggests that someone who was mad could not do that.**)

- Tell students that they are going to do an analysis of the narrator's breakdown. Given the power of **section F**, tell students that together you are going to read those paragraphs aloud. With you leading, and providing the appropriate expression, have the whole class read aloud. Start with *The officers were satisfied. My manner had convinced them.* When you've completed the oral reading, tell students that the narrator's breakdown is actually detailed step-by-step in the part they just read aloud.

• To begin the process of examining the narrator's breakdown, tell students to work with a partner and find and underline all the phrases that describe the sounds that bother the narrator. To have the activities in this section go well, it would be best if you prepared a list on chart paper or the board (which is covered until you reveal each phrase, one at a time). Then start students off by revealing the first phrase.

Sounds the Narrator Hears

I fancied a ringing in my ear

The ringing became more distinct

It continued and became more distinct

It continued and gained definiteness

The noise was not within my ears

The sound increased

It was a low, dull, quick sound

such a sound as a watch makes when enveloped in cotton

but the noise steadily increased

but the noise steadily increased

but the noise steadily increased

but the noise arose over all and continually increased

It grew louder—louder—louder

Louder! louder! louder! louder!

It is the beating of his hideous heart!

• Bring the group together and call on students to read the next item. Then uncover your next item, and have it read. When you have gone through all the items, tell students to look over the phrases and answer the following question: "What do you notice about these sounds as you look down your list?" (Students should notice that the sounds start as just a ringing in his ears but steadily increase and by the end of the story are so loud he can no longer bear the noise of what he now believes is the beating of the old man's heart.)

- Call on several good readers to read the list of sounds and with their voices and expression show the increasing intensity of the narrator's predicament. Tell students that loudness is not the only way to show intensity. Then have the class read the list aloud also demonstrating the increased intensity.

- Tell students that there is a relationship between the sounds the narrator hears and the narrator's actions. They should be able to see that as the sounds increased in intensity, so did the narrator's actions.

- On a large piece of paper or a chalkboard draw two columns as shown below and write the title of each column—**Action words** and **Descriptions of action words**. (The completed chart is provided below.) Tell students that together you are going to complete the chart by finding the narrator's actions and a description of each action in the first paragraph of section F. Tell the class that the first action you found was toward the end, the word *talked*. Have students locate the word in the paragraph. Then, write *talked* under the first column. Now tell students to find the description of how the narrator talked, that is, which words describe how he talked? (**More freely.**) Write those words in the second column of the chart.

How the Author Talked (and Moved)

Action words	Descriptions of action words
talked	more freely
grew	very pale
talked	more fluently and with a heightened voice
gasped	for breath
talked	more quickly
arose and argued	about trifles in a high key and with violent gesticulations

Note: Define *trifles* as things that are not at all important. *Gesticulations* are strong arms and body motions that communicate intense feelings.

- When the chart is complete, have students read across the two columns in each row. Then have students read down the column of actions. Ask students, "What do you recognize when you read down the chart?" (**Students should recognize that the narrator is becoming more and more nervous.**) The actions are a progression from *growing pale* to *arose and argued [with the police] with violent gesticulation*. Reinforce the idea that Poe's word choices allow us to see the increasing anxiety felt by the narrator and how the sequence of the words enable us to see the narrator's behavior increase. Then have the class read the words aloud down the column.

- Now have students work with a partner and, on a sheet of paper, list in a column all the narrator's actions in the next paragraph.

How the Author Moved (and Used his Voice)

paced

foamed

raved

swore

swung

grated

shrieked

admit(ted)

- After students have completed their lists, bring them back together to share their ideas. Call on students to tell what word they listed as first, and then have another student tell what word they have as second and so forth. Have students read aloud the words. Then have them discuss the progression of the words. Tell them that collectively the words tell us about the narrator's state of mind at this point in the story.

- Ask students how the progression of the three sets of words—the sounds that bother the narrator, the way he talks and moves, and then the way he moves and talks, reflect the overall structure of the story. **(Each set of actions starts with milder actions, moves toward stronger actions, and ends with intense actions. The structure of the story also progresses from the narrator's "calm" telling of the situation, his attempt to enter the old man's room, to the killing, and then to the encounter with the police.)**

- Ask students, "How does the end of the story, starting with the police's arrival, show the same structure as the words and phrases in the overall story?" **(At the beginning the narrator is calm and friendly, he then starts hearing the sounds, and from there the section gets more and more intense.)**

Punctuation: Overuse of Dashes and Exclamation Points

Tell students that you are going to examine the effect Poe's use or misuse of punctuation had on the story. Begin by working with Poe's overuse of dashes.

- With you leading, have the students read the first paragraph aloud.

  TRUE!—nervous—very, very dreadfully nervous I had been and am; but why will you say that I am mad? The disease had sharpened my senses—not destroyed—not dulled them. Above all was the sense of hearing acute. I heard all things in the heaven and in the earth. I heard many things in hell. How, then, am I mad? Hearken! and observe how healthily—how calmly I can tell you the whole story.

- Ask: "How does the abundance of dashes affect the reading?" (**A dash typically causes the reader to pause before moving on to the next word. The overuse of dashes interferes with the reader's fluidity and causes the reader to stop and start awkwardly.**)

- Then have students read aloud the beginning of the second paragraph, as it does not contain dashes.

  It is impossible to say how first the idea entered my brain; but once conceived, it haunted me day and night. Object there was none. Passion there was none. I loved the old man. He had never wronged me. He had never given me insult. For his gold I had no desire. I think it was his eye! yes, it was this!

- Ask: "Was there a difference in how we read those lines? What effect did the overuse of dashes have on our reading?" (**The dashes break the flow of the reading. When we read the part without dashes, we read more smoothly. The paragraph with the dashes caused us to start and stop.**)

- After students are able to distinguish between reading with and without dashes, have them work with a partner to respond to the following question: "How does Poe's style of writing, the overuse of dashes, reflect the narrator's state of mind?" (**The narrator is constantly battling between two ideas, that of being insane, and that of being overly clever. The starting and stopping, emphasized by the dashes, may reflect the narrator's struggle with the two ideas.**)

- Tell students that Poe also overuses exclamation points. Together read the second paragraph of **section F.** Then ask students the effect the overuse of exclamation points had on the story. (**This is the most intense part of the story,**

everything is extreme, the narrator is having a breakdown, so Poe uses the exclamation marks to emphasize the intensity of what's going on.)

Vocabulary

Poe's use of rich words is another example of his remarkable prose. There are opportunities for encouraging students to figure out the meaning of words from context. Below we offer several examples in which the contexts provide enough information for students to at least get a sense of what the word means. Examples of supporting students to derive word meaning from context are found in Chapter 6.

- Never before that night had I felt the extent of my own powers—of my sagacity. I could scarcely contain my feelings of triumph.

- But anything was better than this agony! Anything was more tolerable than this derision.

- I brought chairs into the room, and desired them [the police] here to rest from their fatigues, while I myself, in the wild audacity of my perfect triumph, placed my own seat upon the very spot beneath which reposed the corpse of the victim.

Writing Activity

Have students engage in the following independent writing activity. Choose one of the following two claims, and support that claim:

"The narrator was not insane; he was clever and wise."

"The narrator was insane."

Tell students to make sure that they include the three features listed below in their essays, and any other ones they deem useful.

- When you introduce the claim, distinguish it from an alternative claim.
- Support claim with evidence.
- Provide a concluding statement.

John F. Kennedy's Inaugural Address

(January 20, 1961)

Grade Level: 7–8+

Introduction: *John F. Kennedy's Inaugural Address* is considered one of the best inaugural speeches ever given. Both Democrats and Republicans have praised the speech. Some have even said that, although they did not vote for Kennedy, they now would have after hearing his speech.

The main points of the speech deal with the gift of freedom, the doing away of poverty and oppression, the cold war, and, at the end, a call to individuals and the nation to rise to its potential for greatness. Those topics were made meaningful and memorable by Kennedy's amazing use of rhetorical devices. He was a master of rhetoric, and the speech often sounds like poetry.

The background knowledge needed to understand the speech is weighty, but we suggest some important content in this chapter that you can weave into the course of reading with interspersed queries. Our major focus, however, is on some of the rhetorical techniques that Kennedy uses, which have allowed the speech to withstand the test of time and become a classic.

According to our analyses, the speech is appropriate beyond the eighth-grade level, which was influenced by teachers who have taught the speech from sixth through tenth grade. With such a broad range, you must decide at which grade/s the speech is likely to work for your students. Certainly teachers have provided more scaffolding for younger students.

Lesson content	Page
Copy of text for duplication and distribution: *John F. Kennedy's Inaugural Address*	212
Segmented Text and Queries	214
Close Reading	217

John F. Kennedy's Inaugural Address
(January 20, 1961)

Vice President Johnson, Mr. Speaker, Mr. Chief Justice, President Eisenhower, Vice President Nixon, President Truman, reverend clergy, fellow citizens:

We observe today not a victory of party, but a celebration of freedom—symbolizing an end, as well as a beginning—signifying renewal, as well as change. For I have sworn before you and Almighty God the same solemn oath our forebears prescribed nearly a century and three-quarters ago. The world is very different now. For man holds in his mortal hands the power to abolish all forms of human poverty and all forms of human life. And yet the same revolutionary beliefs for which our forebears fought are still at issue around the globe—the belief that the rights of man come not from the generosity of the state, but from the hand of God.

We dare not forget today that we are the heirs of that first revolution. Let the word go forth from this time and place, to friend and foe alike, that the torch has been passed to a new generation of Americans—born in this century, tempered by war, disciplined by a hard and bitter peace, proud of our ancient heritage, and unwilling to witness or permit the slow undoing of those human rights to which this nation has always been committed, and to which we are committed today at home and around the world.

Let every nation know, whether it wishes us well or ill, that we shall pay any price, bear any burden, meet any hardship, support any friend, oppose any foe, to assure the survival and the success of liberty.

This much we pledge—and more.

To those old allies whose cultural and spiritual origins we share, we pledge the loyalty of faithful friends. United there is little we cannot do in a host of cooperative ventures. Divided there is little we can do—for we dare not meet a powerful challenge at odds and split asunder.

To those new states whom we welcome to the ranks of the free, we pledge our word that one form of colonial control shall not have passed away merely to be replaced by a far more iron tyranny. We shall not always expect to find them supporting our view. But we shall always hope to find them strongly supporting their own freedom—and to remember that, in the past, those who foolishly sought power by riding the back of the tiger ended up inside.

To those people in the huts and villages of half the globe struggling to break the bonds of mass misery, we pledge our best efforts to help them help themselves, for whatever period is required—not because the Communists may be doing it, not because we seek their votes, but because it is right. If a free society cannot help the many who are poor, it cannot save the few who are rich.

To our sister republics south of our border, we offer a special pledge: to convert our good words into good deeds, in a new alliance for progress, to assist free men and free governments in casting off the chains of poverty. But this peaceful revolution of hope cannot become the prey of hostile powers. Let all our neighbors know that we shall join with them to oppose aggression or subversion anywhere in the Americas. And let every other power know that this hemisphere intends to remain the master of its own house.

To that world assembly of sovereign states, the United Nations, our last best hope in an age where the instruments of war have far outpaced the instruments of peace, we renew our pledge of support—to prevent it from becoming merely a forum for invective, to strengthen its shield of the new and the weak, and to enlarge the area in which its writ may run. Finally, to those nations who would make themselves our adversary, we offer not a pledge but a request: that both sides begin anew the quest for peace, before the dark powers of destruction unleashed by science engulf all humanity in planned or accidental self-destruction. We dare not tempt them with weakness. For only when our arms are sufficient beyond doubt can we be certain beyond doubt that they will never be employed. . . .

And so, my fellow Americans, ask not what your country can do for you; ask what you can do for your country. My fellow citizens of the world, ask not what America will do for you, but what together we can do for the freedom of man.

Finally, whether you are citizens of America or citizens of the world, ask of us here the same high standards of strength and sacrifice which we ask of you. With a good conscience our only sure reward, with history the final judge of our deeds, let us go forth to lead the land we love, asking His blessing and His help, but knowing that here on earth God's work must truly be our own.

SEGMENTED TEXT AND QUERIES

Text segments	Queries/targeted responses
Vice President Johnson, Mr. Speaker, Mr. Chief Justice, President Eisenhower, Vice President Nixon, President Truman, Reverend Clergy: We observe today not a victory of party, but a celebration of freedom—symbolizing an end, as well as a beginning—signifying renewal, as well as change. For I have sworn before you and Almighty God the same solemn oath our forebears prescribed nearly a century and three-quarters ago. **1**	1. **What is Kennedy saying here?** (He's carrying on the tradition of being sworn into office, but he's telling people that he also represents change and renewal.) Clarify that the word *party,* in this case, refers to political party, such as Democratic and Republican. 1a. **Who are our forebears that Kennedy refers to?** (In this case, it's the people who founded the United States and wrote the Constitution.)
The world is very different now. For man holds in his mortal hands the power to abolish all forms of human poverty and all forms of human life. And yet the same revolutionary beliefs for which our forebears fought are still at issue around the globe—the belief that the rights of man come not from the generosity of the state, but from the hand of God. **2**	2. **Now what is Kennedy saying?** (The world is different now because we have the power to end poverty but also to end human lives. However, in some ways, the world is still the same. The rights that we hold do not come from man. They are our God-given rights.) 2a. **What is the power that could end all human life?** (If students don't know that the power to abolish all forms of life is the atomic bomb, tell them.)
We dare not forget today that we are the heirs of that first revolution. Let the word go forth from this time and place, to friend and foe alike, that the torch has been passed to a new generation of Americans—born in this century, tempered by war, disciplined by a hard and bitter peace, proud of our ancient heritage, and unwilling to witness or permit the slow undoing of those human rights to which this nation has always been committed, and to which we are committed today at home and around the world. **3**	3. **What point is Kennedy making here?** (We are proud of what our previous generations accomplished, especially in terms of human rights, and although we are a new generation, we will continue to be committed to the cause of all human rights.)

Let every nation know, whether it wishes us well or ill, that we shall pay any price, bear any burden, meet any hardship, support any friend, oppose any foe, to assure the survival and the success of liberty.

This much we pledge—and more. **4**

To those old allies whose cultural and spiritual origins we share, we pledge the loyalty of faithful friends. United there is little we cannot do in a host of cooperative ventures. Divided there is little we can do—for we dare not meet a powerful challenge at odds and split asunder. **5**

To those new states whom we welcome to the ranks of the free, we pledge our word that one form of colonial control shall not have passed away merely to be replaced by a far more iron tyranny. We shall not always expect to find them supporting our view. But we shall always hope to find them strongly supporting their own freedom—and to remember that, in the past, those who foolishly sought power by riding the back of the tiger ended up inside. **6**

To those people in the huts and villages of half the globe struggling to break the bonds of mass misery, we pledge our best efforts to help them help themselves, for whatever period is required—not because the Communists may be doing it, not because we seek their votes, but because it is right. If a free society cannot help the many who are poor, it cannot save the few who are rich. **7**

4. **How does this section connect with what we just talked about?**
   (It reinforces the point that we are committed to human rights for all.)

5. **What did we read here?**
   (Kennedy is saying that our nation will continue to be loyal to all of its allies.)

5a. **Find and read the part in which Kennedy talks about being united and divided.**
   (United there is little we cannot do in a host of cooperative ventures. Divided there is little we can do.)

6. **Now what is Kennedy talking about?**
   (He is pledging to new states that the freedom that was fought for will not be lost, and he hopes that even in times when there are differing viewpoints, these new states will support their own freedom.)

Clarify that new states means new countries, not new U.S. states.

7. **How does this new section connect to what we just talked about?**
   (Kennedy is making another pledge. This time he is pledging to people around the world that the United States will provide support in helping these people help themselves.)

7a. **According to Kennedy, what is the purpose of this pledge?**
   (He says it's not to get something out of it, but rather because it's the right thing to do.)

To our sister republics south of our border, we offer a special pledge: to convert our good words into good deeds, in a new alliance for progress, to assist free men and free governments in casting off the chains of poverty. But this peaceful revolution of hope cannot become the prey of hostile powers. Let all our neighbors know that we shall join with them to oppose aggression or subversion anywhere in the Americas. And let every other power know that this hemisphere intends to remain the master of its own house. **8**

To that world assembly of sovereign states, the United Nations, our last best hope in an age where the instruments of war have far outpaced the instruments of peace, we renew our pledge of support—to prevent it from becoming merely a forum for invective, to strengthen its shield of the new and the weak, and to enlarge the area in which its writ may run. **9**

Finally, to those nations who would make themselves our adversary, we offer not a pledge but a request: that both sides begin anew the quest for peace, before the dark powers of destruction unleashed by science engulf all humanity in planned or accidental self-destruction. **10**

8. **What additional information did we learn about this pledge?**
   (Kennedy is pledging to the republics south of the United States to use peaceful ways to assist them in getting rid of poverty and having renewed hope.)

8a. **What point is Kennedy making about using those peaceful methods?**
   (They shouldn't be taken for weakness.)

9. **What is Kennedy saying here?**
   (He is pledging support to the United Nations.)

9a. **What is the United Nations?**
   (An organization of many countries in the world that come together to talk about solving world problems and making the world a better place to live.)

9b. **What does he think of the United Nations?**
   (It's very important because the world is more prepared for war than for peace, so it's important to support the organization that will try to maintain peace.)

10. **What is Kennedy's point here?**
   (He is appealing to the country's adversaries and asking that they start again in their search for peace.)

Clarify that students know what adversaries are.

10a. **What does he mean, " . . . before the dark powers of destruction unleashed by science engulf all humanity in planned or accidental self-destruction"?**
   (Because of scientific advancements, the world could easily be destroyed, so they must work together to prevent that from happening.)

And so, my fellow Americans, ask not what your country can do for you; ask what you can do for your country. My fellow citizens of the world, ask not what America will do for you, but what together we can do for the freedom of man. **11**

Finally, whether you are citizens of America or citizens of the world, ask of us here the same high standards of strength and sacrifice which we ask of you. With a good conscience our only sure reward, with history the final judge of our deeds, let us go forth to lead the land we love, asking His blessing and His help, but knowing that here on earth God's work must truly be our own. **12**

11. **What is Kennedy telling his fellow citizens?**
    (Kennedy is telling Americans to think about what they, personally, can do for their country and what all people can do for freedom.)

12. **What is Kennedy's final point?**
    (He is telling citizens everywhere to expect the same standards from him and the United States government that he is expecting from them.)

CLOSE READING

Language

Antithesis

Explain to students that the purpose of a speech is to deliver a message, and speakers often use a variety of rhetorical devices to make their messages clear, powerful, and engaging. Tell students that the most famous line from President Kennedy's speech is: *And so, my fellow Americans, ask not what your country can do for you; ask what you can do for your country.* Explain that this line is an example of something called *antithesis*, a rhetorical device that puts two contrasting ideas in the same sentence. Speakers often use this device to emphasize a contrast. Because the sentence uses parallel structure, and the contrasting ideas are obvious, they can be easy to recognize but not as easy to understand. Students shouldn't have trouble understanding the notion of contrasting ideas, but you might want to remind them what parallel structure means. Tell them that parallel structure occurs when each idea or item in a sentence repeats the same grammatical pattern.

• As a particularly useful example, tell students that astronaut Neil Armstrong was the first person to land on the moon, and when he put his foot on the moon's surface Armstrong said, "One small step for man, one giant leap for mankind." Ask students what two contrasting ideas are being presented in

Armstrong's statement. **(One small step, one giant leap.)** Then, ask them to describe the parallel structure. **(Five words in each idea; follows the same grammatical pattern, using the same parts of speech.)** Finally, ask them to explain the role of antithesis in the Armstrong quote. **(It emphasizes the contrast between the small step he was literally taking with the huge step he was taking, figuratively, for all of mankind.)**

• Next, have students apply their understanding of antithesis to Kennedy's speech. Reread the famous line from Kennedy's speech, *And so, my fellow Americans, ask not what your country can do for you; ask what you can do for your country.* Ask students what two ideas are being contrasted. **(That you should not think about what your country can do for you; what you really should think about is what you can do for your country.)**

• If students still need more support, read the first paragraph together and ask them if they recognize any additional examples of antithesis. **(There are three: We observe today not a victory of party, but a celebration of freedom; symbolizing an end, as well as a beginning; signifying renewal, as well as change.)** Tell students that together you are going to work through the first example, *We observe today not a victory of party, but a celebration of freedom.* Ask what two things are being contrasted. **(The victory of a political party and a celebration of freedom for everyone.)** Ask them to describe the parallel structure (not a victory of party, but a celebration of freedom). Then, ask if anyone can explain the meaning within the rhetorical device. **(It wasn't just a victory for one party; it was a celebration of freedom for everyone—all parties will benefit.)**

• Have students work in groups of three to four to identify other examples of antithesis, identify the ideas being contrasted, and explain their purpose in the speech. We suggest not spending much time describing the parallel structure pattern, as it is pretty obvious and one of the reasons students will be able to locate examples of antithesis. The table below shows some examples of what students may say.

Example	Explanation of ideas being contrasted
Symbolizing an end as well as a beginning	An end and a beginning: These two ideas are seemingly different, but Kennedy makes the point that being elected is ending what was in place before this day, but on this day it is an opportunity for a new beginning.

United there is little we cannot do . . . divided there is little we can do.	United and divided: Kennedy is emphasizing that if people work together there is little they can't accomplish, but if they don't work together, they won't be able to do much at all.
. . . ask not what America will do for you; but what together we can do for the freedom of man.	You personally and together: Here, Kennedy is addressing the citizens around the world and asking them not to think about what America can do for them, personally. Rather, he asks them to think about how much more they can accomplish for the freedom of all mankind if everyone works together.

- Bring students together and have them share their examples. Then, have a student recap what they learned about antithesis and the impact its role had on Kennedy's speech.

Anaphora

Tell students that you are going to look at another rhetorical device, *anaphora*, that was used in Kennedy's speech. Explain that anaphora is when a word or words are repeated at the beginning of two or more paragraphs, verses, clauses, or sentences.

- With a partner, have students reread the speech and find the phrase that is repeated at the beginning of numerous lines. (**To those. . . .**)

- Have them list all of the lines that begin with the phrase "to those," paying close attention to whom Kennedy is addressing. (**To those old allies, to those new states, to those people in the huts and villages, to those nations who would make themselves our adversary.**) Bring students together and have them share their examples.

- Then, have students work in small groups and discuss the role anaphora played in the speech. Tell them to look specifically at whom Kennedy was addressing, and the purpose of addressing these groups of people. They should come up with ideas such as: its role was to give the people a sense of unity; its purpose was so that every person from any state, country, or hut would not feel alienated; its purpose was to make all people feel important.

Alliteration

Students should be familiar with the meaning of alliteration, so begin by having a student provide a brief explanation. **(When two or more words that begin with the same initial consonant letters or sounds occur close together.)** Although most students are familiar with the term, more than likely their experience with alliteration comes from its use in literary texts. Having them work with alliteration in an informational text will provide a new challenge. Explain that alliteration is often used to emphasize words. When listening to a speech, alliterative words stand out and indicate that the speaker is bringing special attention to those words. There are two kinds of alliterations. One is immediate alliteration, which is when two or more such words are right next to each other. The other kind, nonimmediate alliteration, is when one or several words separate the alliterative words.

Write the following quotation on the board and tell students that it is from Bill Clinton's 1992 Democratic National Convention Acceptance Address:

> Somewhere at this very moment a child is being born in America. Let it be our cause to give that child a happy home, a healthy family, and a hopeful future.

Read it aloud with the class. Then tell students that you will read it aloud again, and they should raise their hands when you get to an alliteration. Underline the alliterations as shown below:

> Somewhere at this very moment a child is <u>be</u>ing <u>b</u>orn in America. Let it <u>be</u> our cause to give that child a <u>h</u>appy <u>h</u>ome, a <u>h</u>ealthy family, and a <u>h</u>opeful future.

Ask which alliterations are immediate and which are nonimmediate.

- Tell students that Kennedy's speech is a gold mine of alliterations. To find them, divide the speech into two parts and divide the class into two groups. Students should work with a partner within their group and find and underline all the alliterations within their part of the speech. Bring students together and have them share the alliterations they found.

- Have students explain their alliterations, how alliteration was used for Kennedy's speech, and how it enhanced the impact of what Kennedy was saying.

Writing Activity

As a concluding activity, have students write a response in which they discuss the impact of the three devices—antithesis, anaphora, alliteration—on Kennedy's speech. Then have students respond to the following question: Which of the three rhetorical devices do you think was most effective in Kennedy's speech? Explain the device, the role it played in the speech, and why you believe it was the most effective device. Cite specific examples from the text to support your ideas.

Reproducible Texts
from Part One

Alice in Wonderland

by Lewis Carroll

Alice was beginning to get very tired of sitting by her sister on the bank, and of having nothing to do: once or twice she had peeped into the book her sister was reading, but it had no pictures or conversations in it, 'and what is the use of a book,' thought Alice 'without pictures or conversations?' So she was considering in her own mind (as well as she could, for the hot day made her feel very sleepy and stupid), whether the pleasure of making a daisy-chain would be worth the trouble of getting up and picking the daisies.

Suddenly a White Rabbit with pink eyes ran close by her. There was nothing so VERY remarkable in that; nor did Alice think it so VERY much out of the way to hear the Rabbit say to itself, 'Oh dear! Oh dear! I shall be late!' (when she thought it over afterwards, it occurred to her that she ought to have wondered at this, but at the time it all seemed quite natural); but when the Rabbit actually TOOK A WATCH OUT OF ITS WAISTCOAT-POCKET, and looked at it, and then hurried on, Alice started to her feet, for it flashed across her mind that she had never before seen a rabbit with either a waistcoat-pocket, or a watch to take out of it and burning with curiosity, she ran across the field after it, and fortunately was just in time to see it pop down a large rabbit-hole under the hedge.

Alice started after the rabbit, never once considering how in the world she was to get out again. The rabbit-hole went straight on like a tunnel for some way, and then dipped suddenly down, so suddenly that Alice had not a moment to think about stopping herself before she found herself falling down a very deep well. Either the well was very deep, or she fell very slowly, for she had plenty of time as she went down to look about her to make out what she was coming to, but it was too dark to see anything. Then she looked at the sides of the well, and noticed that they were filled with cupboards and book-shelves; here and there she saw maps and pictures hung upon pegs.

She took down a jar from one of the shelves as she passed; it was labeled 'ORANGE MARMALADE', but to her great disappointment it was empty: she did not like to drop the jar for fear of killing somebody, so managed to put it into one of the cupboards as she fell past it.

Down, down, down. Would the fall NEVER come to an end! 'I wonder how many miles I've fallen by this time?' she said aloud. 'I must be getting somewhere near the center of the earth. Let me see: that would be four thousand miles down, I think—' (for, you see, Alice had learnt several things of this sort in her lessons in the schoolroom, and though this was not a VERY good opportunity for showing off her knowledge, as there was no one to listen to her, still it was good practice to say it over) '—yes, that's about the right distance—but then I wonder what Latitude or Longitude I've got to?' (Alice had no idea what Latitude was, or Longitude either, but thought they were nice grand words to say).

Presently she began again. 'I wonder if I shall fall right THROUGH the earth! How funny it'll seem to come out among the people that walk with their heads downward! I shall have to ask them what the name of the country is. Please, Ma'am, is this New Zealand or Australia?' (and she tried to curtsey as she spoke—fancy CURTSEYING as you're falling through the air! Do you think you could manage it?) 'And what an ignorant little girl she'll think me for asking! No, it'll never do to ask: perhaps I shall see it written up somewhere.'

Alice in Wonderland *(page 2)*

Down, down, down. There was nothing else to do, so Alice soon began talking again. 'Dinah'll miss me very much to-night, I should think!' (Dinah was the cat.) 'I hope they'll remember her saucer of milk at tea-time. Dinah my dear! I wish you were down here with me! There are no mice in the air, I'm afraid, but you might catch a bat, and that's very like a mouse, you know. But do cats eat bats, I wonder?' And here Alice began to get rather sleepy, and went on saying to herself, in a dreamy sort of way, 'Do cats eat bats? Do cats eat bats?' and sometimes, 'Do bats eat cats?' for, you see, as she couldn't answer either question, it didn't much matter which way she put it.

She felt that she was dozing off, and had just begun to dream that she was walking hand in hand with Dinah, and saying to her very earnestly, 'Now, Dinah, tell me the truth: did you ever eat a bat?' when suddenly, thump! thump! down she came upon a heap of sticks and dry leaves, and the fall was over. Alice was not a bit hurt, and she jumped up in a moment. She looked up, but it was all dark overhead; before her was another long passage and the White Rabbit was still in sight, hurrying down it. Away went Alice like the wind and was just in time to hear it say, as it turned a corner, "Oh, my ears and whiskers, how late it's getting!" She was close behind it when she turned the corner, but the Rabbit was no longer to be seen.

She found herself in a long, low hall, which was lit up by a row of lamps hanging from the roof. There were doors all 'round the hall, but they were all locked; and when Alice had been all the way down one side and up the other, trying every door, she walked sadly down the middle, wondering how she was ever to get out again. Suddenly she came upon a little table, all made of solid glass. There was nothing on it but a tiny golden key, and Alice's first idea was that this might belong to one of the doors of the hall; but, alas! either the locks were too large, or the key was too small, but, at any rate, it would not open any of them. However, on the second time 'round, she came upon a low curtain she had not noticed before, and behind it was a little door about fifteen inches high. She tried the little golden key in the lock, and to her great delight, it fitted!

Black Death

by Janet Callahan

In 1347, a deadly disease swept across Europe. People did not know what caused it. They did not know how to treat it, either. As a result, 25 million people died within five years. About 40 percent of Europe's population was wiped out.

This terrible disease became known as the Black Death. This name suggests the fear that gripped Europe as the disease spread. It also describes the disease's most unmistakable sign: the black or dark purple spots that appeared on victims' bodies just before they died. The disease is also referred to as Bubonic Plague from swellings, called "buboes," that spread over the entire body.

Most experts believed the Black Death was caused by a germ called *Yersinia pestis*. In 2011, scientists studying centuries-old skeletons confirmed that the experts were right about this germ. The germ lived in the bodies of fleas that attached themselves to rats. In the 1300s, rats were a part of everyday life in the cities and villages of people's homes. Infected fleas that bit people passed the disease on to them. People could also catch the disease by coming in close contact with someone who had already fallen ill.

Historians have studied how Black Death germs arrived in Europe. Many believe the flea-ridden rats came from China to Europe on trade ships. Why do they think so? They know that just a few years before the Black Death struck Europe, the same deadly disease broke out in China. Historians think that the flea-ridden rats got aboard European trade ships that visited Chinese ports. When the ships returned to Europe, they brought the rats—with fleas on their bodies—with them.

There is a convincing piece of evidence for this theory. It is an account of an eyewitness from Sicily, an island in Europe off the coast of Italy in the Mediterranean Sea. According to this account, a fleet of trade ships arrived in Sicily in October 1347. Many of the ships' crewmen were already dead when the ships docked. Many more were sick with the disease. When the people of Sicily realized that the Black Death had reached their shores, they ordered the ships out of the harbor. This action came too late to save the people of Sicily, however. Within days, Sicilians began to come down with the disease.

Before long, the Black Death reached other cities along the Mediterranean coast. Historical documents record that the disease spread inland with terrifying speed. In Europe it spread through France, Germany, Spain, and Portugal. It moved on to the British Isles and Scandinavia. It even reached the island of Greenland, near the North Pole, almost wiping out its population.

People felt helpless in the face of such a deadly disease. Although they did not know how to prevent the Black Death, they were willing to try almost anything. Some people washed walls and furniture and even their bodies with rose water or vinegar. Others tried to ward off the illness by wearing garlands of flowers. Many people believed they could stay healthy if they did not eat, drink, or exercise too much. None of these precautions worked. Although a tiny fraction of people who fell ill with the disease were able to recover, most died within a week after their first symptoms appeared.

People who practiced medicine in the 1300s did not know much about diseases or how to treat them. The Black Death was often treated with a warm preparation of butter, onion, and garlic applied to the skin, but it did not help. The most popular remedy of the time was bloodletting, or leeching. In this treatment, the doctor tried to get rid of a disease by taking blood from the patient's body. But this procedure had no effect on the Black Death.

The fear and panic that came with the Black Death was almost as destructive as the death toll. When the Black Death struck a town or village, those who were still healthy often fled for their lives. In the blink of an eye, a town would be left without its shop owners, craftsmen, and other workers. In this way, the Black Death wiped out whole communities.

By 1351, the Black Death had mostly vanished from Europe. In the next 150 years, there would be several more outbreaks of the disease, but none was as bad as the first. Yet fearful memories of the disease's first wave lingered for many years before Europeans finally believed that they had put the Black Death behind them for good.

The Two Brothers

by Leo Tolstoy

Two brothers set out on a journey together. At noon they lay down in a forest to rest. When they woke up they saw a stone lying next to them. There was something written on the stone. It said, "Whoever finds this stone," they read, "let him go straight into the forest at sunrise. In the forest a river will appear; let him swim across the river to the other side. There he will find a she-bear and her cubs. Let him take the cubs from her and run up the mountain with them, without once looking back. On the top of the mountain he will see a house, and in that house he will find happiness."

When they had read what was written on the stone, the younger brother said: "Let us go together. We can swim across the river, carry off the bear cubs, take them to the house on the mountain, and together find happiness."

"I am not going into the forest after bear cubs," said the elder brother. "And I advise you not to go. In the first place, no one can know whether what is written on this stone is the truth; perhaps it was written in jest. It is even possible that we have not read it correctly. In the second place, even if what is written here is the truth, suppose we go into the forest and night comes, and we cannot find the river. We shall be lost. And if we do find the river, how are we going to swim across it? It may be broad and swift. In the third place, even if we swim across the river, do you think it is an easy thing to take her cubs away from the she-bear? She will seize us, and, instead of finding happiness, we shall perish, and all for nothing. In the fourth place, even if we succeeded in carrying off the bear cubs, we could not run up a mountain without stopping to rest. And, most important of all, the stone does not tell us what kind of happiness we should find in that house. It may be that the happiness awaiting us there is not at all the sort of happiness we would want."

"In my opinion," said the younger brother, "you are wrong. What is written on the stone could not have been put there without reason. And it is all perfectly clear. In the first place, no harm will come to us if we try. In the second place, if we do not go, someone else will read the inscription on the stone. Then they will find happiness, and we shall have lost it all. In the third place, if you do not make an effort and try hard, nothing in the world will succeed. In the fourth place, I should not want it thought that I was afraid of anything."

The elder brother answered him by saying, "A proverb says: 'In seeking great happiness small pleasures may be lost.' And also: 'A bird in the hand is worth two in the bush.'" The younger brother then said, "I have heard: 'He who is afraid of the leaves must not go into the forest.' And also: 'Beneath a stone no water flows.'"

The younger brother set off, and the elder remained behind. No sooner had the younger brother gone into the forest, than he found the river, swam across it. And there on the other side was the she-bear, fast asleep. He took her cubs, and ran up the mountain without look-ing back. When he reached the top of the mountain the people came out to meet him. They had a carriage to take him into the city, where they made him their king.

He ruled for five years. In the sixth year, another king, who was stronger than he, waged war against him. The city was conquered, and he was driven out.

Again the younger brother became a wanderer. One day he arrived at the house of the elder brother. The elder brother was living in a village and had grown neither rich nor poor.

The two brothers rejoiced at seeing each other. And at once began telling of all that had happened to them.

"You see," said the elder brother, "I was right. Here I have lived quietly and well, while you, though you may have been a king, have seen a great deal of trouble." The younger brother replied, "I do not regret having gone into the forest and up the mountain. I may have nothing now, but I shall always have something to remember, while you have no memories at all."

Pythons Invade the Florida Everglades

The Florida Everglades teem with life. Migratory and wading birds tiptoe through marshy grasslands. Orchids and ferns dot the hardwood forests. Alligators lounge in the shallows and on muddy riverbanks. Mangrove leaves rustle in the wind as the brackish water laps at their roots. All of this life is made possible by the presence of water. The Everglades are sometimes called the *River of Grass* (1947) after a book of the same name by author Marjory Stoneman Douglas. The phrase illustrates that the Everglades are basically a very wide and shallow river.

Tommy Owen, a tour guide in the Everglades National Park was giving a tour of Florida's famous park wetlands to a group of tourists. He and the tourists were floating in a boat through the shallow water that makes up the Everglades. One of the women in the boat he was steering saw a snake in the water. She got Tommy's attention and pointed the snake out to him. When Tommy saw the snake, he acted fast. He reached into the water and grabbed the animal by the head. He got a good grip and didn't let go. Tourists in the boat were worried when the snake wrapped itself around Tommy's arm. After several minutes, he got control of the animal and removed it from the water. The snake was a ten-foot-long Burmese python. It was a snake not native to Florida and, quite simply, it didn't belong there.

The Burmese python is native to tropical and subtropical zones in Southeast Asia. In their native habitat, Burmese pythons are nocturnal carnivores. When they live close to human habitations, pythons eat rats, mice, and rabbits that are attracted to human dwellings and farms. They can also eat small farm animals like chickens. When they live away from human habitations, pythons eat birds and small wild mammals. The python kills by constricting its body around its prey. Python eggs and hatchlings are a food source for other animals. In the wild, pythons grow to be on average 12 feet long.

In the United States the Burmese python is a popular pet. Docile and beautifully patterned in brown and gold diamond shapes, these snakes can be purchased at pet stores or reptile shows. Owners keep them in cages or tanks and feed them rats or mice. Most people buy pythons when the animals are small. Pythons can grow very quickly. For many pet owners, the pet pythons become too big to manage.

The first Burmese python was found in the Florida Everglades in 1979. It's presumed the animal was originally kept as a pet and then released by its owner. Starting in 1992— when it's thought that numerous Burmese pythons escaped pet stores and cages damaged in Hurricane Andrew—the numbers have grown at a faster rate.

The Burmese pythons that have been released in southern Florida have found a habitat they like in the Everglades. They are breeding in the Everglades and have reached numbers that designate them as an invasive species. Pythons are eating machines. They can eat anything from deer to bobcats, to raccoons to alligators. They especially enjoy dining on small mammals and birds. Studies have shown that since their appearance in the Everglades, the numbers of small mammals in the area are down significantly. Additionally, this population loss is not observed in areas where the python has not established itself.

Many agencies and individuals are trying to put a stop to the python invasion. The National Park Service has begun a program to study these animals in the Florida Everglades. Park Service scientists have implanted tracking devices into seventeen large pythons that were later re-released into the wild. They have provided scientists with information regarding python behavior.

In 2013 the Florida Fish and Wildlife Conservation program issued permits to hunt the snakes within state wildlife-managed areas of the Everglades. Sixty-eight animals were captured.

In the meantime, python records are still being broken.

In May of 2013 Jason Leon was driving in a rural area near Florida City when he spotted a python's head protruding from the brush. The man was a biologist, and was familiar with pythons. He approached the snake and pulled it out of the bush. The animal was bigger than he expected. After a struggle with the animal, Leon killed it. The python was 18 feet long and 128 pounds. Leon contacted the Florida Fish and Wildlife Conservation Commission, who agreed to pick up and examine the snake. The snake was found to be the largest ever in the state of Florida.

The state later issued a statement:

"Jason Leon's nighttime sighting and capture of a Burmese python of more than 18 feet in length is a notable accomplishment that set a Florida record. The Florida Wildlife Commission is grateful to him both for safely removing such a large Burmese python, and for reporting its capture."

The Ecchoing Green
by William Blake

The sun does arise,
And make happy the skies.
The merry bells ring
To welcome the Spring.
The sky-lark and thrush,
The birds of the bush,
Sing louder around,
To the bells' cheerful sound.
While our sports shall be seen
On the Ecchoing Green.

Old John, with white hair
Does laugh away care,
Sitting under the oak,
Among the old folk,
They laugh at our play,
And soon they all say,
'Such, such were the joys.
When we all girls & boys,
In our youth-time were seen,
On the Ecchoing Green.'

Till the little ones weary
No more can be merry
The sun does descend,
And our sports have an end:
Round the laps of their mothers,
Many sisters and brothers,
Like birds in their nest,
Are ready for rest;
And sport no more seen,
On the darkening Green.

Advice to a Young Author

by Arthur Conan Doyle

1. Taking in.
   Cargo stored,
   All aboard,
   Think about
   Giving out.
   Empty ship,
   Useless trip!

2. Never strain
   Weary brain,
   Hardly fit,
   Wait a bit!
   After rest
   Comes the best.

3. Sitting still,
   Let it fill;
   Never press;
   Nerve stress
   Always shows.
   Nature knows.

4. Critics kind,
   Never mind!
   Critics flatter,
   No matter!
   Critics curse,
   None the worse.
   Critics blame,
   All the same!
   Do your best.
   Hang the rest!

Casey at the Bat
A Ballad of the Republic, Sung in the Year 1888
by Ernest Lawrence Thayer

The outlook wasn't brilliant for the Mudville nine that day;
The score stood four to two with but one inning more to play.
And then when Cooney died at first, and Barrows did the same,
A sickly silence fell upon the patrons of the game.

A straggling few got up to go in deep despair. The rest
Clung to that hope which springs eternal in the human breast;
They thought if only Casey could but get a whack at that—
We'd put up even money now with Casey at the bat.

But Flynn preceded Casey, as did also Jimmy Blake,
And the former was a lulu and the latter was a cake;
So upon that stricken multitude grim melancholy sat,
For there seemed but little chance of Casey's getting to the bat.

But Flynn let drive a single, to the wonderment of all,
And Blake, the much despised, tore the cover off the ball;
And when the dust had lifted, and men saw what had occurred,
There was Jimmy safe at second and Flynn a-hugging third.

Then from 5,000 throats and more there rose a lusty yell;
It rumbled through the valley, it rattled in the dell;
It knocked upon the mountain and recoiled upon the flat,
For Casey, mighty Casey, was advancing to the bat.

There was ease in Casey's manner as he stepped into his place;
There was pride in Casey's bearing and a smile on Casey's face.
And when, responding to the cheers, he lightly doffed his hat,
No stranger in the crowd could doubt 'twas Casey at the bat.

Ten thousand eyes were on him as he rubbed his hands with dirt;
Five thousand tongues applauded when he wiped them on his shirt.
Then while the writhing pitcher ground the ball into his hip,
Defiance gleamed in Casey's eye, a sneer curled Casey's lip.

And now the leather-covered sphere came hurtling through the air,
And Casey stood a-watching it in haughty grandeur there.
Close by the sturdy batsman the ball unheeded sped—
"That ain't my style," said Casey. "Strike one," the umpire said.

Casey at the Bat *(page 2)*

From the benches, black with people, there went up a muffled roar,
Like the beating of the storm-waves on a stern and distant shore.
"Kill him! Kill the umpire!" shouted someone on the stand;
And it's likely they'd have killed him had not Casey raised his hand.

With a smile of Christian charity great Casey's visage shone;
He stilled the rising tumult; he bade the game go on;
He signaled to the pitcher, and once more the spheroid flew;
But Casey still ignored it, and the umpire said, "Strike two."

"Fraud!" cried the maddened thousands, and echo answered fraud;
But one scornful look from Casey and the audience was awed.
They saw his face grow stern and cold, they saw his muscles strain,
And they knew that Casey wouldn't let that ball go by again.

The sneer is gone from Casey's lip, his teeth are clinched in hate;
He pounds with cruel violence his bat upon the plate.
And now the pitcher holds the ball, and now he lets it go,
And now the air is shattered by the force of Casey's blow.

Oh, somewhere in this favored land the sun is shining bright;
The band is playing somewhere, and somewhere hearts are light,
And somewhere men are laughing, and somewhere children shout;
But there is no joy in Mudville—mighty Casey has struck out.

Who Has Seen the Wind?

by Christina Rossetti

Who has seen the wind?
Neither I nor you
But when the leaves hang trembling,
The wind is passing through.

Who has seen the wind?
Neither you nor I:
But when the trees bow down their heads,
The wind is passing by.

The Musicians of Bremen

(Retold by Theo Arvenitis, from the Brothers Grimm)

Once upon a time, an old donkey was badly treated by his master. Tired of such unkindness, he decided to run away. He thought he had a pretty good braying voice, so when he heard that Bremen Town was looking for singers he thought he might be accepted.

As he went along the road, the donkey met a skinny dog, covered with sores. "Come with me. If you have a good bark, you'll find a job with the band too. Just wait and see!"

A little later, a stray cat, no longer able to catch mice, joined them and the trio trotted hopefully on towards the town. As they passed a farmyard, they stopped to admire an elderly rooster who was crowing to the skies. "You sing well," they told him. "What are you so happy about?" "Happy?" muttered the rooster with tears in his eyes. "They want to put me in the pot and make broth of me. I'm singing as hard as I can today, for tomorrow I'll be gone." But the donkey told him, "Run away with us. With a voice like yours, you'll be famous in Bremen!" Now there were four of them.

The way was long, night fell, and very frightened, the four creatures found themselves in a thick forest. They scarcely knew whether to press on or to hide in some caves and rest. Suddenly, in the distance they saw a light amongst the trees. It came from a little cottage and they crept up to the window. The donkey placed his front hoofs on the window ledge. Anxious to see, the dog jumped on the donkey's back, the cat climbed onto the dog and the rooster flew on top of the cat to watch what was going on inside.

Now, the cottage was the hideaway of a gang of bandits who were busily celebrating their latest robbery. The hungry donkey and his friends became excited when they saw the food on the table. Upset by the jittery crew on his back, the donkey stuck his head through the window. Then his three companions toppled on to the lamp. The light went out and the room rang with the braying of the donkey, the barking of the dog, and the snarling of the cat. The rooster screeched along with the others.

Taken completely by surprise, the terrified bandits fled screaming: "The Devil! The Devil!" And their abandoned meal ended up in the four friends' stomachs.

Later, however, just as the donkey and his companions were dropping off to sleep, one of the bandits crept back to the now quiet house. He went in to find out what had taken place. The bandit opened the door, and with his pistol in his hand, he stepped trembling towards the fire. However, mistaking the glow of the cat's eyes for burning coals, the bandit dropped a candle next to the cat. Instantly the furious cat sank its claws into the bandit's face. The man fell backwards on to the dog, dropping his gun, which went off. The dog's sharp teeth sank into his leg. When the donkey saw the bandit at the door, he gave a tremendous kick, sending the man flying right through the doorway. The rooster greeted the bandit's action with a grim crowing sound.

"Run!" screamed the bandit. "Run! A horrible witch in there scratched my face. A demon bit me on the leg. A monster beat me with a stick! And . . ." But the other bandits were no longer listening. They had taken to their heels and fled. And so the donkey, the dog, the cat and the rooster took over the house without any trouble. And with the money left behind by the bandits, they always had food on the table, and lived happy and contented for many years.

Dolphins Are Special
by Rita Carboni

Recently, a young girl visited a zoo aquarium and stopped to do some flips in front of a window. A dolphin was swimming on the other side of the window and stopped to watch the girl's performance. The dolphin loved it! The girl kept flipping, and the dolphin kept nodding its head. It seemed to be saying, "Do more flips, please." Scientists explain that humans and dolphins have interacted for years, and this is just another example of that special bond.

One possible reason humans and dolphins may have a special bond is because dolphins are really smart. One study showed that bottlenose dolphins are able to recognize themselves in a mirror. This surprised researchers who thought animals weren't able to recognize themselves. Another study showed that some dolphins use sea sponges as tools. The researchers from the study think this shows that dolphins are able to problem solve, a sure sign of intelligence. Because dolphins are so intelligent, they are able to communicate with people.

Another reason humans may have a special bond with dolphins is because dolphins are entertaining. People love watching dolphins dive down into the water and then jump high in the air. Some dolphins can leap as high as thirty feet in the air. Other dolphins can be trained to do hard tricks. Some dolphins can jump through hoops. Some can play basketball, and others can even paint pictures. People enjoy seeing all of the different things dolphins can do, and dolphins enjoy entertaining people. After watching a dolphin show, one man commented that he was convinced that the dolphins gave the fans a big smile after they finished their performances.

Another reason dolphins share a bond with humans is because they can be helpful, just like people. A British man was in the ocean for an eight-hour swim. The water was freezing, and he didn't think he was going to make it. Then, things got even worse. A shark began to swim near him. It kept swimming next to him and would not leave. The swimmer was very scared and thought the shark was going to attack him, but then a group of dolphins came to his rescue. They stayed by his side and protected him as he continued swimming. The dolphins looked at the man as if to say, "Don't worry, we'll stay with you until you are safe." The man said the dolphins saved his life.

Dolphins also have been known to help other animals. In New Zealand, a group of whales got caught in a terrible storm. The storm washed the whales onto the shore. People tried to get the whales back in the water, but nothing they did worked. Finally, the people got the whales back in the water, but the whales were confused. They didn't know which way to swim. A group of dolphins saw what was happening and hurried to help. It seemed as if the dolphins were actually worried about the whales and didn't want to see them die. They swam next to the whales and guided them back to sea. The dolphins saved the whales!

For years, people told stories about how dolphins saved drowning sailors from the rough waters of the sea. People are now beginning to believe those stories. Today, there are plenty of examples of how dolphins came to the rescue. Dolphins are not only helpful, but they are intelligent and entertaining. It is no wonder that people have a special bond with such special creatures.

Common Core State Standards

Story lesson	Grade level	Standards
The Two Brothers	5–6	**R.**5.1, 5.2, 5.3, 5.4, **W.**5.1, 5.4 **SL.**5.1 **L.**5.1, 5.4, 5.5 **R.**6.1, 6.2, 6.3, 6.4, 6.5 **SL.**6.1 **L.**6.1, 6.5, 6.6
Pythons Invade the Florida Everglades	5–6	**RI.**5.1, 5.2, 5.3, 5.4, 5.8 **SL.**5.1, 5.3 **L.**5.1, 5.4, 5.5 **RI.**6.1, 6.2, 6.3, 6.4, 6.5, 6.6, 6.8 **SL.**6.1 **L.**6.1, 6.4, 6.5
The Ecchoing Green	4–5	**R.**4.1, 4.2, 4.3 **W.**4.1, 4.4 **SL.**4.1 **L.**4.1, 4.4, 4.5 **R.**5.1, 5.2, 5.4 **W.**5.1, 5.4 **SL.**5.1 **L.**5.1, 5.4, 5.5
Advice to a Young Author	6–7	**R.**6.1, 6.2, 6.4 **W.**6.4 **SL.**6.1 **L.**6.1, 6.4, 6.5

Story lesson	Grade level	Standards
		R.7.1, 7.2, 7.4 **W.**7.4 **SL.**7.1 **L.**7.1, 7.4, 7.5
Casey at the Bat	4–5	**R.**4.1, 4.2, 4.3, 4.4, 4.5 **W.**4.1, 4.4, 4.9 **SL.**4.1 **L.**4.1, 4.4, 4.5
		R.5.1, 5.2, 5.3, 5.4, 5.5 **W.**5.1, 5.4, 5.9 **SL.**5.1 **L.**5.1, 5.4, 5.5
Who Has Seen the Wind?	K–2	**R.**K.1, K.3, K.10 **SL.**K.1, K.2, K.3, K.6 **L.**K.1, K.5, K.6
		R.1.1, 1.3, 1.4, 1.10 **SL.**1.1, 1.2, 1.3 **L.**1.1, 1.5, 1.6
		R.2.1 **SL.**2.1, 2.2, 2.3 **L.**2.1, 2.5, 2.6
The Musicians of Bremen	K–2	**R.**K.1, K.2, K.3, K.10 **W.**K.3 **SL.**K.1, K.2, K.3, K.4, K.6 **L.**K.1, K.6

Story lesson	Grade level	Standards
		R.1.1, 1.2, 1.3, 1.4 **W.**1.3 **SL.**1.1, 1.2, 1.3, 1.4, 1.6 **L.**1.1
		R.2.1, 2.2, 2.3, 2.5 **W.**2.3 **SL.**2.1, 2.2, 2.3, 2.4, 2.6 **L.**2.1, 2.6
Dolphins Are Special	K–2	**R.**K.1, K.2, K.3, K.8, K.10 **SL.**K.1, K.2, K.3, K.4, K.6 **L.**K.1, K.6
		R.1.1, 1.2, 1.3, 1.4, 1.8, 1.10 **SL.**1.1, 1.2, 1.3, 1.4, 1.6 **L.**1.1
		R.2.1, 2.2, 2.3, 2.4, 2.6, 2.8 **SL.**2.1, 2.2, 2.3, 2.6 **L.**2.1

TEXTS IN PART TWO

Story lesson	Grade level	Standards
Does an Elephant Never Forget?	3–4	**RI.**3.1, 3.2, 3.4 **SL.**3.4 **W.**3.2
		RI.4.1, 4.2, 4.8 **W.**4.2 **SL.**4.1, 4.3 **L.**4.4

Story lesson	Grade level	Standards
Li Ju and the Magic Tapestry	3–4	**RL.**3.1, 3.2, 3.3 **L.**3.5 **RL.**4.1, 4.3 **W.**4.9.a **SL.**4.1 **L.**4.5
Arachne, the Spinner	5–6	**RL.**5.1.b, 5.2, 5.3, 5.6 **W.**5.1.b.c.d, 5.5 **SL.**5.1 **L.**5.3 **RL.**6.1, 6.2 **W.**6.3 **SL.**6.1.b.c.d **L.**6.2
Tribute to a Dog	5–6	**RI.**5.1, 5.2, 5.3 **W.**5.3.a.d.e **SL.**5.5.a.b **L.**5a.b, 5.6 **RI.**6.1, 6.4, 6.6 **W.**6.1.b.e, 6.3.a.e **SL.**6.1 **L.**6.2, 6.4
The Lady, or the Tiger?	5–6	**RL.**5.1, 5.4 **W.**5.1a, 5.1c, 5.3 **SL.**5.1c **L.**5.4, 5.5a

Story lesson	Grade level	Standards
		RL.6.1,6.4 W.6.1.a.b.e, 6.2.f SL.6.1.c L.6.4.a
The Hound of the Baskervilles	7–8	RL.7.1, 7.3, 7.4 W.7.1.a.b.e, 7.2.b.f SL.7.1 L.7.4.a.c
		RL.8.1, 8.3, 8.4 W.8.1.a.b.e SL.8.1 L.8.4
The Tell-Tale Heart	7–8	RL.7.1.a.b.e, 7.3, 7.4 W.7.1a.b.e SL.7.1.b.d L.7.4
		RL.8.1, 8.2, 8.3, 8.4, 8.6 W.8.1a.b.e SL.8.1.b.d L.8.4.a.c.d
John F. Kennedy's Inaugural Address	7–8+	RI.7.1, 7.4 W.7.1.a.b.e SL.7.4 L.7.4, 7.5a
		RI.8.1, 8.4 W.8.1a.b.e SL.8.4 L.8.5

References

Beck, I. L., & McKeown, M. G. (1981). Developing questions that promote comprehension: The story map. *Language Arts, 58*(8), 913–918.

Beck, I. L., & McKeown, M. G. (2001). Text talk: Capturing the benefits of read-aloud experiences for young children. *The Reading Teacher, 55*(1), 10–20.

Beck, I. L., & McKeown, M. G. (2006). *Improving comprehension with questioning the author: A fresh and expanded view of a powerful approach*. New York: Scholastic.

Beck, I. L., McKeown, M. G., & Gromoll, E. W. (1989). Learning from social studies texts. *Cognition and Instruction, 6*(2), 99–158. Hillsdale, NJ: Erlbaum.

Beck, I. L., McKeown, M. G., Hamilton, R., & Kucan, L. (1997). *Questioning the author: An approach for enhancing student engagement with text*. Newark, DE: International Reading Association.

Beck, I. L., McKeown, M. G., & Kucan, L. (2013). *Bringing words to life: Robust vocabulary instruction* (2nd ed.). New York: Guilford Press.

Beck, I. L., McKeown, M. G., & Omanson, R. C. (1987). The effects and uses of diverse vocabulary instructional techniques. In M. G. McKeown & M. E. Curtis (Eds.), *The nature of vocabulary acquisition* (pp. 147–163). Hillsdale, NJ: Erlbaum.

Beck, I. L., McKeown, M. G., Omanson, R. C., & Pople, M. T. (1984). Improving the comprehensibility of stories: The effects of revisions that improve coherence. *Reading Research Quarterly, 19*(3), 263–277.

Beck, I. L., Omanson, R. C., & McKeown, M. G. (1982). An instructional redesign of reading lessons: Effects on comprehension. *Reading Research Quarterly, 17*(4), 462–481.

Black, J. B. (1985). An exposition on understanding expository text. In B. K. Britton & J. B. Black (Eds.), *Understanding expository text: A theoretical and practical handbook for analyzing explanatory text* (pp. 249–267). Hillsdale, NJ: Erlbaum.

Burkins, J., & Yaris, K. (2013). Defining close reading. Retrieved from *www.burkinsandyaris.com/defining-close-reading*.

Callahan, J. (2013). Black Death. In L. Kucan & A. S. Palinscar (Eds.), *Comprehension instruction through text-based discussion* (pp. 46–49). Newark, DE: International Reading Association.

Carpenter, P. A., & Daneman, M. (1981). Lexical retrieval and error recovery in reading: A model based on eye fixations. *Journal of Verbal Learning and Verbal Behavior, 20*(2), 137–160.

Common Core State Standards Initiative. (2015). Retrieved from *www.corestandards.org/about-the-standards/development-process*.

Fisher, D., & Frey, N. (2012). Close reading in elementary schools. *The Reading Teacher, 66*(3), 179–188.

Goerss, B. L., Beck, I. L., & McKeown, M. G. (1999). Increasing remedial students' ability to derive word meaning from context. *Reading Psychology, 20*(2), 151–175.

Hallden, O. (1986). Learning history. *Oxford Review of Education, 12*, 53–66.

Hayes, D., & Ahrens, M. (1988). Vocabulary simplification for children: A special case of "motherese"? *Journal of Child Language, 15*, 395–410.

Kintsch, W. (1998). *Comprehension: A paradigm for cognition*. New York: Cambridge University Press.

Kintsch, W., & van Dijk, T. A. (1978). Towards a model of text comprehension and production. *Psychological Review, 85*, 363–394.

McKeown, M. G., Beck, I. L., & Blake, R. G. K. (2009). Rethinking reading comprehension instruction: A comparison of instruction for strategies and content approaches. *Reading Research Quarterly, 44*(3), 218–253.

Nagy, W., Herman, P., & Anderson, R. (1985). Learning words from context. *Reading Research Quarterly, 20*, 233–253.

National Center for Education Statistics. (2013). A first look: 2013 mathematics and reading. The Nation's Report Card. Retrieved from *http:nationsreportcard.gov/reading_math_2013*.

Omanson, R. C., Beck, I. L., Voss, J. F., & McKeown, M. G. (1984). The effects of reading lessons on comprehension: A processing description. *Cognition and Instruction, 1*(1), 45–67.

Prose, F. (2006). *Reading like a writer*. New York: HarperPerennial.

Rothkopf, E. Z. (1966). Learning from written instructive materials: An exploration of the control of inspection behavior by test-like events. *American Educational Research Journal, 3*, 241–249.

Rothkopf, E. Z. (1972). Structural text features and the control of processes in learning from written materials. In J. B. Carrp & R. O. Freedle (Eds.), *Language comprehension and the acquisition of knowledge* (pp. 315–335). Washington, DC: Winston.

Sandora, C., Beck, I., & McKeown, M. (1999). A comparison of two discussion strategies on students' comprehension and interpretation of complex literature. *Reading Psychology, 20*(3), 177–212.

Shanahan, T. (2012). What is close reading? Retrieved from *www.shanahanonliteracy.com/2012/06/what-is-close-reading.html*.

Swanborn, M. S. L., & de Glopper, K. (1999). Incidental word learning while reading: A meta-analysis. *Review of Educational Research, 69*(3), 261–285.

Teale, W. H., & Martinez, M. G. (1996). Reading aloud to young children: Teachers' reading styles and kindergartners' text comprehension. In C. Pontecorvo, M. Orsolini, B. Burge, & L. B. Resnick (Eds.), *Children's early text construction* (pp. 321–344). Mahwah, NJ: Erlbaum.

Valencia, S. W., & Wixson, K. K. (2013). CCSS-ELA: Suggestions and cautions for implementing the reading standards. *The Reading Teacher, 67*(3), 181–185.

Watts, G. H., & Anderson, R. C. (1971). Effects of three types of inserted questions on learning from prose. *Journal of Educational Psychology, 62*, 387–394.

Whitehurst, G. J., Arnold, D. S., Epstein, J. N., Angell, A. L., Smith, M., & Fischel, J. E. (1994). A picture book reading intervention in day care and home for children from low-income families. *Developmental Psychology, 30*(5), 679–689.

Wright, J. (n.d.) How to teach close reading: Demystifying literary analysis for undergraduates. Retrieved April 2014, from *http://teachingcollegelit.com/tcl/?page_id=255.n.*

Literature Cited

Babbitt, N. (1985). *Tuck everlasting.* New York: Farrar, Straus, & Giroux.

Blake, W. (2015). *The ecchoing green* [Public domain]. Retrieved from *www.poemhunter.com/poem/the-ecchoing-green-3.*

Bogaerts, R., & Bogaerts, G. (1992). *Socrates.* San Francisco: Chronicle Books.

Brett, J. (1996). *The mitten.* New York: Putnam.

Brothers Grimm. (1857). *The musicians of Bremen* [Public domain], Retold by Theo Arvanitis (unpublished). Original text available at *www.gutenberg.org/files/19068/19068-h/19068-h.htm#illus-155.*

Carboni, R. (n.d.). *Does an elephant never forget?* Unpublished article.

Carboni, R. (n.d.). *Dolphins are special.* Unpublished article.

Carroll, L. (1865). *Alice in Wonderland* [Public domain]. Retrieved from *www.gutenberg.org/cache/epub/11/pg11.txt.*

Douglas, M. S. (1947). *The Everlades: River of grass.* New York: Rinehart.

Doyle, A. C. (1902). *The hound of the Baskervilles* [Public domain]. Retrieved from *www.gutenberg.org/files/2852/2852-h/2852-h.htm.*

Doyle, A. C. (1911). *Advice to a young author* [Public domain]. Retrieved from *www.scottish-poetrylibrary.org.uk/poetry/poems/advice-young-author.*

du Maurier, D. (1952). The birds. In *The apple tree.* (Reprinted in 1963 as *The Birds and Other Stories*, London: Penguin.)

Henry, O. (1906). *The gift of the Magi, The Four Million.* New York: Doubleday, Page & Company.

Hughes, L. (1951). Harlem. Retrieved June 1, 2015, from *www.poemhunter.com/poem/dream-deferred/.*

Kennedy, J. F. (1961). *Inaugural address* [Public domain]. Retrieved from *www.bartleby.com/124/pres56.html.*

Keyes, D. (1966). *Flowers for Algernon.* New York: Harcourt, Brace & World.

Millman, L. (1987). The raven and the whale. In *A kayak full of ghosts: Eskimo tales.* Santa Barbara, CA: Capra Press.

O'Connor, F. (1953). A good man is hard to find. In *A good man is hard to find and other stories*. New York: Harcourt.

Poe, E. A. (1843). *The tell-tale heart* [Public domain]. Retrieved from *www.gutenberg.org/files/2148/2148-h/2148-h.htm#link2H_4_0019*.

Prose, F. (2006). *Reading like a writer*. New York: HarperCollins.

ReadWorks. (2013, November 26). Pythons invade the Florida Everglades. Retrieved from *www.readworks.org/passages/pythons-invade-florida-everglades*.

Rey, H. A. (1975). *Curious George takes a job*. Boston: Houghton Mifflin.

Root, P. (1996). *Mrs. Potter's pig*. Somerville, MA: Candlewick Press.

Rossetti, C. (1872). Who has seen the wind? [Public domain]. Retrieved from *www.poetry-foundation.org/poem/171952*.

Seeger, P. (1986). *Abiyoyo*. New York: Simon & Schuster.

Silverstein, S. (1964,1992). *The giving tree*. New York: Harper & Row.

Steig, W. (1982). *Doctor De Soto*. New York: Farrar, Straus & Giroux.

Steig, W. (1986). *Brave Irene*. New York: Farrar, Straus & Giroux.

Stevenson, R. L. (1883). *Treasure Island*. Cambridge, MA: University Press Cambridge, John Wilson and Son.

Stockton, F. R. (1882). The lady, or the tiger? [Public domain]. Retold by Shirley Hazlett (unpublished). Original text available at *www.gutenberg.org/files/25549/25549-h/25549-h.htm#tiger*.

Thayer, E. L. (1888). Casey at the bat [Public domain]. Retrieved from *www.poetryfoundation.org/poem/174665*.

Tolstoy, L. (2015, April). The two brothers [Public domain]. Retrieved from *www.populationme.com/All/Literature/TwoBrothersTolstoyActivity.pdf*.

Vest, G. G. (1855). Tribute to a dog [Public domain]. Retrieved from *www.historyplace.com/speeches/vest.htm*.

White, E. B. (1952). *Charlotte's web*. New York: Harper & Row.

Zion, G. (1956). *Harry the dirty dog*. New York: HarperCollins.

Index

Page numbers followed by *n* indicate note